AP® U.S. GOVERNMENT AND POLITICS CRASH COURSE®

Katherine Olson-Goldman, J.D.
Nancy Fenton, M.A.

Research & Education Association
www.rea.com

Research & Education Association
258 Prospect Plains Road
Cranbury, New Jersey 08512
Email: info@rea.com

AP® U.S. GOVERNMENT AND POLITICS CRASH COURSE®, 2nd Edition

Published 2022
Copyright © 2020 by Research & Education Association.
Prior edition copyright © 2010 by Research & Education Association.
All rights reserved. No part of this book may be reproduced in any form without permission of the publisher.

Printed in the United States of America

Library of Congress Control Number 2019946648

ISBN-13: 978-0-7386-1249-2
ISBN-10: 0-7386-1249-9

AP® U.S. GOVERNMENT AND POLITICS CRASH COURSE TABLE OF CONTENTS

Introduction

Content Review

UNIT 1: FOUNDATIONS OF AMERICAN DEMOCRACY

UNIT 2: INTERACTIONS AMONG BRANCHES OF GOVERNMENT

ABOUT OUR BOOK

REA's *AP® U.S. Government and Politics Crash Course* is designed for the last-minute studier or any student who wants a quick refresher on the AP® course. This *Crash Course* is based on the 2020–2021 AP® U.S. Government and Politics course and exam and focuses only on the topics tested, so you can make the most of your study time.

Written by veteran AP® exam experts, our *Crash Course* gives you a concise review of the major concepts and important topics tested on the AP® U.S. Government and Politics exam.

- **Part I** gives you **Keys for Success**, so you can tackle the exam with confidence. It also gives you a list of the **Key Terms** that you absolutely must know.

- **Part II** offers **Key Content Review**, which covers every critical aspect of today's exam.

- **Part III** zeros in on the exam's **Required Foundational Documents** and **Required Supreme Court Cases**, along with a succinct overview of important laws enacted by Congress.

- **Part IV** gives you specific **Test-Taking Strategies** to conquer the multiple-choice and free-response questions, along with AP®-style practice questions to prepare you for what you'll see on test day.

ABOUT OUR ONLINE PRACTICE EXAM

How ready are you for the AP® U.S. Government and Politics exam? Find out by taking **REA's online practice exam** available at *www.rea.com/studycenter*. This test features automatic scoring, detailed explanations of all answers, and diagnostic score reporting that will help you identify your strengths and weaknesses so you'll be ready on exam day.

Whether you use this book throughout the school year or as a refresher in the final weeks before the exam, REA's *Crash Course* will show you how to study efficiently and strategically, so you can boost your score.

Good luck on your AP® U.S. GoPo exam!

ABOUT OUR AUTHORS

Katherine Olson-Goldman, J.D., has spent the last two decades developing and teaching numerous courses in government and politics, law, and history, including AP® United States Government and Politics, AP® Comparative Government and Politics, and Practical Law.

Ms. Olson-Goldman holds a bachelor's degree in political science from DePaul University, a secondary teaching certification from the University of Wisconsin, and a Juris Doctor from Marquette University Law School where she was a Thomas Moore scholar and served on law review.

Nancy Fenton, M.A., teaches AP® U.S. Government and Politics at the award-winning Adlai E. Stevenson High School in Lincolnshire, Illinois. She has been teaching government and politics since 2003. Ms. Fenton is also a College Board consultant and has served as a reader for AP® Psychology since 2008 and a table leader since 2017. She has a bachelor's degree in history and holds two master's degrees, one in psychology and one in curriculum and instruction technology.

ABOUT REA

Founded in 1959, Research & Education Association (REA) is dedicated to publishing the finest and most effective educational materials—including study guides and test preps—for students of all ages.

Today, REA's wide-ranging catalog is a leading resource for students, teachers, and other professionals. Visit *www.rea.com* to see a complete listing of all our titles.

ACKNOWLEDGMENTS

We would like to thank Pam Weston, Publisher, for setting the quality standards for production integrity and managing the publication to completion; Larry B. Kling, Editorial Director, for his overall guidance; John Paul Cording, Technology Director, for managing the REA Study Center; Diane Goldschmidt, Managing Editor, and Wayne Barr, Test Prep Project Manager, for shepherding this book through development and production; Alice Leonard, Senior Editor, for editorial review; and Jennifer Calhoun for file prep.

We also extend our appreciation to Larry Krieger and Amy Skonberg-Reznicek for technical review; Karen Lamoreux for copyediting; and Kathy Caratozzolo of Caragraphics for typesetting.

PART I
INTRODUCTION

Seven Keys for Success
on the AP® U.S. Government and Politics Exam

The AP® U.S. Government and Politics course and exam cover the U.S. political system, including the foundations of American government, its institutions, entities that help connect the government and the governed, public policy, and the interactions that sustain and define the workings of the federal constitutional system. You will be expected to have a command of nine key foundational documents and fifteen key U.S. Supreme Court cases, as well as be able to interpret various other relevant primary and secondary source materials.

1. UNDERSTAND THE EXAM STRUCTURE AND SCORING

The exam consists of two sections described in the following table:

Section	Total Number of Questions	Time Limit	Percentage of Overall Exam Score
Section I: Multiple-Choice Questions	55 Multiple Choice Questions	1 hour and 20 minutes	50%
Section II: Free-Response Questions	4 Free-Response Questions	1 hour and 40 minutes	50%

There will be a short break between the multiple-choice and free-response sections. Detailed information on the types of multiple-choice and free-response exam questions—as well as practice questions—is available in Part IV: Test-Taking Strategies.

The machine-scored multiple-choice section awards points for each correct answer. No points are lost for skipped or incorrect answers. Experienced high school and college instructors grade the free-response questions by hand. The College Board combines the multiple-choice and free-response scores to create a total exam score using this 5-point scale:

AP® Score	Recommendation
5	Extremely well qualified
4	Well qualified
3	Qualified
2	Possibly qualified
1	No recommendation

2. REVIEW THE FIVE AP® U.S. GoPo UNITS

The course is organized into five content units, which are reviewed in this *Crash Course* book. Here are some of the main concepts from each unit:

UNIT 1: FOUNDATIONS OF AMERICAN DEMOCRACY (15%–22% of the exam)

- Fundamental concepts of American government and democratic ideals
- Founding documents and the motivations of the authors of the Constitution
- Three models of representative democracy
- Weaknesses of the Articles of Confederation addressed by the Constitution
- Federalist and Anti-Federalist views on the Constitution
- Key compromises during the Constitutional Convention
- Separation of powers and checks and balances
- Division of federal/state powers in the Constitution
- Development of federalism, including key U.S. Supreme Court rulings
- Amendment procedure and federalism

UNIT 2: INTERACTIONS AMONG BRANCHES OF GOVERNMENT
(25%–36% of the exam)

- Effect of structure, functions, powers, and procedures of the three federal branches on the policy-making process
- Influence of checks and balances, competing policy-making interests, ideological differences, and public opinion on the interactions of the branches
- Cooperation and competition among the branches
- Changes in the exercise of the powers of each branch and the impact on the federal government today
- Structure, organization, and functions of the federal bureaucracy
- Effect of elections, interest groups, and citizens on the federal branches

UNIT 3: CIVIL LIBERTIES AND CIVIL RIGHTS
(13%–18% of the exam)

- Court interpretation of the Bill of Rights and the process of selective incorporation and its implications
- Due Process and Equal Protection clauses of the Fourteenth Amendment
- Influence of the Constitution and court rulings on social movements
- Response of the government to social movements, including the drafting of legislation and court rulings

UNIT 4: AMERICAN POLITICAL IDEOLOGIES AND BELIEFS
(10%–15% of the exam)

- Influence of demographics, political culture, social change, and the interpretation of democratic values on the development of political beliefs
- Cultural influences on political socialization, efficacy, and participation
- Scientific polling
- Impact of political ideologies and political parties on public policy
- Government's role in the economy and social issues

UNIT 5: POLITICAL PARTICIPATION
(20%–27% of the exam)

- Constitutional and legislative protections of voting rights
- Role of linkage institutions—elections, political parties, interest groups, media
- Organization and functions of political parties
- Influence of campaign finance, realignment, and advances in communication technology on political parties
- Impact of and structural barriers to the success of minor political parties
- Functions and impact of interest groups and social movements on elections and public policy
- Presidential election process and the Electoral College
- Congressional election process
- Campaign organization and impact of federal law and court rulings on campaign finance
- Functions and impact of the media on elections and public policy

3. APPLY THE BIG IDEAS

While reviewing each of the five units, reference the 5 big ideas, discussed below, in the context of U.S. government and politics as well as how political scientists study political behavior.

BIG IDEA 1. Constitutionalism: The structure and policies of the U.S. government involve both federalism and separation of powers, among the three independent branches that provide checks and balances on each other. Government is based on the rule of law and respect for majority rule and minority rights.

- The Constitution was a product of compromises to overcome the weaknesses in the Articles of Confederation. It remains a model of representative democracy and limited government.
- Principles of federalism, popular sovereignty, separation of powers, and checks and balances are reflected in the Constitution.
- The legislative branch was designed to reflect the ideals of republicanism.

- Powers of the executive branch have been expanded beyond those outlined in the Constitution.

- The judicial branch as created by the Constitution and the power of judicial review are an independent check on the other branches.

- Supreme Court's judicial review of laws and government actions based on the Constitution is influenced by the composition of the justices on the court and citizen–government interactions.

BIG IDEA 2. Liberty and Order: The structure and policies of the U.S. government involve a balance between individual freedom and collective security based on the Constitution. The Bill of Rights has been interpreted by the judicial branch to balance the need for government authority and the protection of civil liberties. Examples in this book show how the Bill of Rights has been selectively incorporated to limit the authority of the states over its citizens under the Due Process Clause of the Fourteenth Amendment.

- Models of participatory, pluralist, and elitist democracy illustrate the ambivalence of the founders and political theorists toward unrestricted mass participation in governance.

- The Constitution and its Bill of Rights have long been interpreted by the courts to balance individual liberties with societal requirements for order and stability.

BIG IDEA 3. Civic Participation in a Representative Democracy: The ideals of popular sovereignty, individualism, and republicanism influence laws and policy-making and are based on the idea that citizens will be involved.

- Several provisions of the Constitution, including the Fourteenth Amendment's Equal Protection Clause, have been interpreted to ensure equality in American society.

- Federal laws and policies on elections, voting, and campaign finance are viewed differently across the political spectrum.

- Today's media outlets provide citizens with information about public policy and influence how citizens participate in government.

BIG IDEA 4. Competing Policy-Making Interests: Public policy results from input from various public and private institutions and individuals at the federal, state, and local levels.

- The Constitution uses the doctrines of separation of powers and checks and balances to preserve individual rights and make sure the government represents the will of the people.

- The massive federal bureaucracy has a vital role in the implementation of public policy, which is sometimes challenged for lacking accountability.

- Public policy on civil rights has been shaped by public opinion, social movements, legislation, and court rulings.

- Major political ideologies influence public policy debates and decisions.

- Linkage institutions (e.g., political parties, interest groups, elections, and the media) create pathways for political participation and policy input.

BIG IDEA 5. Methods of Political Analysis: Political scientists use scientific polling and data analysis to evaluate political participation, ideologies, and government institutions. This data influences policy and often electoral outcomes. Citizen attitudes about government, including political ideology, efficacy, and participation, are based on the influence of many actors: demographic characteristics, family culture, social events, education, and the media.

Test Tip

The big idea of methods of political analysis applies across the entire AP® course and thus appears on both multiple-choice and free-response questions on the exam. You will be expected to analyze data sets, graphs, charts, and political science reading passages.

4. FOCUS ON THE CONSTITUTION

Though nine foundational documents are represented on the exam, none is more important than the Constitution. It is the one most frequently cited in free-response answers. The Constitution consists of three main parts:

- Preamble

- Articles (7)

- Amendments (27) including the Bill of Rights

5. ANALYZE SOURCES LIKE A POLITICAL SCIENTIST

Both the multiple-choice and free-response questions require analysis of various primary and secondary sources. Primary sources include the nine foundational documents and opinions from the fifteen required Supreme Court cases. Detailed information aiding in this analysis are found throughout this book. Secondary sources include quotes from political science research articles, editorials, and books in which various political theories are presented.

Foundational Documents: This book connects the nine foundational documents to the philosophical underpinnings of U.S. government and American political values. It also applies them to key political science terminology and concepts. The nine foundational documents are:

- The *Declaration of Independence*

- The *Articles of Confederation*

- The *Constitution of the United States* including the *Bill of Rights*

- *Brutus No. 1*

- *Federalist Nos. 10, 51, 70, 78*

- *Letter from a Birmingham Jail* (Martin Luther King, Jr.)

Required Supreme Court Cases: An understanding of the fifteen required Supreme Court cases includes the facts of the case, constitutional issues raised, the holding and its reasoning, and any important implications or related vocabulary. Each decision should be considered in relation to the idea of precedent and the impact on public policy, as well as the relationship between the branches of government and between the government and the citizens and residents of the United States. The required cases will be included on the SCOTUS comparison free-response question as well as in multiple-choice questions. The cases, which follow, represent seven legal categories.

1. Federalism

    - *McCulloch v. Maryland* (1819)

    - *United States v. Lopez* (1995)

2. Bill of Rights

    - *Engel v. Vitale* (1962)

    - *Wisconsin v. Yoder* (1972)

    - *Tinker v. Des Moines Independent Community School District* (1969)

- *New York Times Co. v. United States* (1971)
- *Schenck v. United States* (1919)

3. Selective Incorporation

- *Gideon v. Wainwright* (1963)
- *Roe v. Wade* (1973)
- *McDonald v. Chicago* (2010)

4. Civil Rights

- *Brown v. Board of Education* (1954)

5. Campaign Finance

- *Citizens United v. Federal Election Commission* (2010)

6. Representative Government

- *Baker v. Carr* (1962)
- *Shaw v. Reno* (1993)

7. Role of the Court

- *Marbury v. Madison* (1803)

Test Tip

Some of the SCOTUS cases fall into multiple categories. For example, Gideon is a Sixth Amendment (Bill of Rights) case, but it is also an example of selective incorporation.

Text-Based Sources: The exam requires you to analyze documentary sources in terms of how they relate to key principles of U.S. government. These sources include historical documents or modern writings by political scientists and historians. You may be asked to analyze the perspective of the author, identify the author's thesis and reasoning in your own words, explain evidence to support the argument, or describe an alternate perspective. Be prepared to explain the potential implications of the author's reasoning.

Quantitative Sources: Both the multiple-choice and free-response questions require analysis of quantitative data (measured numerically) presented in graph or chart form. You will be asked to identify similarities, differences, and trends, as well as reach accurate conclusions that apply your knowledge of course material. You will also be asked to explain the importance of the information in the data.

Visual Sources: The exam will include various visual sources, including cartoons, maps, and infographics. Thus, you will need to interpret information presented graphically, which means familiarizing yourself with the concepts of viewpoint, data point, trends, implications, limitations, and sources.

6. USE THIS *CRASH COURSE* TO BUILD A PLAN FOR SUCCESS ON THE AP® U.S. GoPo EXAM

This book is the result of a detailed analysis of the most recent College Board AP® U.S. Government and Politics Course and Exam Description. This *Crash Course* includes the key political science terminology, a summary of each of the five units, descriptions of the nine foundational documents and the fifteen required Supreme Court cases.

You are advised to review each chapter that covers the material for each of the units, focusing on units or sections about which you feel more uncertain. Each chapter outlines the essential knowledge for each unit as determined by the College Board. Pay special attention to the Test Tips that highlight difficult topics and help you make important distinctions that will give you the edge you need on exam day.

Study the chapters that discuss specific strategies for tackling the six styles of multiple-choice questions and the four types of free-response questions. In addition, be sure to take the online practice exam that comes with this book.

After completing the online exam, which mimics the actual exam in the number and type of questions, be sure to read the detailed explanations to deepen your connection with the material. Notice what distinguishes the best answer from the inferior distractors.

7. SUPPLEMENT *CRASH COURSE* WITH COLLEGE BOARD MATERIALS

This *Crash Course* has everything you need to succeed on the exam. However, the College Board's website is also a valuable resource. The site provides information about the test structure, question types, FAQs, and more importantly, additional study materials and sample questions.

Key Terms

AMICUS CURIAE BRIEF: Legal documents filed by outside groups not directly involved with a case in an attempt to influence the decision of the SCOTUS.

BIPARTISAN: Agreement between the two major political parties about a particular bill, policy, or issue.

CAUCUS. (1) A group of members of Congress with shared goals or interests, such as the Democratic or Republican caucuses. (2) A method for choosing delegates to the national nominating convention used in some states instead of a primary election, in which voters meet in person to discuss and vote on candidates for president.

CIVIL LIBERTIES: The guarantees in the Constitution and especially the Bill of Rights that protect individuals from interference by the federal government. These constitutional protections have been applied to the state governments through the process of selective Incorporation under the Fourteenth Amendment's Due Process Clause.

CIVIL RIGHTS: The obligation of the federal government to protect citizens from discrimination; based on the Equal Protection Clause of the Fourteenth Amendment.

CLOTURE: A Senate rule that can be used to end a filibuster with a supermajority of 60 votes.

COMMERCE CLAUSE: Provision of Article I that gives Congress the expressed power to regulate interstate and international trade, which is the basis for much of the legislation passed by Congress.

COMMITTEE OF THE WHOLE: A procedure in the House of Representatives in which the entire House becomes a committee. The group cannot pass legislation, but may debate and propose amendments under a more relaxed and efficient set of rules.

CONCURRENT POWERS: Powers that are granted to both federal and state governments, such as the power to tax, spend, and borrow money.

CONFERENCE COMMITTEE: A temporary committee of members of both the House and Senate created to resolve differences in a bill that has passed both chambers of Congress.

CONSTITUENT ACCOUNTABILITY: The duty of elected officials to act in the best interest of the citizens they represent.

COOPERATIVE FEDERALISM: A model of federalism that involves the shared state and federal exercise of power. Often called *marble cake federalism* to emphasize the complex interplay between the levels of government.

DARK MONEY: Political campaign contributions made under legal circumstances where donors' names are not required to be disclosed.

DEALIGNMENT: The general decline in party identification and loyalty to the major parties among the electorate, leading to an increase in the number of individuals who identify as independent.

DELEGATE MODEL: The theory that the role of an elected representative is to vote in a manner consistent with the views of his or her constituents.

DEVOLUTION: The process of transferring responsibility for policy development and implementation from the federal government to state and local governments.

DISCHARGE PETITION: A tool for releasing a bill from a committee in the House, requiring the signatures of 218 members (a majority).

DUAL FEDERALISM: A model of federalism that involves creating distinct state and federal exercises of power; often described as *layer cake federalism* to emphasize the sharp division of powers between the two levels of government.

DUE PROCESS CLAUSE: A clause found in both the Fifth and Fourteenth Amendments designed to ensure that laws and the judicial process are fair and impartial. The Fourteenth Amendment's Due Process Clause has been used as the vehicle to apply federal civil liberties protections against state actions through selective incorporation.

ELITE DEMOCRACY: The theory that power in a democracy is controlled by a few powerful people who have the greatest influence on policy decisions.

ENTITLEMENT: Mandatory spending on government programs that provide benefits to qualified individuals. Examples include Social Security, Medicare, and Medicaid.

ENUMERATED (EXPRESSED) POWERS: The powers or areas of authority of the federal government that are directly listed in the Constitution.

EQUAL PROTECTION CLAUSE: Fourteenth Amendment clause that forms the basis for civil rights claims. Courts have interpreted the clause to require the federal government to address and prevent discriminatory practices.

ESTABLISHMENT CLAUSE: First Amendment clause preventing the government from supporting or associating with any religion, except in the most limited ways.

EXCLUSIONARY RULE: A rule established by the Supreme Court providing that otherwise admissible evidence cannot be used in a criminal trial if it was the result of illegal action by the government.

EX POST FACTO LAW: A type of law, prohibited by the Constitution, that punishes individuals for actions committed before the law was enacted.

EXECUTIVE AGREEMENT: An agreement entered into by the president and a foreign head of state. It is similar to a treaty, but does not require Senate ratification.

EXECUTIVE ORDER: A declaration by the president that impacts policy and has the force of law without congressional approval.

EXECUTIVE PRIVILEGE: The idea that the president can keep conversations and documents within the executive branch confidential from the other branches of government and the public.

FEDERALISM: A system of government with a written constitution in which power is divided among national, state, and local governments.

FILIBUSTER: The practice of using the Senate rule allowing continuous debate to delay legislative action.

FISCAL POLICY: An area of government policy controlled by Congress, related to the management of the economy through taxing and spending.

FREE EXERCISE CLAUSE: The First Amendment freedom of religion clause that has been interpreted by the Supreme Court to mean that the government may not interfere with citizens' practice of their chosen religion unless there are important reasons for restricting it.

FRONTLOADING: The tendency for states to hold primary elections and caucuses earlier in the election season in order to have greater influence over the choice of candidates and get increased media coverage.

FULL FAITH AND CREDIT CLAUSE: Provision found in Article IV that requires all states to recognize the legal records and acts of other states.

GERRYMANDERING: The process by which the majority party in a state legislature may draw congressional or state legislative district boundaries to favor that party. The intended result is a disproportionate number of members of that party being elected and creating "safe" seats for the party.

HARD MONEY: Political campaign contributions that are donated directly to candidates.

HOLD: A procedure in which a senator delays consideration of a bill or nomination in the Senate.

HORSE RACE JOURNALISM: Media reporting of an election that focuses on polling and speculates about the eventual winner, as opposed to a discussion of policy differences between the candidates.

IMPLIED POWERS: Powers of the national government that are not directly written in the Constitution, but are reasonably suggested based on expressed powers and are allowed under the Necessary and Proper Clause.

INDEPENDENT EXPENDITURES: Outside political campaign spending by unaffiliated groups to promote a candidate. The amounts are unlimited as a result of the decision in *Citizens United v. FEC,* as long as there is no direct coordination with the campaign.

INHERENT POWERS: Powers of the national government that are not mentioned in the Constitution, but are recognized as belonging to all sovereign states.

IRON TRIANGLE: A long-lasting, mutually advantageous, and strong (iron) relationship involving three components: an interest group, a congressional committee, and an executive branch agency.

ISSUE NETWORK: A group of individuals, elected officials, and interest groups that all focus on the same policy issue.

JOINT COMMITTEES: Congressional committees with members from both chambers that have limited authority and frequently handle administrative housekeeping tasks or keep tabs on specific policy areas. They inform Congress but do not introduce legislation.

JUDICIAL ACTIVISM: The idea that the judicial branch should freely use the power of judicial review to protect the rights and liberties of individuals and minorities. This philosophy recognizes that the legislative and executive branches may not always act fairly for all because they are elected officials and may have overriding loyalties to their constituents.

JUDICIAL RESTRAINT: The principle that the judicial branch should defer to the judgment of the elected branches of government whenever possible, and should use the power of judicial review to invalidate laws or executive actions only when absolutely necessary.

JUDICIAL REVIEW: The power of the courts to determine the constitutionality of any actions of federal or state government. This power is not explicitly granted in the Constitution, but was established by *Marbury v. Madison.*

LINKAGE INSTITUTION: Organizations or systems that connect people with the government and create channels for the flow of information and interaction in policy development. Political parties, interest groups, elections, and the media are all linkage institutions.

LOBBYING: The efforts by interest groups to influence public policy through targeted interactions with government officials, including providing information, writing legislation, and offering support for political campaigns.

LOGROLLING: A method of compromise in which members of Congress agree to support bills they would normally oppose in exchange for support from other members on bills that are of importance to them.

MIRANDA RULE: As a result of the case *Miranda v. Arizona,* the SCOTUS held that suspects must be informed of their Fifth and Sixth Amendment rights before being interrogated by the police if the prosecution wants to use any information from their statements against them in court.

MONETARY POLICY: An area of government policy related to the management of the economy through the control of the money supply and interest rates. The Federal Reserve Board manages this area of economic policy.

NECESSARY AND PROPER CLAUSE (ELASTIC CLAUSE): A clause in Article I of the Constitution that gives Congress the authority to create any laws related to the expressed powers, thus creating implied powers.

OPINION: A written document created by an appellate court indicating the facts of the case and an analysis of the legal reasoning behind a decision. (1) A majority opinion represents the ruling of the court. (2) A concurring opinion indicates the reasoning of a justice(s) that agrees with the ruling of the court but for different reasons. (3) A dissenting opinion indicates the reasoning of a justice(s) that disagrees with the ruling of the court.

OVERSIGHT: The authority of Congress to ensure that the executive branch bureaucracy implements laws correctly by holding hearings, investigating, and using the power of the purse to increase or decrease agency budgets.

PARTICIPATORY DEMOCRACY: The theory that citizens hold the power in a democracy, emphasizing their widespread participation in politics, civic engagement, and the principle of majoritarianism.

PARTY-LINE VOTING: Theory that voters with a strong party identification are likely to make voting decisions based on the party affiliation of the candidates.

PARTY PLATFORM: A formal statement of a political party's positions on major issues and policy goals.

PLURALIST DEMOCRACY: Theory that the power in a democracy incorporates the influence of various groups of individuals with shared beliefs, without allowing any one group to dominate.

PLURALITY VOTE: An electoral outcome in which one candidate has more votes than the others, but no candidate has a majority. Single-member legislative districts and electoral votes at the state level can be won by a plurality, which results in a disadvantage for third party candidates. The candidate with the most votes wins the election, even if no candidate wins a majority of votes.

POLITICAL ACTION COMMITTEE (PAC): A private group created by a corporation, union, or interest group that raises and distributes funds to be used in election campaigns.

POLITICAL EFFICACY: The belief that one's actions can affect government policies and that a single vote matters.

POLITICAL SOCIALIZATION: The process through which an individual adopts a political identity, political party affiliation, beliefs, and values. The most important influence on the process is family.

POLITICO MODEL: The theory that the role of an elected representative is to vote based either on the preferences of his or her constituents (delegate model) or on his or her conscience (trustee model). The choice depends on the issue and the degree of public concern about a particular policy decision.

PORK BARREL: Funding for specific projects that is added to appropriations bills, often without debate, that usually benefits the district or state of a particular member of Congress. Pork barrel spending is essentially synonymous with the less pejorative "earmarks," although there are small technical differences.

POWER OF THE PURSE: The unofficial term for the power of Congress to fund various agencies in the executive branch, which serves as a powerful check.

PRECEDENT: An earlier appellate decision that guides courts in deciding later similar cases.

PROSPECTIVE VOTING: Theory that voters evaluate the promises and proposals made by candidates and predict how their priorities will be affected when choosing between candidates.

RANDOM SAMPLE: A subset of a population chosen to take part in a poll based on the principle of equal probability of selection.

RATIONAL-CHOICE VOTING: Theory that voters seek out information about candidates and issues, then vote for the person they believe will advance their policy preferences.

REALIGNMENT: A significant change in the membership of the base of a political party resulting in a changed political landscape.

REAPPORTIONMENT: The redistribution of the 435 House seats among the 50 states to account for population shifts. This occurs every ten years following the national census.

REDISTRICTING: The redrawing of new district boundaries within states for congressional districts to account for an increase or decrease in the total number of representatives each state has, and to make sure each district is roughly the same in total population.

RESERVED POWERS: Areas of government authority that are not specifically granted to the federal government and not denied to states. These powers belong to the states and the people, according to the Tenth Amendment and the principle of division of powers.

RETROSPECTIVE VOTING: Theory that voters consider the track record of each candidate and party to determine how effectively that candidate or party has governed when choosing between candidates.

REVOLVING DOOR: The movement of individuals who have worked in government into positions within the industries they previously regulated and affiliated interest groups or lobbying firms, or vice versa.

RULES COMMITTEE: Important standing committee in the House of Representatives responsible for putting bills on the calendar, setting limits for the amount of time for debate, and deciding if amendments can be added.

SAMPLING ERROR (MARGIN OF ERROR): The predicted difference between a poll's results and the opinion of the larger population. In general, a larger sample size will decrease the margin of error in a poll.

SELECTIVE INCORPORATION: The piecemeal (one case at a time), rather than complete, process of applying the civil liberties in the Bill of Rights to the states through the Due Process Clause of Fourteenth Amendment.

SIGNING STATEMENT: A written document that a president may create when signing a bill into law that outlines how the administration will interpret and enforce the law.

SOFT MONEY: Political campaign contributions donated directly to political parties for party-building activities that were banned by the Bipartisan Campaign Reform Act (BCRA), but that have been replaced by independent expenditures.

SPECIAL (SELECT) COMMITTEE: Usually temporary congressional committees formed for specific purposes, such as to investigate a particular issue. These committees rarely work on legislation and often focus on collecting data and examining potential policy options.

SPLIT-TICKET: A method of voting for candidates from different parties for various offices in the same election.

STANDING COMMITTEE: Permanent groups of legislators that continue from one Congress to the next that focus on all bills related to a particular policy area.

STARE DECISIS: The practice by courts of following established precedent in deciding subsequent cases.

STRAIGHT-TICKET: The practice of voting for one party's candidates for all offices on a ballot.

STRICT SCRUTINY: Legal doctrine that government actions that infringe on a fundamental liberty or affect a protected class of individuals—such as race or gender—must be based on a compelling government interest, be narrowly tailored to achieve that interest, and utilize the least restrictive method to achieve that interest.

SUPERDELEGATE: Individuals who are delegates to the presidential nominating convention who were not chosen by primary elections or caucuses. Superdelegates are typically members of Congress or party leaders who are free to vote for any candidate (as opposed to pledged delegates, who are not). Mostly associated with the Democratic nominating convention.

SUPPLY-SIDE THEORY: Economic theory that advocates the reduction of taxes, primarily on businesses and wealthy individuals, in order to stimulate investment in capital, which will stimulate job creation and economic growth.

SUPREMACY CLAUSE: A section of Article VI of the Constitution, which states that the Constitution and federal laws overrule any state laws.

TRUSTEE MODEL: The theory that the role of an elected representative is to vote based on his or her conscience in the best interest of society, even if this results in choices that do not please a majority of his or her constituency.

UNANIMOUS CONSENT: A procedure allowing a rule to be bypassed at the request of a senator with the approval of all 100 senators.

UNFUNDED MANDATE: A rule made by the national government that forces the states to comply with federal guidelines without offering money to help the states meet the requirement.

WAYS AND MEANS COMMITTEE: An influential standing committee in the House of Representatives responsible for reviewing all bills that would raise or lower revenue (taxes).

WINNER-TAKE-ALL METHOD: Under the Electoral College system, the candidate who wins the largest number of votes within a state (with a small number of exceptions) receives all of that state's electoral votes.

WRIT OF CERTIORARI (CERT): A legal document issued by the Supreme Court to a lower court to provide the case records for review when a case is selected to be heard on appeal.

PART II
CONTENT REVIEW

UNIT 1

FOUNDATIONS OF AMERICAN DEMOCRACY

Foundational Concepts and Documents

I. FUNDAMENTAL CONCEPTS OF AMERICAN GOVERNMENT

A. LIMITED GOVERNMENT - restrict to protect rights

The theory that the power of the government and political leaders would be restricted in order to protect natural rights was built into the Constitution by specifically listing the powers of government, the powers denied to the government, and the rights of the people. The following ideas represent various aspects of the concept of limited government:

1. **Natural Rights** - born w/i protected

   According to the Enlightenment-era philosophers such as John Locke, certain freedoms are guaranteed to all citizens. The authors of the Constitution believed that governments existed not only to provide order, but also to protect the natural rights of citizens. Natural rights are referred to as "unalienable Rights" in the Declaration of Independence.

2. **Popular Sovereignty** - government 4 the ppl

   The power and authority of government belong to the people.

   a. Popular sovereignty is evident in the Declaration of Independence with the phrase, "Governments are instituted among men, deriving their just powers from the consent of the governed."

   b. Popular sovereignty is found in the Constitution, specifically in the well-known opening phrase, "We the people."

Test Tip

A helpful way to remember the meaning of the term popular sovereignty:

> *Popular = people*
>
> *Sovereign = ruler*
>
> *Popular sovereignty = the people rule*

3. **Social Contract** - let gov. control you to keep ur rights

   The Enlightenment philosopher John Locke indicated that power and authority belonged to the people (popular sovereignty). As a result, Locke proposed, government existed because the people voluntarily gave up some power to the government in exchange for security in what he called a social contract. However, the government was required to protect the natural rights of the people. If the government failed to uphold the agreement, the people had the right to rebel. Locke's social contract represented a shift from the accepted theory of the time—the divine right of kings to rule. The social contract became the foundation of the argument presented in the Declaration of Independence.

4. **Republicanism** - B reps

   A system of government in which citizens vote for individuals to represent their interests and make decisions about policy. The term *republicanism* is essentially synonymous with representative or indirect democracy.

5. **Separation of Powers**

   The Constitution implements the concept of separation of powers by granting each branch of government specific areas of authority (power). This idea is based on the work of Enlightenment philosopher Baron de Montesquieu.

6. **Checks and Balances**

   The Constitution grants specific mechanisms to each branch of government for limiting the actions of the other branches. This is called checks and balances. The idea behind checks and balances is that when a written constitution gives each branch of government the authority to block actions by the other branches,

know chart

no one branch or individual accumulates too much power. Checks and balances is another democratic ideal that originated with Baron de Montesquieu and is related to the separation of powers.

7. **Federalism (Division of Powers)** *States ♈ Federal*

A system of government in which a constitution assigns different types of authority and responsibility to national and state governments. The Constitution created a government based on federalism, replacing the confederate style of government that existed under the Articles of Confederation.

8. **Rule of Law**

A system that holds all individuals, including leaders, accountable to the same laws, and which applies all laws to everyone regardless of their position. The foundation of the law is a document, the Constitution, as opposed to an individual, the king. Under such a system, every person, including government officials, is accountable to the law, and the process of justice is fair, equitable, and available to all citizens.

9. **Majority Rule and Minority Rights**

This concept addresses the possibility of tyranny by the majority— a situation in which a majority may oppress the minority. The Constitution protects minority rights from being violated, even when such violation is broadly supported by voters. The Bill of Rights, advocated by the Anti-Federalist movement and adopted shortly after the Constitution itself, establishes individual rights, or "liberties," as part of fundamental law. The Framers relied upon an independent judiciary (the courts) to enforce these protections.

Test Tip

The distinction between the terms **separation of powers** *and* **division of powers** *is frequently confusing for students.* **Separation of powers** *refers to the allocation of powers among the three branches of government (horizontally).* **Division of powers** *refers to the fact that powers are divided vertically, between federal and state (and local) governments. Pay attention to these terms in multiple-choice questions and use them correctly in the FRQs.*

B. FOUNDING DOCUMENTS

1. **Declaration of Independence**

   Signed by the Second Continental Congress, the Declaration of Independence announces the political separation of the colonies from Great Britain. Primarily authored by Thomas Jefferson, it is based significantly on the philosophy of John Locke and his ideas relating to natural rights and the social contract.

   a. Natural rights and the social contract are evident in the statement in the Declaration of Independence that

      all men are created equal, that they are endowed by their Creator with certain unalienable rights, that among these are Life, Liberty, and the pursuit of Happiness. That to secure these rights, Governments are instituted among Men, deriving their just powers from the consent of the governed.

   b. The Declaration goes on to proclaim a right to rebel against and replace an unjust government. It provides an extensive list of grievances, or "repeated injuries and usurpations" to justify the separation. For this reason, the Declaration is often referred to as a "breakup letter."

   c. The Declaration has served as the inspiration for numerous similar documents, including the Seneca Falls Declaration of Sentiments (1848) and the United Nations Universal Declaration of Human Rights (1948). It is regarded as the inspiration for many modern countries' founding statements.

2. **U.S. Constitution**

   The Constitution is a relatively brief document that sets out the structure and functions of this new republican form of government. It is frequently vague and lacking in detail. The Framers anticipated that future adaptation would be necessary to adjust this radical experiment in government to real-world conditions. Its simple provisions have been expanded and interpreted since its adoption. For this reason, the Constitution is often referred to as a "living document."

   <u>Preamble</u>

   This introduction to the Constitution states the six legitimate purposes of the government created in the document.

Article I: The Legislative Branch

This article creates a bicameral legislature, lays out electoral requirements and legislative procedures, and specifies the powers of Congress. *section 8: elastic clause, enumerated powers, powers denied*

Article II: The Executive Branch

This article defines the qualifications for office and describes powers and duties of the president. It describes the process for choosing the president through the Electoral College, the presidential oath of office, and the Office of the Vice President.

Article III: The Judicial Branch

This article creates the Supreme Court of the United States and defines its jurisdiction. It grants Congress broad powers with regard to creating and structuring lower federal courts.

Article IV: Relations Among States

state rights →

This article includes several key clauses that regulate relationships among the states, and between the states and the national government.

Article V: Amendment Process

This article reflects federalism by describing how the U.S. Constitution may be changed through proposal at the national level and ratification by the states. *2/3 congress or states vote*

Article VI: National Supremacy

supreme law →

This article states that federal laws and treaties are the highest law of the land and are binding on states. It requires that certain government officials swear an oath to support the Constitution and prohibits a religious test for holding office.

Article VII: Ratification Process

This article required nine states to initially ratify the Constitution in order for it to become effective as to those states.

3. **Amendments to the Constitution**

Amendments 1–10: The Bill of Rights

The first ten amendments were added to the document as a compromise to address the concerns of the Anti-Federalists. The Federalists, on the other hand, felt that individual rights were already protected by the state constitutions.

10 - reserves rights 2 states

<u>Amendments 11–27</u>

These amendments were added after the Bill of Rights and address the needs of a changing nation, procedural concerns, civil rights, and the expansion of suffrage.

A common mistake students make is confusing the Declaration of Independence with the Preamble to the U.S. Constitution. The Declaration describes unalienable (natural) rights: life, liberty, and the pursuit of happiness; and provides justification for the colonies to politically separate themselves from England. The Constitution creates and defines our government. The Preamble is the first paragraph of the Constitution, which lays out the purposes of the new government.

II. MODELS OF REPRESENTATIVE DEMOCRACY

The writers of the Constitution sought a compromise among the three main competing models of representative democracy: participatory democracy, pluralist democracy, and elite democracy. Democracy in the United States today includes elements of each of these theories.

A. PARTICIPATORY DEMOCRACY

1. This is a type of democracy that focuses on popular sovereignty and the idea that governmental authority should be in the hands of individuals selected by the people. Authority in a representative democracy is based on the will of the numerical majority in what is called majoritarianism. This type of democracy emphasizes the wide-ranging participation of citizens as individuals, rather than as group members or powerful elites.

2. The clearest example of participation in democracy is voting for public officials.

3. Citizens in democracies, however, have numerous options for participation in government, including engaging in political discussions, signing petitions, attending town hall meetings, contacting officials, and participating in various forms of political protest, such as demonstrations and walkouts.

B. PLURALIST DEMOCRACY

1. Pluralism is the idea that democracy should incorporate the influence of various groups of individuals with shared beliefs, without allowing any one group to dominate. Various groups compete for power and influence, but no one group is able to establish long-term control.

2. Pluralism today is evidenced by the large number of interest groups active in influencing policy because they are concerned about a particular issue or issues.

3. Interest groups today impact policy by donating to campaigns, lobbying, testifying at hearings, providing research, and helping to write laws.

C. ELITE DEMOCRACY

1. Elite democracy embodies the idea that government authority in a democracy tends to migrate to the hands of a small group of educated and wealthy individuals and reduce popular participation.

2. It can be argued that the influence of elites is reflected in the membership of our governmental institutions. Many members of Congress, for example, have a net worth of $1 million or more, and very few members come from a working-class background. Supreme Court justices are usually graduates of prestigious law schools.

D. THE CONSTITUTION AND MODELS OF DEMOCRACY

1. **Participatory Democracy** – voting

   a. The Constitution's method for selecting members of the House of Representatives, which has always been by popular vote, is a clear example of participatory democracy.

   b. The First Amendment enables participation by citizens because it protects freedom of speech, religion, assembly, press, and petition.

2. **Pluralist Democracy**

   a. The Constitution advances pluralism through a complex system of power-sharing. By spreading power among states and the three federal branches, the Framers intentionally created an environment in which competing groups could influence policy through different access points.

b. For example, advocacy groups for farmworkers, commercial farming interests, and consumers of agricultural products may advance their interests through different branches of state and federal governments. This ensures a process of give-and-take resulting in compromise, with no single group dominating.

3. **Elite Democracy** ~supreme court, senate originally

a. The method for selecting the president through the Electoral College, first established in Article II of the Constitution, provided originally for the selection by states of independent electors, who would take the citizens' wishes into consideration but vote conscientiously for the best choice of leaders. (This system has evolved so that electors are now determined by the popular vote in each state.)

b. Senators were originally chosen by state legislatures, not by popular vote. These legislatures were likely to be controlled by members of the elite class.

E. "BRUTUS NO. 1" AND MODELS OF DEMOCRACY

1. Participatory Democracy

Anti-Federalists favored participatory democracy. Their views were well-expressed in "Brutus No. 1," an essay written by the prominent Anti-Federalist Robert Yates of New York under the pen name "Brutus" in 1787. In the essay, he argued that creating a powerful central government would be a danger to personal liberty.

2. Pluralist Democracy

The essay argued that democracy is most effective if there are few competing factions. It warned that the large republic contemplated by the Constitution would involve far too many different interests (pluralism), which posed a threat to the interests of individual citizens.

In a republic, the manners, sentiments, and interests of the people should be similar. If this be not the case, there will be a constant clashing of opinions. . . . This will retard the operations of government, and prevent such conclusions as will promote the public good. [excerpted from "Brutus No. 1"]

3. Elite Democracy

Brutus argued that the large size of the republic would make the rulers under the proposed Constitution too distant from the interests of the people they represented, presenting an elitist threat to participatory democracy. The Anti-Federalists feared that the leaders would become elites who were not accountable to the people.

> In so extensive a republic, the great officers of government would soon become above the control of the people, and abuse their power to the purpose of aggrandizing themselves, and oppressing them. The trust committed to the executive offices, in a country of the extent of the United States, must be various and of magnitude. [excerpted from "Brutus No. 1"]

F. "FEDERALIST NO. 10" AND MODELS OF DEMOCRACY

1. Participatory Democracy

"Federalist No. 10" is an essay written by James Madison in *The Federalist Papers,* a collection of 85 essays and articles written by Madison, Alexander Hamilton, and John Jay to promote the ratification of the Constitution. In the essay, Madison pointed out that the principle of popular vote would prevent any group (faction) from dominating if it held less than majority support. "If a faction consists of less than a majority, relief is supplied by the republican principle, which enables the majority to defeat its sinister views by regular vote," he wrote in the essay. (It is noteworthy that only white, male property owners were permitted to vote under state laws at the time the Constitution was adopted.)

2. Pluralist Democracy

Madison was extremely concerned with the problem of factions, associations of people with common interests, which he realized were a threat to democracy. In these groups, he saw the possibility that fundamental rights and liberties could be violated. Madison found the solution to the problem of factions in two places.

a. Madison found the first solution to the factions problem in the effect of representative government by which highly qualified leaders make policy decisions (see item C, "Elite Democracy," in the "Models of Representative Democracy" section above).

b. Second, Madison argued that the problem of factions could be overcome through the creation of a large republic in which many groups compete for influence. Under such a system, no single group would be able to dominate the others.

> Extend the sphere, and you take in a greater variety of parties and interests; you make it less probable that a majority of the whole will have a common motive to invade the rights of other citizens. . . . [James Madison in "Federalist No. 10"]

Furthermore, the federalist framework allowed for concerns to be addressed at a local or national level, depending upon the issue involved.

3. **Elite Democracy**

Whereas elite democracy is often viewed negatively today, Madison believed that elites should have weighted influence in making public policy. This idea is reflected in his assertion that a republic (representative democracy) was superior to a democracy (direct or pure democracy) because educated and thoughtful people would be elected to make policy. He argued that a republic would

> refine and enlarge the public views, by passing them through the medium of a chosen body of citizens, whose wisdom may best discern the true interest of their country, and whose patriotism and love of justice will be least likely to sacrifice it to temporary or partial considerations. Under such a regulation, it may well happen that the public voice, pronounced by the representatives of the people, will be more consonant to the public good than if pronounced by the people themselves. [James Madison, in "Federalist No. 10"]

III. EVOLUTION OF CONSTITUTIONAL PRINCIPLES

A. THE ARTICLES OF CONFEDERATION

1. The Articles of Confederation was the newly independent colonies' first attempt at creating a central government. It established the government of the former colonies as a sovereign country by distributing power mainly among the 13 independent states with a weak central government. This government allowed the states to cooperate on some issues but remain independent.

> Each state retains its sovereignty, freedom, and independence, and every Power, Jurisdiction and right, which is not by this Confederation expressly delegated to the United States, in Congress assembled.

The said States hereby severally enter into a firm league of friendship with each other, for their common defense, the security of their liberties, and their mutual and general welfare, binding themselves to assist each other, against all force offered to, or attacks made upon them, or any of them, on account of religion, sovereignty, trade, or any other pretence whatever. [Article II, The Articles of Confederation, 1781]

B. **SHAYS' REBELLION**

1. Following the Revolutionary War, many farmers in Massachusetts found themselves burdened with crushing debt and facing the foreclosure of their property.

2. The government, under the Articles of Confederation, did not have the power to tax and, as a result, could not pay the veterans the money they were owed for their military service.

3. Daniel Shays led an uprising of farmers who were facing the loss of their land. The rebellion proved difficult for the government to control due to the lack of a standing military force.

4. Shays' Rebellion convinced leaders that a stronger national government was needed to maintain order and protect property.

C. **HOW THE CONSTITUTION ADDRESSED THE WEAKNESSES OF THE ARTICLES OF CONFEDERATION**

Weaknesses of the Articles of Confederation	How Addressed in the Constitution
Single-branch national government; no national executive to enforce laws or judiciary to settle disputes between the states.	Created a three-branch national government consisting of a legislative branch with power to make laws, an executive branch to enforce laws, and a judicial branch to interpret and apply laws.
Congress lacked power to tax and raise money to run the national government.	Congress was given the authority to tax and borrow.
Congress lacked the power to regulate interstate commerce, which led to an unstable and ineffective economy.	Congress was given the authority to regulate interstate and international trade.
Congress did not have the power to maintain an army and navy.	Congress was given the authority to raise and maintain military forces.

(continued)

Weaknesses of the Articles of Confederation	How Addressed in the Constitution
Unicameral Congress gave each state one vote regardless of population.	A bicameral Congress gave each state representation proportional to its population in the House of Representatives and equal representation (two seats per state) in the Senate.
A supermajority (two-thirds, or 9 of 13 states) was required in order to pass laws.	A simple majority of both houses was required in order to pass laws.
The Articles could not be amended without the unanimous support of the states.	Proposed amendments to the Constitution required a two-thirds affirmative vote in each chamber of Congress. Ratification of amendments needs affirmative votes from three-quarters of the states.

IV. WRITING THE CONSTITUTION: A BUNDLE OF COMPROMISES

between virginia & NJ plans

A. THE GREAT (CONNECTICUT) COMPROMISE

1. Balancing Large and Small States' Needs

   A fundamental issue in drafting the Constitution was resolving the question of how states should be represented in Congress. More populous states, led by Virginia, favored a scheme in which representation would be based on population. Smaller states, led by New Jersey, favored a plan that guaranteed equal representation for all states regardless of size. The Great Compromise incorporated both positions.

2. A Bicameral Congress

   a. In the Senate, power is distributed equally among the states, with each state holding two seats for a total of 100 senators.

   b. In the House of Representatives, representation is based on population.

      ➤ The total number of House seats is fixed at 435 today, and each state is allocated a proportion of seats according to its proportion of the population.

➤ The minimum number of seats a state may hold is one; there is no maximum.

B. THE ELECTORAL COLLEGE

1. The debate over the method for selecting the executive required a compromise among many competing interests and ideas.

   a. Some delegates feared that in the largely rural nation, in which information traveled slowly, voters choosing the executive through popular election would lack information about candidates and thus could be misled.

   b. Selection of the executive by Congress was rejected due to concerns about separation of powers because the executive could be controlled by the legislative branch.

   c. Selection of the executive by state legislatures was also a concern for delegates from small states, who feared that large states would dominate the process.

   d. Concerns about slavery were also at play. Many southern states, which had small, rural populations and large populations of slaves, saw a disadvantage in many of the proposals.

2. The compromise for choosing the executive was the creation of the Electoral College (a term not used in the Constitution), in which each state is entitled to a number of electors equal to its total number of seats in Congress (House seats + Senate seats). The electors chosen in each state would vote for the president and vice president.

3. The procedure for choosing electors would be left to the states.

4. The design of the Electoral College allowed the Three-Fifths Compromise to operate to the advantage of slaveholding states by amplifying their influence in selecting the president based on their slave populations.

C. SLAVERY AND THE CONSTITUTION

1. The existence of slavery was a formidable problem in negotiating a document acceptable to both free and slave states. Many citizens and leaders firmly opposed the toleration of slavery under the new Constitution, but it was widely agreed that achieving a union of all or most states was critical to the success of the young nation. Although the word "slave" appears nowhere in the document, the conflicting interests of slaveholding states and free states

required significant compromise in order to make the Constitution acceptable to all 13 states.

2. **The Slave Trade Compromise:** Slaveholding states feared that a strong new federal government would prohibit the slave trade. As a result, the Constitution included a provision denying Congress the power to act on the slave trade for 20 years.

3. **The Three-Fifths Compromise:** Because many states had significant numbers of slaves, the Great Compromise required the Framers to address the question of whether slaves would be counted as part of a state's population in determining representation in the House. The result was the Three-Fifths Clause, under which 60% of a state's slave population ("three-fifths of all other Persons") was calculated into its allocation of House seats.

D. AMENDMENT PROCEDURE

1. The Framers recognized that a major flaw in the Articles of Confederation was the inability of the document to be amended, or changed, without the unanimous approval of the states. At the same time, they recognized that the nation's foundational document should provide stability and should not be easily modified.

2. They settled on a system that would allow for amendment with supermajority approval at both the state and national levels.

   a. The Constitution established an amendment process in two stages: a proposal stage and a ratification stage.

   b. An amendment may be proposed by either:

   ➤ a two-thirds vote of both houses of Congress; or

   ➤ a national convention called by Congress at the request of two-thirds of state legislatures. (The second method has never been used.)

   c. A proposed amendment may then be ratified by either:

   ➤ approval by three-quarters of state legislatures; or

   ➤ approval by three-quarters of special conventions called by Congress in each of the states (The second method has been successfully used only once, in the adoption of the Twenty-First Amendment, which repealed the Eighteenth Amendment prohibiting liquor distribution.)

   d. The Constitution has been amended 27 times.

   e. Neither the president nor the federal courts have any
       constitutional powers or duties with regard to amendments.

AMENDING THE U.S. CONSTITUTION

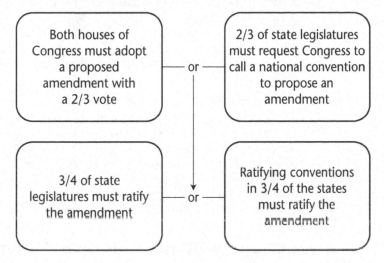

Both houses of
Congress must adopt
a proposed
amendment with
a 2/3 vote

— or —

2/3 of state legislatures
must request Congress to
call a national convention
to propose an
amendment

3/4 of state
legislatures must ratify
the amendment

— or —

Ratifying conventions
in 3/4 of the states
must ratify the
amendment

E. PRESENT-DAY CONSTITUTIONAL CONTROVERSIES

1. **Electoral College problems.** Presidents are not chosen by direct
    popular vote, but rather through the Electoral College system,
    under which states are allocated a number of votes not directly
    proportional to their populations. For this reason, it is possible for
    a candidate to win the popular vote but lose the Electoral College
    vote, a problem that occurs with increasing frequency as the
    population shifts within the United States. The Framers failed to
    foresee how population growth coupled with migration patterns
    would lead to states with increasingly different populations.

2. **Representation in the Senate.** In 1790, two years after the
    Constitution was ratified, there were substantial differences in
    state populations, with Virginia, the most populous state, having
    almost 10 times the population of Delaware, the least populous
    state. These differences meant that, under the Great Compromise,
    less populous states received power in the Senate that was vastly
    disproportionate to their shares of the population. As of 2019,
    Wyoming is the least populous state. California has the largest
    population, nearly 70 times that of Wyoming. As our population
    grows and moves, control of the Senate can be achieved with an

increasingly small minority of the population, resulting in counter-majoritarian policies.

3. **Reserved powers.** Because the Constitution required striking a balance between states' rights and a powerful national government, tension exists today regarding the appropriate role of the federal government in shaping policies not directly related to enumerated powers. Debate continues over how much influence the federal government should have regarding public education, civil rights, and environmental protections.

4. **Individual rights.** The Constitution creates compromises between the responsibility of the government to provide security ("provide for the common defense and ensure domestic tranquility") and the protection of natural rights, which are guaranteed in the Bill of Rights. This tension between liberty and order is present in the modern debate about the limits of government power to intrude into the privacy of individual citizens. The increased scrutiny of communications following the 9/11 attacks intensified this debate.

V. ALLOCATION OF POWER IN THE CONSTITUTION

A. SEPARATION OF POWERS

1. Separation of powers is the concept of creating independent branches of government and assigning to each a specific set of duties and powers. The reasoning is that, since each branch of government is limited in which powers it may exercise, no single branch can become too powerful. Separation of powers is intended to prevent authoritarianism.

2. The Framers created three branches of government: a legislative branch with the power to make laws; an executive branch charged with enforcing laws; and a judicial branch to interpret and apply laws.

B. CHECKS AND BALANCES

1. Separation of power created a problem: how to ensure one branch did not overpower the other two?

2. This solution was devised to allow each branch specific powers, or "checks," by which it could limit the actions of the other branches.

SOME IMPORTANT CHECKS AND BALANCES

Congress	
Checks Over President	**Checks Over Court**
passes laws which president is charged with enforcing	may change number and jurisdiction of federal courts
authorizes funding for agencies & programs (power of the purse)	sets lower federal court jurisdiction
veto override with 2/3 vote of both houses	may change number of justices on Supreme Court
Senate approval of presidential appointments (judicial & executive branch)	approval of judicial appointments
Senate approval of treaties (negotiated by president)	removal of judges through impeachment
removal of president by impeachment	initiating constitutional amendments
oversight of executive agencies	

President	
Checks Over Congress	**Checks Over Court**
legislative veto	appointment of federal judges
discretion with regard to enforcing legislation	discretion with regard to enforcing court decisions
executive orders	pardon power
executive agreements	
appealing to the people (bully pulpit)	

Supreme Court	
Checks Over Congress	**Checks Over President**
may declare laws unconstitutional (judicial review)	power to declare executive branch actions unconstitutional (judicial review)

*This does not represent an exhaustive list of checks and balances.

C. "FEDERALIST NO. 51"

1. Madison recognized that the success of the new government could not rest on the character or morals of individuals who might come to hold positions of power. He believed that controls on government power must be built into the system.

   > If men were angels, no government would be necessary. If angels were to govern men, neither external nor internal controls on government would be necessary. In framing a government which is to be administered by men over men, the great difficulty lies in this: You must first enable the government to control the governed; and in the next place, oblige it to control itself. [James Madison, "Federalist No. 51"]

2. Madison argued that separation of powers, along with checks and balances, would provide a way for "ambition to counteract ambition" by granting each branch of government weapons to effectively prevent self-interested abuses of power by the other branches.

3. Furthermore, Madison assumed that the legislative branch, with its lawmaking power, would be the most powerful of the branches, and therefore more problematic to control through external checks alone. He considered the bicameral structure of Congress to be an internal check, since each house would have distinct interests and legislative action would require agreement of both houses.

   > But it is not possible to give each department an equal power of self-defense. In republican government, the legislative authority, necessarily, predominates. The remedy for this inconvenience is, to divide the legislative into different branches; and to render them by different modes of election and different principles of action, as little connected with each other, as the nature of their common functions, and their common dependence on the society, will admit. [James Madison, "Federalist No. 51"]

You do not need to memorize quotes or passages from the required documents.

Instead, focus on being able to recognize key themes.

➤ *"Brutus No. 1" is an Anti-Federalist argument; it criticizes the Constitution because it creates a national government that has too much power, which is a threat to liberty.*

➤ *"Federalist No. 10" is a Federalist argument that the large republic created by the Constitution is the best defense against the problems created by factions.*

➤ *"Federalist No. 51" is a Federalist argument that the Constitution protects liberty by utilizing a system of checks and balances.*

Federalism

HOW THE FEDERAL AND STATE GOVERNMENTS SHARE POWER

A. FEDERALISM AND THE CONSTITUTION

1. Federalism is a system of government in which more than one government holds governing authority over people within the same territory at the same time. This system was devised by the Framers as a way to reconcile the demands and interests of many states into a single political entity. An important debate at the Philadelphia Convention in 1787 involved the sharing of powers between the state and national governments. While the general form of a federal government, featuring a division of power between state and federal levels, was broadly accepted, exactly how government power was to be divided had to be hammered out. In the end, some powers were granted by the Constitution to either the federal or state governments, while some powers were shared.

2. Exclusive powers are those powers that are held entirely by either the federal government or state governments. A power that is exclusively held by the federal government may not be exercised by the states, and vice versa.

3. Concurrent powers are those powers that are shared by the federal and state governments and may be exercised by both.

Examples of Powers Held by State & Federal Governments*

Exclusive Powers of Federal Government	Concurrent Powers	Exclusive Powers of State Governments
coin and regulate money	taxation	regulate education
conduct foreign relations	enact laws	regulate marriage
naturalization	define crimes and enforce punishments	regulate intrastate (within the state) commerce
declare war	establish courts ✓	establish local governments
maintain army and navy	borrow money ✓	conduct elections
regulate interstate and foreign commerce	charter banks and corporations	
establish postal system	build infrastructure (roads, dams, bridges, etc.)	
	exercise eminent domain	

*This list includes examples only and is not inclusive of all powers.

Conflicts often arise relating to state vs. federal power in specific areas. Questions about gun regulation and marijuana legalization, for instance, may lead to disagreement between state and federal laws. In these cases, the judicial branch determines which government holds authority in each particular circumstance. Considerations include the type of power in question and how the Constitution assigns (or denies) it, as well as the role of the Necessary and Proper Clause and the Supremacy Clause.

B. FEDERALISM IN PRACTICE

1. As with most aspects of government, the distinctions between exclusive and concurrent powers are not always clear. They are most commonly represented by two models or ideal types: dual federalism and cooperative federalism.

a. Dual federalism portrays power within the federal system as clearly delineated between those powers exercised by the federal government and those held by the states. Under this analysis, each level of government holds and exercises specific powers within its own sphere of influence, and there is very limited overlap between the spheres. Dual federalism is often called *layer cake federalism* because, like a layer cake, the layers are distinctly separate from each other.

b. The model of cooperative federalism envisions a system in which there is extensive overlap and interplay between state and federal exercises of power. In this view, the state and federal governments share concerns involving many of the same issues and policy areas, and often act, both independently and cooperatively, within the same spheres. This model is often referred to as *marble cake federalism*, to emphasize the complex interaction between the levels of government.

Test Tip

The history of the United States reflects an evolving view of the appropriate exercise of power by each level of government. Overall, the trend has been an expansion of federal power into state and local areas, although, during certain periods, the ideal of dual federalism has been favored.

2. Federal Grants (Grants-in-Aid). A primary avenue through which the federal government has extended its influence into state and local matters has been through the use of grants. These are transfers of money from one level of government (in this case, federal) to another to be used for a specified purpose. Federal grants may take several forms, some of which come with many requirements attached, some with few.

   a. Categorical grants are grants of money to state and local governments that must be used in compliance with highly specific instructions.

   b. Block grants are transfers of money to state and local governments given for broad purposes with few strings attached.

   c. Federal revenue-sharing was a practice under which the federal government collected taxes nationally and then distributed a portion of that national tax revenue to state and local governments without specific policy requirements attached. It was implemented in 1972 and reflected a movement away from what was perceived as the burdensome requirements of categorical grants. It was argued that local officials were in a better position than federal officials to determine how best to address issues on a local level. From a federal enforcement perspective, such a program was also easier and more efficient to administer. The revenue-sharing program was discontinued in 1986.

d. Mandates are federal directives that generally require the recipient state or local government to comply with specific requirements in return for federal aid money. In other words, the grant of money is *conditional* on the recipient's compliance with specific federal requirements.

   ➤ Some mandates may be unfunded. An unfunded mandate is one that imposes duties and associated costs on state or local governments without providing federal money to cover those costs.

e. Federal incentives are monies offered to state and local governments and individuals for various purposes that serve the national interest.

Models of Federal Assistance to State and Local Governments

	Key Features	Examples
Categorical Grant	– money transferred between levels of government – recipient must comply with specific requirements	– Head Start program grants provide money for early childhood education. – Medicaid program provides healthcare funding for eligible low-income families and individuals.
Block Grant	– money transferred between levels of government – recipient must comply with only broad purpose; few requirements	– Community Development Block Grant from the U.S. Department of Housing and Urban Development – The Temporary Assistance to Needy Families (TANF) program provides a block grant to states to provide limited financial support for low-income families.

	Key Features	Examples
Revenue Sharing	– revenue collected by federal government and transferred to state and local governments – spending at discretion of local officials	– 1986 revenue-sharing grants ranged from $201 for the smallest town to $41,957,530 for New York City
Mandate	– federal rule that imposes an obligation on state or local government – frequently associated with receipt of federal funding	– The Civil Rights Act of 1964 outlawed discrimination based on race, color, religion, sex, or national origin. – The National Minimum Drinking Age Act of 1984 conditioned receipt of federal highway funding on state compliance with raising the drinking age to 21.
Unfunded Mandate	– federal rule that imposes an obligation on state or local government without providing funds to help pay associated costs	– The Americans with Disabilities Act of 1990 prohibits discrimination against disabled Americans and requires states to comply with costly access requirements. No federal funds are provided.

Test Tip

Expect to encounter questions asking you to differentiate between block and categorical grants. In the case of a block grant, the states must spend federal funds on a broadly defined area of policy. For example, transportation block funds could be used for building roads, airports, train systems, or ports. However, with a categorical grant, states must use the money for a more specific policy area such as a categorical transportation grant that can only be used for building airports.

3. *Devolution* is a federal effort to return authority temporarily to the states, including decisions about administering federal programs and spending federal money.

C. MULTIPLE ACCESS POINTS

1. An important concept with regard to both separation of powers as well as federalism, is the idea of access to power, or the ability of citizens to influence policy through multiple avenues. In this context, an *access point* is a place where individuals or groups can interact with government to affect government actions.

2. The separation of powers among the three branches of government creates numerous access points by giving each branch specific powers and making each branch responsible to the public in specific ways.

Examples of Access Opportunities*

Legislative Branch	Executive Branch	Judicial Branch
– Citizens vote for representatives whom they believe will represent their political views and interests.	– Citizens vote for an executive whom they believe will represent their political views and interests.	– Citizens vote for judges at the state level.
– Citizens share opinions with their legislators in many ways, such as phone calls, emails, social media, and town hall meetings.	– Citizens share opinions with the executive through phone calls, emails, and social media.	– Citizens may file lawsuits to enforce or dispute laws or regulations.
– Interest groups lobby legislators on behalf of their members.	– Citizens and interest groups interact with various agencies to influence regulatory policy.	– Interest groups may file *amicus curiae* briefs to influence court decisions.

*This chart is not intended to include all of the many ways citizens and groups can access government.

3. The federal system allows for citizens to impact policy at both the state and federal government levels. The 50 state governments replicate the federal structure, allowing access to three branches at both levels of government.

II. THE EVOLUTION OF FEDERALISM

A. HOW POWER IS DIVIDED BY THE CONSTITUTION

1. Several sections and clauses within the Constitution address the sharing of power between the federal and state governments, but it is not always clearly defined. Under the federal system, states generally hold broad lawmaking authority within their borders, so long as they do not contradict federal law or infringe on individual rights. The power relationship between the state and federal governments has changed over time through several mechanisms, especially court decisions, and continues to evolve.

2. **Article 1, Section 8.** This section of the Constitution lists 17 specific (enumerated) powers of Congress, including the power to tax, the power to borrow on the credit of the United States, and the power to maintain military forces. This specific and rather narrow list reflects the concept of limited government. Congress was intended to be limited in its exercise of power to the 17 specific areas described.

3. **Necessary and Proper Clause.** The list of specific powers in Article 1, Section 8 concludes with the Necessary and Proper Clause. This clause grants Congress the power to "make all Laws which shall be necessary and proper for carrying into Execution the foregoing Powers. . . ." In other words, Congress holds powers, which are not specified in the Constitution, that may be reasonably related to the use of those powers that are listed. These are known as implied powers. It would be futile to try to list a power for everything Congress might need to do in order to effectively exercise its enumerated powers. For example, maintaining military forces involves contracting for the manufacture of weapons, procuring housing and food for troops, providing education, and numerous other actions not specified in the Constitution. The Necessary and Proper Clause allows these and thousands of other (not enumerated) powers to be exercised by Congress.

Remember that the Necessary and Proper Clause is called the Elastic Clause because it expands the power of Congress.

4. **Regulate Interstate (and Foreign) Trade.** One of the most expansive powers listed in Article 1, Section 8 is the power of Congress to regulate interstate (and foreign) trade. This authority is found in the Commerce Clause, which grants Congress the power to "regulate Commerce with foreign Nations, and among the several states, and with the Indian Tribes . . .." (Commerce is the movement of goods and services in an economy.) This brief clause has been the subject of intense controversy and has served as the primary basis for the expansion of federal power.

   a. Note that the Constitution gives Congress the power to regulate *interstate* commerce, or business between and among the states, but not *intrastate* commerce, the regulation of which is a power retained by the states.

   b. Because it can be very difficult to determine what economic transactions are interstate versus intrastate, this power has been interpreted very broadly. With a few notable exceptions, most commercial activities have been found by the Court to be a part of the stream of interstate commerce.

Test Tip

Scenarios in which the power of the federal government is expanded are very frequently related to the commerce power (through the Necessary and Proper Clause). This power has been used to prohibit discrimination, regulate controlled substances, prohibit human trafficking, and many other activities that do not obviously relate to interstate commerce. Also, when you see the term **interstate,** *think of commerce power!*

5. **Article IV: Relations Among States**

   a. The Full Faith and Credit Clause requires states to accept the public acts, records, and judicial outcomes of the other states. For example, if two people are married in one state, their marriage must be recognized by the other states.

   b. The Privileges and Immunities Clause prohibits states from discriminating unreasonably against citizens of other states. For example, a state's police force may not focus exclusively on out-of-state drivers for ticketing, but a state may charge higher tuition rates to out-of-state students, who do not support the state's university system through their taxes.

   c.   Extradition is the return of a fugitive from justice from one state to another. This is guaranteed by Article IV.

   d.   Congress admits new states to the union and governs U.S. territories.

   e.   The federal government must intervene militarily to protect states when needed.

6. **Article VI: Supremacy**

   a.   The Supremacy Clause makes clear that the Constitution and all laws and treaties made by the federal government take precedence over state laws.

   b.   All state and federal officers must swear by oath or affirmation to uphold the Constitution, but religious requirements are prohibited as a requirement for holding office.

7. **The Tenth Amendment** states that "[t]he powers not delegated to the United States by the Constitution, nor prohibited by it to the States, are reserved to the states respectively, or to the people." This amendment represents a counterweight to the broad interpretation of the Necessary and Proper Clause, and is critical to understanding the states' rights arguments that historically tend to arise when states oppose a particular national policy. The Supreme Court does not have a strong tradition of recognizing specific rights or powers as belonging to the states. However, at times the Tenth Amendment has been referenced in decisions limiting federal power, and it is generally the basis for arguments asserting that specific powers are held by the states.

8. **The Fourteenth Amendment**, adopted in 1868 following the Civil War, has also had a profound impact on the allocation of power between the states and the federal government. Conceived to address the oppression of former slaves by southern state governments, its adoption was a requirement for those states' readmission to the union and congressional representation. Section 1 defines citizenship and guarantees due process and equal protection to all persons. Specifically, the amendment prohibits any state from depriving any person of due process or equal protection. The Due Process Clause of the *Fourteenth* Amendment (not the Due Process Clause of the *Fifth* Amendment) has been used by the Supreme Court to prohibit states from infringing upon most rights guaranteed to citizens by the Bill of Rights, which was previously interpreted as solely limiting the power of the federal government.

Constitutional Clauses Related to Federal and State Power

Constitutional Section or Clause	What It Says	How It Affects the Distribution of Government Power
Article I, Section 8	– lists 17 specific enumerated powers of Congress	– limits power of federal legislature (Congress)
Necessary and Proper Clause	– grants numerous additional unspecified powers to Congress if needed to carry out 17 enumerated powers	– expands power of Congress (Elastic Clause)
Commerce Clause	– grants Congress the power to regulate interstate and foreign trade	– expands power of Congress through Necessary and Proper Clause because "interstate commerce" is so broad
Supremacy Clause	– states that the Constitution and federal laws and treaties are the supreme law of the land	– limits state power by prohibiting states from acting contrary to federal laws and treaties
Tenth Amendment	– reserves all rights not explicitly granted by the Constitution to the federal government to the states	– enhances state power; limits federal power
Fourteenth Amendment	– Due Process Clause requires states to ensure due process of law – Equal Protection Clause requires that states afford equal treatment to all persons	– prohibits states from violating individual rights guaranteed by the U.S. Constitution – prohibits unequal treatment based on group membership

B. THE SUPREME COURT AND THE EVOLUTION OF FEDERAL POWER

1. *McCulloch v. Maryland* (1819)

Questions around federal power and the extent of the Necessary and Proper Clause arose early in United States history. *McCulloch* was a result of Maryland's attempt to impose a tax on the Second Bank of the United States. The cashier of the Baltimore branch, James McCulloch, refused to pay the tax. The Supreme Court held that the power to establish a national bank was implied by the enumerated powers of Congress. The case produced two important rulings with regard to federal/state power sharing:

a. **Facts of the Case:** In 1816, Congress chartered the Second Bank of the United States, which was the target of significant political opposition. Several states enacted anti-Bank laws. Maryland's law placed a tax on all banks operating in the state that were not chartered by the state. This tax was aimed squarely at the federal Bank. When the Bank failed to pay the tax, Maryland sued the Bank and its cashier, James McCulloch.

b. **Constitutional Issue(s):** Does the federal government have the constitutional authority to charter a national bank? If so, does the state of Maryland have the authority to tax the bank?

c. **Holding(s):** The federal government does have the constitutional authority to charter a national bank. States do not have the authority to tax a federal bank.

d. **Reasoning:** The establishment of a national bank is a legitimate exercise of congressional power under the Necessary and Proper Clause of Article I. The Constitution grants Congress several powers, including the power to borrow, tax, coin money, and regulate commerce, that may be facilitated through a national bank. Although the establishment of a bank is not one of Congress's specifically enumerated powers, it is clearly within the category of actions anticipated by the Necessary and Proper Clause. The national bank is a helpful and appropriate means for Congress to implement its enumerated powers. Furthermore, under the Supremacy Clause, the state of Maryland did not have the authority to tax the bank. "[T]he power to tax involves the power to destroy." According to the Supremacy Clause, the state of Maryland may not impede the legitimate actions of the federal government.

Test Tip

McCulloch v. Maryland is important because it is the foundational case broadly interpreting the scope of the Necessary and Proper Clause. The Court held that the Necessary and Proper Clause granted Congress implied powers, which it may use to carry out its enumerated powers. Secondarily, the Court relied on the Supremacy Clause to invalidate the state law to tax the national bank, which contradicted the federal law chartering the bank.

2. *United States v. Lopez* (1995)

    a. **Facts of the Case:** Alfonso Lopez was a twelfth-grade student who carried a gun and ammunition into his Texas high school. He was convicted of violating the federal Gun-Free School Zones Act of 1990 which made it illegal "for any individual knowingly to possess a firearm [in] a school zone." He was sentenced to six months in prison and an additional two years of probation.

    b. **Constitutional Issue(s):** Does the federal government have the authority to regulate firearms through the Gun-Free School Zones Act within the states under the Commerce Clause?

    c. **Holding(s):** No, the Commerce Clause does not allow Congress the power to regulate the carrying of handguns within states and the Gun-Free School Zones Act is unconstitutional.

    d. **Reasoning:** The Court held that the Gun-Free School Zones Act was unconstitutional because Congress lacked the power to regulate the carrying of handguns within states under the Commerce Clause. The court ruled that the law was criminal in nature and not related to commerce or economic activity.

    e. *United States v. Lopez* marked a departure from the Court's willingness, throughout most of the 20th century, to accept a very broad range of activities as legitimate subjects of regulation by Congress under the commerce power. Lopez marks the limit of commerce power.

Test Tip

On the AP® exam you will be asked about two required cases related to federalism: McCulloch v. Maryland *(1819)* and United States v. Lopez *(1995). The Supreme Court in* McCulloch v. Maryland *ruled in favor of an expansion of federal power, but in* United States v. Lopez *the Court ruled in favor of states' rights. The overall trend in the late 20th century was for the courts to side with the federal government, but since the ruling in the* Lopez *decision, the Supreme Court has been less consistent.*

UNIT 2

INTERACTIONS AMONG BRANCHES OF GOVERNMENT

Chapter 5

The Legislative Branch

I. POWERS OF CONGRESS

A. Congressional authority is limited to those powers enumerated, or expressed, in the text of the Constitution. They may also be referred to as delegated powers. The enumerated powers of Congress are found in Article 1, Section 8.

B. Additionally, congressional power extends to legislation that is necessary and proper in order to effect policy under one or more of the enumerated powers. The Necessary and Proper (Elastic) Clause allows Congress to make laws related to a wide range of public policy issues using its implied powers.

Powers of Congress

Enumerated Power	Description	Examples of Implied Powers
1. The power to tax and spend.	Congress may collect money through taxes and may spend money to pay down the national debt, provide for the common defense and general welfare of the United States.	– Every year, Congress creates and approves a budget for federal expenditures. – Congress provides funding for medical care programs for the elderly (Medicare) and persons whose income falls below a minimum threshold (Medicaid). – Federal funds are used for infrastructure projects, such as roads, bridges, and dams.

Continued →

Powers of Congress (continued)

Enumerated Power	Description	Examples of Implied Powers
2. To borrow money on the credit of the United States.	Congress may borrow money that the United States is then obligated to repay.	– The U.S. Treasury Department issues marketable securities (such as bonds) that guarantee a specific return.
3. To regulate commerce with foreign nations, among the several states, and with the Indian tribes (Commerce Clause).	Congress may make rules and laws to protect and promote the economic health of the United States as it relates to the stream of economic activity among the states and with other countries.	– The Civil Rights Act of 1964 allowed the federal government to prohibit discrimination based on race, color, religion, sex, or national origin. – Congress may ban the production of marijuana (Controlled Substances Act).
4. To establish uniform rules for naturalization and to establish a uniform system of bankruptcy.	a. Congress creates rules and procedures for non-citizens to acquire United States citizenship. b. Congress creates a system of bankruptcy, which allows individuals or corporations to discharge their debts when they cannot pay.	– Federal law prohibits the granting of U.S. citizenship to persons advocating world communism or the violent overthrow of the United States government. – The Bankruptcy Abuse Prevention and Consumer Protection Act of 2005 was passed in order to protect creditors. It places restrictions on people and companies filing for bankruptcy.
5. To coin money and regulate its value.	Only the national government may make U.S. currency. This function is carried out by the United States Mint.	– In 1791, the federal government chartered a federal bank to produce a standard form of currency.

Enumerated Power	Description	Examples of Implied Powers
6. To provide for the punishment of counterfeiting the coin or securities of the United States.	In order to protect the value and integrity of U.S. currency, Congress has enacted criminal laws to try and punish counterfeiters.	– Crimes relating to the crime of counterfeiting include possession or passing of a counterfeit document or possessing counterfeiting tools.
7. To establish post offices and post roads.	Congress may create and fund a system of post offices for the distribution of mail.	– Numerous federal crimes, such as fraud and mailing controlled substances, relate to illegal uses of the postal service.
8. To promote science and the useful arts by guaranteeing to scientists, inventors, authors, and artists the exclusive right to profit from their creation for a period of time.	Congress has created protections for various types of intellectual property, including copyrights, patents, and trademarks. The purpose is to encourage technological growth and cultural expression.	– Under Title 35 of the U.S. Code, patent holders may sue violators for patent infringement. – Internet file sharing without the permission of the copyright holder is a crime under federal law.
9. To create lower federal courts.	Congress may and has created numerous federal courts below the United States Supreme Court.	– Congress may set judicial salaries, make administrative decisions about the location and operations of courts, and fund judicial administration.

Continued →

Powers of Congress (continued)

Enumerated Power	Description	Examples of Implied Powers
10. To define and punish piracy, crimes committed on the high seas, and offenses against the Law of Nations.	Danger on the seas has always presented a threat to national security and commercial traffic. Congress has also been historically concerned with upholding international law.	– The Foreign Sovereign Immunities Act creates guidelines for when foreign governments or their agents may be sued in U.S. courts. – The Torture Victim Protection Act allows torture victims to file suit against foreign governments in U.S. courts.
11. To declare war	Only Congress may declare war on another country. The president, however, may commit military forces without congressional authorization under the War Powers Act.	– The War Powers Act clarifies the relationship and powers of Congress v. the president with regard to use of the armed forces.
12. To raise and support an army; and 13. To raise and support a navy. 14. To administer the armed forces. 15. To make rules for calling forth the militia as necessary. 16. To organize, arm, and discipline the militia.	– Congress holds the power to establish and maintain a military force. The power to fund military activities is an important check on the executive branch. – The militia (local groups of armed volunteers) were considered part of the national defense apparatus at the time the Constitution was written.	– Congress has created other branches of the military to carry out specialized functions. Examples include the Air Force and the Coast Guard. – The GI Bill (Servicemen's Readjustment Act of 1944) funded educational benefits for veterans and their families.

Enumerated Power	Description	Examples of Implied Powers
17. To govern the territory of the seat of the U.S. government.	This provision removed control of the seat of the federal government (what would become Washington, D.C.) from any state. It required that the seat of the U.S. government would be a separate territory, governed directly by Congress.	– The District of Columbia Home Rule Act (1973) allocated direct governing responsibility for the District of Columbia to an elected mayor and city council.

C. Inherent powers are those held by Congress that are neither enumerated nor implied. This category can be defined as those powers that obviously and automatically belong to the government of every sovereign state. They are understood to inherently (by nature) belong to every nation's government. Examples include the powers to:

   1. control national borders

   2. acquire new territory

   3. put down revolutions

D. The Constitution, in Article I Section 9, specifically prohibits the national government taking certain actions that are referred to as denied powers. For example, Congress is denied the authority to:

   1. tax exports

   2. pass ex post facto laws or bills of attainder or violate the Bill of Rights

   3. suspend habeas corpus other than during times of rebellion or invasion

   4. grant titles of nobility

E. Article I, Section 9, also contains the Emoluments Clause, which states that federal officials may not "accept of any present, Emolument, Office, or Title, of any kind whatever, from any King, Prince, or foreign State," without the approval of Congress.

   1. An emolument is a payment or any thing of value.

   2. The prohibition is broadly interpreted as barring any gift or thing of value "of any kind whatever."

F. In addition, the Constitution, in Article I Section 10, outlines the specific powers that are denied to the states. The states may not:

1. tax imports or exports

2. pass ex post facto laws, bills of attainder, or violate the Bill of Rights

3. make treaties with other nations or declare war

4. print money

5. grant titles of nobility

Test Tip

The many names for the different types of powers are often confusing for students (and teachers!). Enumerated, or expressed, powers are those that are specifically listed in the Constitution. These are also sometimes called delegated powers, because they were delegated or given to the federal government by the states. The term implied powers refers to the thousands of powers that are not explicitly listed in the Constitution, but that are suggested by those powers that are listed. Also, keep in mind that every implied power must be reasonably related to one or more of the enumerated powers. If Congress wants to claim an implied power under the Necessary and Proper Clause, it must be clearly related to at least one enumerated power. Many implied powers are based on multiple enumerated powers.

II. CONGRESSIONAL STRUCTURE AND ELECTIONS

A. SENATE

1. Senate Qualifications to Serve

   a. 30 years old

   b. 9 years' citizenship

   c. residency in the state represented

2. Term length: 6-year term (<u>S</u>enate = <u>S</u>ix); there are no limits on the number of terms that a senator may serve.

3. Senators are elected at-large, that is, they are elected by voters throughout an entire state. Senators serve as representatives of

all people living within the geographic boundaries of their state, rather than as representatives of smaller divisions within the state.

4. Rather than hold elections for all 100 Senate seats every 6 years, the Framers designed a staggered election scheme in which one-third of Senate seats are up for election every 2 years. This concept created a continuous body, a system that promotes stability by ensuring that at least two-thirds of the membership would not change in any given election cycle.

B. HOUSE OF REPRESENTATIVES

1. House Qualifications to Serve

    a.   25 years old

    b.   7 years citizenship

    c.   residency in state (not district) in which their district is located

2. Term length: 2-year term; there are no limits on the number of terms a representative may serve.

3. Unlike the Senate, the House is not designed as a continuous body; all 435 seats are up for election every 2 years. Since most members are reelected, massive membership changes do not generally occur.

4. Representatives (also sometimes called Congress members) are elected from single-member districts within states. They represent the residents of their districts.

C. CONGRESSIONAL DISTRICTS

1. The Constitution directs that each state shall receive in the House a number of seats proportional to its share of the population. Beyond this, states have the reserved power to determine the "Times, Places and Manner of holding Elections for Senators and Representatives."

2. The number of House seats allocated to each state is recalculated every 10 years, based on the census count. The census is a national survey designed to quantify and collect data on the United States population.

3. Following each census, the number of House seats allocated to each state is reapportioned, or redistributed, based on the percentage of the population living in each state. States may gain or lose seats.

4. Each state legislature then divides the state into congressional districts, a number of geographical areas with roughly equal populations, corresponding to the number of House seats held by the state. For the least populated states, with only one House seat, the district is the entire state.

5. State legislatures have broad discretion in how district boundaries are constructed. Districts must be roughly equal in population and drawn based on racial considerations that are subject to strict scrutiny.

6. Because state legislatures draw district maps, a party holding a majority in a given state legislature may draw the map to its advantage. That is, a majority party in a state legislature may manipulate district boundaries to elect to Congress a disproportionate number of members of that party. This practice is called gerrymandering.

7. Gerrymandering is based on two basic principles: packing and cracking. Packing is the process of creating districts that include a large proportion of opposition voters, limiting their voting power by concentrating them in one or a small number of districts. Cracking is the process of spreading opposition voters among many districts, preventing them from having a majority in any of them.

8. Some states use independent commissions to conduct the process of redistricting and avoid partisan gerrymandering.

Test Tip

*Be sure you know and understand the difference between reapportionment, redistricting, and gerrymandering. **Reapportionment** is the redistribution of the 435 House seats among the 50 states following the census. **Redistricting** is the drawing of new district boundaries within states. **Gerrymandering** is redistricting in such a way as to create an advantage for a party.*

D. THE SUPREME COURT AND GERRYMANDERING

1. *Baker v. Carr* (1962)

   a. **Facts of the Case:** The district boundaries for the state legislature in Tennessee in the 1950s were based on outdated census data that did not reflect population shifts. As a result, there were substantial differences in the population sizes of each district, with rural districts having smaller populations than urban districts. The 7 constitution required redrawing districts every on population shifts, but that requirement had not been followed. This resulted in malapportionment, or the creation of voting districts with significantly unequal populations. Because the votes of residents of different districts were of unequal weight in selecting political representation, Charles Baker, a resident of an urban district, argued that he and other voters in his district were being denied "equal protection" guaranteed by the Fourteenth Amendment.

b. **Constitutional Issue(s):** Does a Fourteenth Amendment equal protection challenge to a legislative districting plan represent a political question, which cannot be decided by the Court?

c. **Holding:** A Fourteenth Amendment equal protection challenge to the constitutionality of a districting plan does not present a political question. The federal district court may hear the case.

d. **Reasoning:** A political question is one that may not be decided by the courts for a variety of reasons. For example, the Constitution may grant final authority on a matter to another branch of government, or the courts may not be able to offer an appropriate remedy (solution). Although the Court had previously declined to decide the merits of cases related to redistricting, here the Court held that the issue of malapportionment did not present a political question. Because the case had been dismissed by the District Court without a trial, the Supreme Court did not consider whether the Tennessee districting scheme actually violated the plaintiffs' rights in this case. Importantly, *Baker v. Carr* established the precedent that districting plans could be challenged as a violation of the Equal Protection Clause of the Fourteenth Amendment, leading to the "one person, one vote" principle later articulated in *Reynolds v. Sims* (1964), which stated that electoral districts in state legislatures must be equal in population. The equal population precedent would later be applied to congressional districts in *Wesberry v. Sanders* (1964).

2. *Shaw v. Reno* (1993)

a. **Facts of the Case:** Following the 1990 census, North Carolina gained one seat in the House of Representatives, and a new congressional district map was drawn consisting of 12 districts. Under the Voting Rights Act of 1965, states, counties, and municipalities with a history of racial discrimination in voting rules were required to obtain the approval of the United States Attorney General before implementing new voting rules, including new congressional districts. (This provision of the Voting Rights Act of 1965 is no longer in effect.) In this case, North Carolina attempted to create two *majority-minority districts*, or districts in which a racial minority (African Americans) would compose more than half of the district. One of these districts was 160 miles long, primarily following a highway. The district bisected several existing communities and was, in some places, only as wide as the highway it followed. Five white voters sued, claiming that the district was drawn based on racial motivation in violation of the Equal Protection Clause.

b. **Constitutional Issue(s):** Does a plan of congressional redistricting drawn with the purpose of favoring a racial minority group violate the Equal Protection Clause of the Fourteenth Amendment?

c. **Holding:** Congressional districts drawn solely on the basis of race violate the Equal Protection Clause of the Fourteenth Amendment.

d. **Reasoning:** Although racial considerations may be a legitimate concern in many state-level decisions, efforts to segregate the voting public based on race alone may be divisive and have unintended negative consequences. The drawing of district boundaries based solely on race is a violation of the Fourteenth Amendment. The test for determining whether a district is based on race alone is whether its design can be reasonably understood as being based on other factors.

> **Note:** In *Rucho v. Common Cause* (2019), SCOTUS ruled that *partisan* gerrymandering claims (those involving districts drawn purely to advantage a political party) are political questions and may not be decided by federal courts. Federal courts may address districting cases involving population disparities (*Baker*) and racial gerrymandering claims (*Shaw*) because these violate Equal Protection guarantees. Partisan gerrymandering claims are nonjusticiable because a judicially manageable standard for resolving such claims does not exist. Furthermore, the Constitution assigns responsibility for districting decisions to state legislatures and Congress.

Test Tip

Expect to encounter questions asking you to differentiate between the two required Supreme Court cases related to redistricting and the Equal Protection Clause of the Fourteenth Amendment:

➤ **Baker v. Carr (1962):** *Courts may hear cases involving redistricting, leading ultimately to the one person one vote rule that district populations be roughly equal.*

➤ **Shaw v. Reno (1993):** *Race may not be the only factor in drawing district boundaries.*

III. HOW CONGRESS FUNCTIONS

A. UNIQUE POWERS AND DUTIES OF EACH CHAMBER

1. Although both houses have similar legislative duties and follow broadly similar procedures, the Framers allocated to each house of Congress specific duties related to its unique nature.

2. The Senate represents broader constituencies (entire states) and offers more experience and stability, while House members are regarded as being closer, and therefore more responsive, to the people.

**Unique Constitutional Powers and Duties
of the Senate and the House of Representatives**

Senate	House of Representatives
ratifies treaties with a two-thirds vote	initiates all revenue bills (taxes)
conducts trials of impeached officials (needs a two-thirds vote for removal from office)	has the authority to charge officials with impeachment by a majority vote
chooses the vice president in case the Electoral College fails to produce a winner	chooses the president in case the Electoral College fails to produce a winner
ratifies presidential appointments (e.g., judges, ambassadors, cabinet secretaries) by majority vote	

B. THE COMMITTEE SYSTEM

1. The vast majority of the work related to the development of legislation is the result of work in congressional committees, especially standing committees.

2. Every member of Congress is assigned to at least one standing committee. Long-term participation in specific standing committees allows members of Congress to develop expertise around particular policy areas.

3. Note that the majority party holds a majority of votes in every committee, and a member of the majority party is always the chair of each committee.

4. Committees also conduct hearings related to both the lawmaking and oversight functions of Congress.

Committees in Congress

Type of Committee	Functions
Standing (permanent)	Permanent groups that continue from one Congress to the next and focus on all bills related to a particular policy area. Membership in standing committees allows members to develop expertise around specific issues. Examples: Agriculture, Armed Forces, Budget, Education, Foreign Relations, Judiciary, Veterans Affairs
Subcommittee	Smaller specialized divisions of larger committees that are created to divide the work and more efficiently work out details in bills.
Joint (permanent)	A limited number of committees with members from both chambers that have limited authority and frequently handle administrative housekeeping tasks or keep tabs on specific policy areas. They inform Congress, but do not introduce legislation. Examples: Joint Economic Committee, Joint Committee on the Library of Congress, Joint Committee on Taxation
Conference (temporary)	Temporary groups composed of members of both the House of Representatives and the Senate created to reconcile different versions of the same bill. This is necessary because bills must pass the House and Senate with identical wording.

Type of Committee	Functions
Select or Special (generally temporary)	Usually temporary groups formed for specific purposes such as to investigate a particular issue and that rarely work on legislation. Often focus on collecting data and examining potential policy options. Some select committees are more permanent in nature such as the ones on Aging, Ethics, and Intelligence.

Examples: The Watergate Select Committee (officially the Select Committee on Presidential Campaign Activities, established in 1973) and the House Select Committee on Energy Independence and Global Warming, which existed from 2007–2011. |

Test Tip

It is important that you are familiar with a few of the important standing committees in Congress. There will definitely be questions related to them on the exam.

Important Standing Committees in Congress

House of Representatives	Senate
Rules: responsible for putting bills on the calendar; setting limits for the amount of time for debate; and specifying whether amendments can be added	**Armed Services:** oversees issues relating to the military and Department of Defense
Ways and Means: responsible for reviewing all bills that would raise or lower revenue (taxes)	**Foreign Relations:** plays a key role in establishing international policy, evaluating treaties, and approving appointments related to foreign policy and diplomacy
Judiciary: responsible for beginning the process for impeachment of federal officials	**Judiciary:** responsible for the initial steps in the confirmation of all federal judges

C. LEADERSHIP

1. Before each new Congress convenes, the Democratic Caucus and the Republican Conference (membership of each party in each house) meet to select leaders and committee chairs. Leadership positions in Congress are then determined by strict party votes. The majority party holds all of the key leadership positions, including committee chairs, and the majority party has the most members on every committee. The leadership teams of each party work to advance the party's platform and coordinate deal-making efforts when issues result in a division within the party or within the House or Senate.

2. **Leadership of the House of Representatives**

   a. The presiding officer is the Speaker of the House, who controls the calendar, sets the agenda, and assigns bills to committees. The Speaker is second in the order of presidential succession according to the Twenty-Fifth Amendment.

   b. The majority floor leader manages the legislative process and coordinates the party strategy to get bills important to the party caucus passed.

   c. The majority whip assists the party by building coalitions, counting potential votes, and influencing members to vote with party leadership. No vote is held before the whip informs party leadership of the likely outcome.

   d. Committee chairs are the powerful leaders of the standing committees who have the power to kill a bill by not reporting it to the full House.

   e. The minority party leadership consists of a minority party floor leader and a minority whip that coordinate the legislative strategy of the party out of power.

3. **Leadership of the Senate**

   a. The presiding officer of the Senate, according to the Constitution, is the president of the Senate, who is also the U.S. vice president. The position of president of the Senate is largely ceremonial. The U.S. vice president appears in the Senate on opening day and for the State of the Union Address, and casts a vote only in the instance of a tie.

   b. The president pro tempore ("for the time") presides over the Senate in the absence of the vice president (almost always) and is third in the order of presidential succession, after the vice president and the Speaker of the House. This largely symbolic role is typically given to the longest- of the majority party.

c. The most powerful position in the Senate is t leader, who schedules legislation and coordinate party strategy along with the majority whip.

d. Committee chairs are the leaders of the standing committees who have the power to kill a bill by not reporting it to the full Senate.

e. The Senate minority party leadership consists of a minority party floor leader and a minority whip that coordinate the legislative strategy of the party out of power.

IV. THE LEGISLATIVE PROCESS: HOW A BILL BECOMES A LAW

A. Bills may only be introduced by members of Congress. (The president may not introduce legislation; he or she may only request that Congress do so.) Both houses follow similar procedures in processing legislation. Each house, however, has its own unique rules and procedures, so the path that legislation follows from introduction to passage can vary widely.

1. Bills may be introduced in either house, although revenue bills, those that propose to generate government income through the imposition of taxes or fees, must constitutionally be introduced first in the House.

2. Members of the House introduce bills by putting them into the *hopper*, a box on the floor of the House. In the Senate, bills are introduced by submission to clerks on the Senate floor.

3. A bill must be passed by each house of Congress in identical form before it may be submitted to the president to be signed into law.

4. Incumbent members of both houses derive an advantage in campaigning for re-election as a result of their ability to direct federal funds to their states and districts. The practice of generating legislation that produces income for their districts is known as *pork barrel spending*, as it is often excessive and unnecessary, but proves a member's ability to "bring home the bacon."

5. The term *logrolling* refers to trading votes, or "you vote for my bill and I will vote for yours." This practice is a feature of both chambers.

B. In both houses, bills are next assigned to the standing committee with the appropriate jurisdiction and subject matter expertise to evaluate and work on the bill. Occasionally, most often in the House, multiple committees may work on parts of bills.

C. **Committee Consideration**

    1. Committee chairs set each committee's agenda. That is, they decide which bills the committee will attempt to pass through Congress during the session. Committees are always chaired by a member of the majority party in the chamber.

    2. For practical and political reasons, most bills are not reported by the committee. Bills that are not placed on a committee's agenda (or pigeonholed) normally die in committee. In the House, a bill can be removed from committee and brought directly to the floor using an instrument called a discharge petition, which requires majority support of the full membership. The process is rarely successful, however, as it requires disloyalty to the party agenda on the part of at least some majority party members.

    3. Committee action generally begins with a hearing, during which policy experts and interested parties may give testimony about the subject under consideration. Hearings inform members of Congress, the press, and the public about proposed legislation and its impact. Committee members, of course, also seek input on legislation from other sources.

    4. Subcommittees—smaller, more specialized subgroups within committees—may play roles in revising proposed bills.

    5. A *markup* follows. This is a meeting in which the committee discusses the proposed legislation, makes changes, and produces a final draft for floor consideration. The bill that comes out of the committee may be essentially the same as the original bill, or it may be substantially rewritten in committee.

D. Following committee consideration, bills are placed on calendars for floor debate. This is done through different mechanisms in each house, but in both cases, the process is directed by the majority party.

E. Procedures for debating and passing bills on the floor of each chamber are similar. In both houses, a quorum, or a majority of the membership, must be present in order to conduct business. Each chamber, however, has its own set of procedural rules. Following are the most significant differences in debate between the two houses of Congress.

1. **House Procedures**

   a. Procedures in the House, because of its membership size (435), are more formal and debate more limited than in the Senate.

   b. Most bills are considered under the suspension of the rules procedure, which limits debate to 40 minutes, does not allow members to propose amendments to bills, and requires two-thirds approval for passage of legislation.

   c. Other bills are debated under a special rule created by the House Rules Committee, sometimes called the traffic cop committee of the House.

   d. Each special rule sets forth specific limitations on debate for the bill in question, including time limits and restrictions on offering amendments.

   e. After a special rule is adopted, the House generally considers the bill as the Committee of the Whole. That is, the entire House becomes a committee, allowing for consideration of amendments under a more relaxed and efficient set of rules. (This procedure also allows for work to take place without a quorum present.) The Committee of the Whole then reports to the full House of Representatives (itself) where amendments may be adopted and the bill voted on.

   f. In the House, some votes may be taken by voice (members vote "aye" or "nay" in response to the question, and the Speaker announces the winner of the vote), but most votes are taken via an electronic voting system, which records each member's vote.

2. **Senate Procedures**

   a. Procedures in the Senate are characterized by less formality than those of the House. In fact, there is no formal limit on debate in the Senate, which proudly considers itself to be the most democratic body in the world.

   b. In terms of legislative procedure, the Senate must first agree to bring a bill to the floor, usually through unanimous consent.

c. Because Senate rules do not allow for a simple majority to terminate debate, senators may engage in a filibuster. The filibuster is a tactic by which one or more senators may threaten to extend debate on an issue to prevent a vote. A senator signals the intent to filibuster by placing a hold—a request to delay floor debate—on a bill.

d. Originally, a filibuster would bring a halt to Senate business through sustained debate. Starting in 1970, however, Senate rules were changed to create a two-track system, under which the chamber could consider other business while filibustered bills are pending.

e. A filibuster may be ended using cloture, a procedure under which debate may be terminated by a 60-vote supermajority. The practical effect of these procedures, particularly in a partisan environment, is that bills frequently require sixty votes for passage in the Senate.

f. Votes may be taken by voice, standing, or by roll call, in which each senator's vote is on the record.

Test Tip

You may encounter a question that requires you to identify constitutional powers unique to each house. Be aware that most House and Senate procedures and rules, e.g., filibuster, cloture, Committee of the Whole procedures, Rules Committee procedures, discharge petitions, and others, are not discussed in the Constitution. How the houses of Congress conduct business is only broadly described in the Constitution. For unique constitutional powers of each house, see the "Unique Constitutional Powers and Duties of the House and the Senate" chart earlier in this chapter.

F. Before a bill can become law, it must be passed in identical form in both houses. Most often, however, House and Senate versions of a bill have differences, which must then be reconciled. This is done in a conference committee, a committee made up of members of both houses who work out a compromise bill that can be passed in identical form in both houses.

G. Once a bill has been passed in identical form in both houses, it goes to the president for a signature. There are four possible scenarios at this point.

1. If the president signs the bill, it becomes law.

2. The president may veto the bill, or refuse to sign the bill and return it to Congress with an explanation of his or her objections. A veto may be overridden by a two-thirds vote of both houses. In the event of an override, the bill becomes law without the president's signature. Otherwise, the bill dies.

3. The president may refuse to sign or veto the bill, in which case it will become law in 10 days without his or her signature.

4. If Congress adjourns within the 10-day period, however, the bill dies. This is called a pocket veto.

Comparing the Senate and the House

	Senate	House of Representatives
Representation	states	population
Membership	100	435
Election	at-large	single-member districts
Qualifications	30 years old 9 years' citizenship resident of state	25 years old 7 years' citizenship resident of state
Term Length	6 years	2 years
Unique Powers	advice & consent: ratifies treaties, confirms judicial appointments, confirms other executive appointments, conducts impeachment trials	revenue bills, brings impeachment charges, chooses president in event of Electoral College failure
Debate Rules	filibuster, cloture, holds, unanimous consent	Rules Committee, Committee of the Whole, discharge petitions
Procedures	less formal	more formal
Partisanship	less partisan	more partisan
Policy Focus	focus on foreign policy	focus on taxes and revenues
	proposed amendments to bills generally do not need to be related to bill content	proposed amendments must be related to bill content

Questions that ask you to integrate material from different units are common on the AP® exam, so be aware of these relationships as you study. Also, certain themes, or principles, are applicable to many areas of content. For example, be prepared to describe examples of majoritarian and pluralist features of Congress today.

Majoritarian examples:

- *A majority (of those present) is required for the passage of a bill in the House and Senate.*

- *Quorum in the form of a majority is needed for debate and vote.*

- *The majority party in each chamber holds the chairs of all committees and dominates the legislative process.*

Pluralist examples:

- *Lawmaking often depends on compromise between competing interests through logrolling, bargaining, and coalition building.*

- *Pork barrel legislation benefits only specific groups rather than the majority.*

- *The filibuster allows minority interests in the Senate to have a greater influence.*

- *Standing committee memberships and the formation of iron triangles leads members to focus on specific policy areas and influences them to support specific interests.*

V. THE FEDERAL BUDGET

A. BUDGET PROCESS

1. Working with the executive branch, Congress must generate a budget each year to fund all of the activities, programs, and services carried out by the federal government. The budget includes three broad categories of spending.

   a. Discretionary spending, or federal agency spending, is funding for various agencies and programs, which the government is not obligated to fund to a certain level. Congress has discretion, or the ability to decide how much federal money should be spent. Discretionary spending accounts for about one-third of federal spending.

b. Interest on the national debt, which Congress must pay and cannot change, generally makes up less than 10 percent of the budget.

c. Mandatory spending is spending required by law. It includes Social Security, Medicare, veterans' benefits, and other entitlements, or benefits to which certain people are guaranteed by law, and makes up over half of all funding.

2. The Office of Management and Budget (OMB): The OMB, part of the executive branch, begins the budget process by reviewing all of the monetary requests from each of the federal agencies and combining them into the president's proposed budget. The OMB estimates, based on taxes and spending, whether the government will have a surplus or budget deficit and sends the proposed budget to Congress. Although Congress has the power to reduce entitlements, this is extremely politically difficult and rarely done.

3. Congressional Budget Office (CBO): The CBO, which was created by Congress, analyzes the president's proposed budget and provides economic data to Congress.

4. Congressional Review: Standing budget committees in each chamber make changes and create budget resolutions. Budget resolutions are passed by each house.

5. House and Senate versions of the budget go to conference committee for reconciliation (compromise).

6. The budget resolution is not a law. It provides guidelines or goals for spending. Spending bills, also called appropriations bills, are passed to fulfill the budget targets.

7. Appropriations bills are then sent to the president for approval.

B. FACTORS INFLUENCING THE BUDGET

1. All money the government spends must come from either revenue (government income, mostly produced by taxes) or borrowing (the government takes on debt).

2. Each annual budget passed by Congress produces either a surplus (the government spends less than it is generating in revenue) or a deficit (the government spends more than it is generating in revenue).

3. A defining feature of the modern budget process is the tension between mandatory spending, which increases over time, and discretionary spending.

4. As entitlement costs increase, discretionary spending must decrease unless taxes are raised, or the government is willing to take on more debt.

5. Reducing discretionary spending is unpopular because discretionary spending pays for many important programs that benefit citizens and businesses.

6. Taking on debt is politically difficult because both debt and interest must be paid in the future and this may hamper economic growth.

7. Raising taxes is unpopular.

Test Tip

Students are sometimes confused by the relationship between "deficit" and "debt." A budget deficit is the amount by which the government's expenditures exceed its revenues in a given year. The national debt is the total amount the government owes. Each year of deficit spending contributes to the national debt.

VI. IDEOLOGY IN THE POLITICAL PROCESS

A. IDEOLOGICAL DIVISIONS (PARTISANSHIP)

1. Members of Congress usually try to support their political party's goals if possible, and partisanship in Congress has been increasing.

2. Congress is organized by political party. The majority party leaders dominate the workings of Congress and ensure most benefits come to majority party members.

B. DIVIDED GOVERNMENT

1. When the majority party in Congress is different from the party of the president, it is often difficult to pass legislation, resulting in gridlock.

2. The president may convince members of Congress to compromise on legislation because it is unlikely that Congress would have the two-thirds supermajority needed to override a veto.

C. COALITIONS IN CONGRESS

1. Coalitions are formed when groups and individuals within Congress join together to advance a set of policy goals that they could not successfully promote alone. Coalitions may be based on ideology, economics, geography, or other factors. Winning alliances are able to place issues on the legislative agenda and guide their policies through Congress.

2. Coalitions tend to form more readily in the Senate than in the House. This is due in part to term lengths. House members count on being re-elected every two years and may be more hesitant to displease their constituencies, which may be more partisan. Senators, on the other hand, serve for six years, and they serve entire states, which may encompass greater diversity of opinion.

D. VIEWS OF THE PROPER ROLE OF A REPRESENTATIVE

1. **Delegate:** A member of the House or Senate votes based on the preferences of the majority of his or her constituents. This view reflects participatory democracy.

2. **Trustee:** A member of the House or Senate votes based on his or her conscience in the best interest of society, even if this results in choices that do not please a majority of his or her constituency. Members of Congress may have more access to information about issues from hearings and debate and may be better informed than their constituents. This view reflects elite democracy.

3. **Politico:** This model is a hybrid of the trustee and delegate models of representation. A member of the House or Senate follows the preferences of his or her constituents (delegate model) or his or her conscience and informed decision (trustee model), depending on the issue and the degree of public concern about a particular policy decision.

Test Tip

Members of Congress may not always be acting on some combination of the delegate and trustee models. You may encounter questions relating to the motivations of legislators in various situations. Be aware that lawmakers are also influenced by the goals of their political party (partisanship) and the effect of interest groups. However, be cautious of answers that appear cynical (distrustful of the integrity or sincerity of a person or thing). For example, legislators are not "bribed" by interest groups; interest group campaign donations help them to gain "access" to lawmakers.

The Executive Branch

ARTICLE II OF THE CONSTITUTION

A. **THE EXECUTIVE**

1. Article II of the U.S. Constitution creates and defines the executive branch of the federal government.

2. Section 1 states that "the executive Power shall be vested in a President of the United States of America," which forms the basis for most of the formal and informal powers of the president.

3. Section 1 outlines the process for choosing the president through the Electoral College, and not by direct popular vote.

B. **QUALIFICATIONS AND TERMS**

1. The Constitution mandates that a president meet three specific qualifications.

   a. Natural-born citizen (born on U.S. soil or born to a parent who is a citizen)

   b. 35 years of age

   c. 14 years of residency in the United States

2. The president and the vice president serve four-year terms. Although the original Constitution placed no limit on the number of terms an individual could serve, this was limited by passage of the 22nd Amendment.

C. **COMPENSATION AND OATH OF OFFICE**

1. Congress determines the salary of the president. Congress may not raise or lower the salary of a serving president.

2. The Constitution spells out the oath of office for the presidency in which the elected individual may either choose to swear or affirm.

"I do solemnly swear (or affirm) that I will faithfully execute the Office of President of the United States, and will to the best of my Ability, preserve, protect and defend the Constitution of the United States."

D. REMOVAL FROM OFFICE

1. The president, vice president, and other civil officers can be removed from office through impeachment and conviction.

2. Article II provides that "[t]he President, Vice President, and all civil Officers of the United States shall be removed from Office on Impeachment for, and on Conviction of, Treason, Bribery, or other high Crimes and Misdemeanors."

   a. The role of the House in impeachment is to bring charges. Once articles of impeachment are passed by the House, the officer charged has been "impeached" (but not convicted).

   b. The role of the Senate in impeachment is to conduct a trial. In the event of impeachment of the president, the Chief Justice of the Supreme Court presides over impeachment trials in the Senate.

   c. The impeachment trial results in conviction or acquittal. Conviction requires a two-thirds vote of the Senate.

   d. The penalty for conviction on impeachment charges is removal from office.

   e. The term "high Crimes and Misdemeanors" is a traditional legal term meaning any serious crime.

3. Only two presidents have been impeached (Andrew Johnson and Bill Clinton). Neither was convicted and removed from office.

E. OFFICE OF THE VICE PRESIDENT

1. According to the Constitution, the duties of the vice president include serving as the president of the Senate (largely ceremonial and usually a role served by the president pro tempore), breaking any tie votes in the Senate, helping to decide questions of presidential disability (Twenty-Fifth Amendment), and taking over the presidency if the president is unable to finish his or her term.

2. Informally, the role of the vice president is determined by the president and can involve either a domestic or international focus, often serving ceremonial purposes.

3. The vice president often plays a role in the election process, and presidential candidates often choose running mates that differ from them in areas such as geographic region, party subgroup, or experience in order to balance the ticket and expand their electoral appeal.

II. ROLES AND POWERS OF THE PRESIDENT

A. PRESIDENTIAL ROLES

1. **Chief Executive:** The president directs the activities of the several million federal employees to implement and carry out federal laws.

2. **Chief of State:** The president is a symbol of the nation, representing the American people to the world.

3. **Chief Legislator:** The president plays a leading role in setting the country's legislative agenda by attempting to successfully shepherd his or her party's policy initiatives through Congress.

4. **Chief Diplomat:** The president conducts relations with the other countries of the world and sets U.S. foreign policy agenda.

5. **Commander-in-Chief:** The president holds decision-making authority and operational control over all branches of the armed forces.

6. **Party Chief:** The president is the de facto leader of his or her political party, leading in policy development and electoral strategy.

B. PRESIDENTIAL POWERS

1. Each president takes office with a policy agenda, a set of policies that he or she would like the government to pursue. Accompanying the president's roles are numerous powers, both formal and informal, that he or she may use to attempt to achieve adoption of his or her policy agenda.

2. Formal powers are also called constitutional powers, because they are areas of authority granted to the president by the Constitution.

   a. **Executing the Law:** The president is charged with taking care that laws be faithfully carried out (executed). The president oversees the fulfillment of legislation passed by Congress and manages relevant agencies and programs.

b. **Appointing Power:** The president appoints candidates (often with Senate approval required) for public office, including:

➤ the heads of executive departments and their top aides

➤ the heads of independent agencies

➤ ambassadors and other diplomats

➤ all federal judges

➤ U.S. marshals and attorneys

c. **Recess Appointments:** The president may appoint people to fill administrative vacancies that occur when Congress is not in session. This type of appointment is called a recess appointment because it occurs when Congress is in recess. These appointments are not permanent; they last until the end of the next congressional session or until the Senate confirms a replacement.

d. **Requesting Written Opinions:** The president may request the written opinion of government officials.

e. **State of the Union:** The president must periodically address Congress to report on the country's needs and conditions. The State of the Union address is given annually (by tradition) to a joint session of Congress, normally in late January or early February. Presidents use this opportunity to generate support for their policy agendas.

f. **Power to Recommend Legislation:** The president may recommend legislation to Congress. Note that this is a "soft" power. The president may not demand or require that any particular legislation be introduced or enacted.

g. **Power to Convene Congress:** The president may convene Congress. That is, he or she may call Congress into session while it is in recess.

h. **Power to Adjourn Congress:** The president may adjourn Congress in cases where the two houses cannot agree on a time of adjournment. This power has never been exercised by the president.

i. **Veto Power:** The president may veto legislation passed by Congress. (Congress may override with a two-thirds vote.)

The line item veto is a long-debated power, but not currently held by the president. This power would allow the president to cancel individual spending items in a budgeting or appropriations bill, thereby vetoing part, but not all, of the bill. Its purpose is to allow the executive to reduce wasteful spending (pork) by Congress. Although Congress granted this power to the president by statute in 1996, it was struck down as unconstitutional in **Clinton v. City of New York** *(1998). Many state governors have this power.*

j. **Commander-in-Chief Power:** The president serves as commander-in-chief of the armed forces. That is, he or she is the supreme commander of all branches of the United States military. Civilian control of the military is a critical feature of liberal democracy. The actual extent of the president's military powers has been a subject of contention throughout our history.

➤ The Constitution grants Congress the power to declare war, but names the president as the commander-in-chief of the armed forces.

➤ The War Powers Resolution of 1973 (also known as the War Powers Act) was enacted in response to growing congressional concern about presidential overreach in use of the military, both during the Korean War and the Vietnam War. The law, which was passed over Nixon's veto, includes the following requirements:

— The president must inform Congress within 48 hours of committing military forces to action.

— If Congress does not authorize the action within 60 days, forces must be withdrawn.

— An additional 30 days are allowed for the troops to make a safe withdrawal.

k. **Treaty Power:** The president may make treaties with other countries. This requires approval by a two-thirds vote of the Senate.

Test Tip

Remember that the Senate alone approves treaties and appointments (not Congress as a whole; the House has no role in these procedures). Treaties must be approved by a two-thirds vote of the Senate. Presidential appointments of cabinet officers, ambassadors, federal judges, and other officials may be approved by a simple majority (51%).

l. **Recognition Power:** The president receives ambassadors, which means that the president chooses whether to formally recognize a foreign government. Recognition simply means that the United States acknowledges the legitimacy, or legal basis, of a government and agrees to do business with it. The United States recognizes many governments that are not democratic or that do not meet modern western standards in other respects, such as individual rights and freedoms.

m. **Pardon Power:** The president may grant pardons (legal forgiveness) for federal crimes, except in cases of impeachment. The president's formal pardoning power can take several forms, including individual pardons, amnesty, commutations, and reprieves, which all serve as checks on the judicial branch. Presidents may only pardon federal offenses, and not crimes charged under state laws.

➤ **Pardon:** An order from the president granting a person release from punishment and total legal forgiveness for a crime. The only exception to the pardon power involves cases of impeachment. The most famous pardon was granted by President Ford to former President Richard Nixon for any misconduct related to the Watergate affair. Ford justified his actions by expressing a desire for closure, saying, "It could go on and on and on, or someone must write the end to it. I have concluded that only I can do that, and if I can, I must." Nixon had resigned to avoid impeachment, thereby allowing for a pardon from Ford.

➤ **Amnesty:** Amnesty allows the president to grant pardons to a group of individuals all convicted of the same crime. For example, President Carter granted amnesty to all of the individuals who avoided the draft during the Vietnam War, either by not registering or leaving the country.

➤ **Commutation:** The power of a president to reduce the punishment (e.g., time in jail, fines) without removing the guilty verdict of the courts.

      ➤ **Reprieve:** The power of the president to delay punishment, without removing the guilty verdict of the courts.

3. Informal powers are those powers not explicitly granted by the Constitution. Article II of the Constitution states that "[t]he executive power shall be vested in a President of the United States of America." Known as the "Vesting Clause," this clause, along with the directive requiring the president to ensure that the laws are faithfully executed, forms the basis for the president's informal powers.

    a. **Executive Orders:** In many circumstances, the president may issue executive orders, directives that have the force of law.

      ➤ Executive orders are normally used in the process of carrying out the president's duties—for example, by enforcing the Constitution or legislation passed by Congress.

      ➤ Executive orders are often used when Congress refuses to enact the president's agenda or negotiate a solution.

      ➤ Some presidents have issued executive orders that seem to exceed their constitutional authority or contradict the legislature.

      ➤ Congress has several checks on the use of executive orders, including the ability to refuse to fund these directives or to invalidate them through the passage of legislation.

      ➤ Executive orders may be challenged in the courts as well. They may be found unconstitutional or in conflict with federal law (judicial review).

    b. **Signing Statements:** When signing a bill into law, a president may issue a written statement offering his or her interpretation of the law and how it is to be executed.

      ➤ Signing statements are advisory in nature and do not have the force of law.

      ➤ Signing statements give presidents the opportunity to express their interpretations and plans for execution of laws to the public and the legislative branch.

      ➤ Signing statements may be used by a president to indicate disapproval of all or part of a bill in the event that a veto would likely face an override.

> ➤ Signing statements are not mandatory. Most legislation is not accompanied by a signing statement.

c. **Executive Agreements:** Presidents may make executive agreements with heads of government of other countries.

> ➤ These agreements are similar to treaties, but do not require Senate approval.

> ➤ They are typically made under the authority of an existing treaty to deal with bureaucratic issues and minor details.

> ➤ Occasionally, a president may conclude significant international business in the form of an executive agreement.

> ➤ Since executive agreements are not approved by the Senate, they may be altered or canceled by subsequent presidential administrations. They may also be altered or canceled by heads of state in countries that are party to the agreement.

d. **Removal Power:** Generally, the president has the power to remove, or dismiss, without cause, any high-level federal official that he or she has the power to nominate. Although not mentioned in the Constitution, it has been inferred from the appointment power and the power to execute the law. Supreme Court rulings have placed restrictions on the president's ability to fire various types of executive officers, especially without cause. The president does not have the power to dismiss federal judges, or the heads of regulatory commissions.

e. **Power of Persuasion:** The president's central role in the federal government requires that he or she is at the center of constant negotiations. The president is expected to demonstrate bargaining skills and to persuade other members of the executive and legislative branches to support his or her party's policies.

f. **The Bully Pulpit:** The president has the ability to speak directly to the American people at will, which is an important informal power. The term "bully pulpit" was coined by Theodore Roosevelt to refer to the presidency as a highly visible position that could be used to speak out and persuade. Note that "bully" in the usage of the early twentieth century was used as an adjective meaning "excellent," or "superior." A pulpit, of course, is an elevated position from which preachers speak.

g. **Global Leader:** The president is recognized as an important global leader, holds discussions with other world leaders, and builds international coalitions.

h. **Crisis Manager:** The president is required to respond to crises, both international and domestic. The president's role as crisis manager provides the opportunity to enhance his or her reputation, power, and agenda.

i. **Emergency Powers:** Presidents have claimed various emergency powers to deal with situations of rebellion, war, and terrorism. These have included the suspension of habeas corpus (Lincoln), internment of Japanese Americans (Franklin D. Roosevelt), and holding enemy combatants without trial (George W. Bush).

Presidential Powers

Type of Power	Formal	Informal
Executive	– execute laws – nominate officials – request written opinions – make recess appointments	– executive orders – signing statements – crisis manager – emergency powers – removal power
Legislative	– give State of the Union address – recommend legislation – call special sessions – adjournment – veto	– bargaining/negotiation bully pulpit
Foreign Policy/Military	– command military (Commander-in-Chief) – make treaties – nominate ambassadors – recognize diplomats and foreign governments	– executive agreement – bargaining/negotiation – world leader – meets with heads of foreign governments – coalition builder – crisis manager
Judicial	– nominate judges – pardon federal crimes, except involving impeachment	

Be aware that various sources use different names for types of presidential powers, which can be confusing. The two main categories of presidential powers are:

➤ formal or constitutional powers, which are defined in the Constitution

➤ informal or inherent powers, which are not spelled out in the Constitution, but based on the Vesting Clause and the president's duty to execute laws passed by Congress

III. EXECUTIVE INTERACTIONS WITH CONGRESS AND THE COURTS

A. DIVIDED GOVERNMENT/POLICY CONFLICTS

1. Each president enters office with a policy agenda, or set of initiatives, which he or she would like Congress to enact into law. In the event that Congress is uncooperative, the president may sometimes enact his or her preferred policies through executive orders.

2. The president often clashes with Congress over a policy initiative or executive order. This happens most frequently when one or both houses of Congress are controlled by the opposition party to the president (divided government).

3. Although the president's position is the most untenable when both houses of Congress are controlled by the opposition party (often resulting in gridlock), each house also has specific areas of authority which it may use to impede the president's agenda.

    a. With sufficient opposition in both houses, the president's policies, including executive orders, may be countered by the passage of legislation. The president's veto of legislation may be overridden by a two-thirds vote in both houses. Sometimes the threat of an override may be sufficient to dissuade the president from using the veto.

    b. The House holds unique powers to restrain the president's agenda, including limiting taxation and spending (power of the purse).

    c.   Unique powers of the Senate to check the president include the ability to refuse to confirm appointments and treaties.

B. THE SENATE AND PRESIDENTIAL APPOINTMENTS

1. The president has the responsibility of appointing thousands of federal officials, including the heads of the executive departments, federal judges, military leaders, and many other categories of employees within the federal bureaucracy. About 1,200–1,400 of these positions require Senate approval.

2. When a new president takes office, he or she has the formidable task of immediately appointing qualified individuals to thousands of positions. Most significant are the positions that form the president's team: the top leadership of the executive departments (the president's cabinet), the staff of the Executive Office of the President, and other high-level positions.

3. The level of Senate scrutiny applied to presidential nominations can vary with the type of appointment. Higher-level, critical appointments, such as Supreme Court justices, receive the most intense examination and may involve Senate hearings and investigations.

4. Senate confirmations may be more contentious when the Senate is not controlled by the president's political party.

    a.   Generally, the president has the right to assemble his or her own administrative team. The Senate has traditionally shown considerable deference to the president's choices for top-level administrative officials, particularly White House staff, regardless of party.

    b.   The president's cabinet includes the heads of the 15 executive departments and various other officials, including top intelligence officers. The role of the cabinet is to serve as an advisory body to the president. Cabinet members are generally afforded considerable deference by the Senate in recognition of their key roles in the president's executive responsibilities. Very rarely is this type of appointment seriously challenged in the Senate.

    c.   The president appoints ambassadors, top-level diplomats assigned to conduct relations with foreign governments. Ambassadors are often political appointees who have supported the president's election campaign financially, but lack diplomatic or other relevant experience. In spite of this, ambassadors are almost always confirmed.

C. JUDICIAL APPOINTMENTS

1. Judicial nominations, particularly those for the Supreme Court, receive the highest levels of Senate scrutiny. This is true because federal judges receive life tenure and may only be removed through the impeachment process.

2. For presidents, the appointment of federal judges is an important power, as it gives them the ability to install like-minded individuals who will continue to influence policy for decades to come.

3. In Supreme Court confirmation hearings, nominees are questioned regarding their political views and their positions on high-profile issues. Judicial nominees with extremely liberal or conservative views are less likely to be confirmed, particularly when the Senate is controlled by the other party.

4. Although not in the Constitution, the custom of senatorial courtesy requires that any judicial nomination for a district (trial level) judge must be acceptable to senators of the president's party from the state where the judge will serve. Note that this is a custom, or tradition, and not a rule or law, but one that has a long history and is generally followed.

5. Prior to 2013, all presidential appointments were subject to filibuster, effectively requiring 60% support for approval. In that year, a Democratic-controlled Senate, frustrated by Republican filibusters of President Obama's judicial nominees, changed the rule. (The filibuster is a Senate rule, not a law or constitutional procedure.) The new rule allowed approval of presidential appointments by a simple majority, with the exception of Supreme Court justices. In 2017, a Republican-controlled Senate, facing a filibuster of Trump Supreme Court nominee Neil Gorsuch, changed the rules so that a simple majority vote would be sufficient to confirm Supreme Court nominees.

6. The Senate has increasingly sought input from interest groups during judicial confirmation hearings, especially for appointments to the Supreme Court. For example, the American Bar Association (an interest group for lawyers) has published ratings for potential judges as Highly Qualified, Qualified, or Not Qualified.

7. During judicial confirmation hearings (particularly those for Supreme Court nominees), senators frequently ask probing questions of nominees to elicit information regarding their judicial philosophies and political tendencies (liberal or conservative). Often referred to as litmus tests, these are questions about controversial and polarizing issues, which can be utilized as a kind

of shorthand to describe the judge's political viewpoint and to anticipate how he or she would rule on a variety of issues.

8. The Constitution gives the Senate the power to reject a presidential nominee to the federal courts, including the Supreme Court. But can the Senate refuse to even consider a presidential nominee? In 2016, Supreme Court Justice Antonin Scalia died. With 10 months left in his term of office, President Obama nominated Judge Merrick Garland. The Republican-controlled Senate refused to hold any hearings on Garland and announced that the process would be delayed until after the next presidential election. President Trump was elected and nominated Neil Gorsuch for the Supreme Court position, who was confirmed by the Senate.

D. PUBLIC PERCEPTION OF THE PRESIDENT

1. The president's approval ratings—the percentage of the public that approves of the president's job performance—have been monitored by polling organizations for decades.

2. Factors that tend to increase approval ratings include:

   a. Honeymoon period: the time immediately following election when the president is granted greatest deference in terms of policy and performance

   b. foreign policy successes

   c. rally-around-the-flag effect: crises that create feelings of national unity

   d. strong economic growth and low unemployment

   e. positive media coverage

3. Factors that tend to decrease approval ratings include:

   a. scandals involving the president or his or her top aides

   b. expectations gap: the president does not achieve anticipated success

   c. foreign policy failures/extended armed conflict without resolution or success

   d. weak economic growth and high unemployment

4. A president's approval rating affects his or her relationship with Congress. High approval ratings can enhance the president's bargaining power, as a popular president can more effectively

use the bully pulpit to appeal to voters. Low approval ratings can reduce a president's ability to push his or her agenda through Congress.

Test Tip

The AP® Exam requires you to be able to interpret graphs and charts and relate them to course concepts. Be prepared to identify trends in presidential approval ratings when presented in a graph.

IV. IMPORTANT DOCUMENTS RELATING TO THE EXECUTIVE BRANCH

A. **"Federalist No. 70: The Executive Department Further Considered" (1788)** is an essay written by Alexander Hamilton defending the creation of a single president, as described in Article II of the Constitution, against critics who feared that the president would become, in effect, a king. Hamilton, writing under the pen name Publius, argues that a single executive is the best method to lead the government with efficiency and energy.

1. **Efficiency:** A single president is able to respond to a crisis faster and work with more secrecy (if necessary) than an executive branch run by a group of individuals. Spreading executive authority among several individuals will reduce effectiveness and decisiveness in executing the law.

   > That unity is conducive to energy will not be disputed. Decision, activity, secrecy, and dispatch will generally characterize the proceedings of one man in a much more eminent degree than the proceedings of any greater number; and in proportion as the number is increased, these qualities will be diminished.

2. **Accountability:** A single president is preferred because one corrupt or ineffective leader cannot hide within a group, and he or she would be easy to identify and vote out of office.

   > It is evident from these considerations that the plurality of the executive tends to deprive the people of the two greatest securities they can have for the faithful exercise of any delegated power, first, the restraints of public opinion, which lose their efficacy, as well on account of the division of the censure attendant on bad measures among a number

as on account of the uncertainty on whom it ought to fall; and, second, the opportunity of discovering with facility and clearness the misconduct of the persons they trust, in order either to their removal from office or to their actual punishment in cases which admit of it.

The argument essay requires you to state a defensible claim that is supported with evidence from one of the required foundational documents including the Constitution. Be prepared to utilize information from "Federalist No. 70," Article II of the Constitution, and the constitutional amendments related to the presidency (12th, 20th, 22nd, 23rd, and 25th) if you are given an argumentative essay related to the executive branch. Excerpts from "Federalist No. 70" are also likely to be used for qualitative analysis questions related to the justifications for creating a single executive.

B. CONSTITUTIONAL AMENDMENTS AND THE PRESIDENCY

1. **Twelfth Amendment:** An early correction to the procedures of the Electoral College so that electors voted separately for president and vice president.

2. **Twentieth Amendment:** Moved the date for the start of the terms for the new Congress and the new president from March to January 20, thus reducing the lame duck period.

*The term **lame duck** refers to the time period in which an elected leader (often the president) is holding his or her position after having lost a bid for reelection or not seeking reelection. The time period during which an official is a lame duck often results in reduced effectiveness. However, lame duck presidents or members of Congress are still able to exercise their constitutional powers. At the same time, the lame duck period may also liberate an officeholder to use powers or act in ways that he or she would not if anticipating future time in the office.*

3. **Twenty-second Amendment:** Limits individuals to a maximum of two terms of office or a total of 10 years as president. Because George Washington served only two terms, subsequent presidents

followed that example until Franklin D. Roosevelt (FDR) was elected four times, creating impetus for an amendment.

4. **Twenty-fifth Amendment:** Clarifies vice presidential succession to the presidency, vice presidential vacancies, and the procedures related to cases of presidential inability.

    a. Makes clear that the vice president actually assumes the office of the president in the event of presidential death or disability.

    b. Establishes a procedure for filling a vice presidential vacancy whereby a new vice president is appointed by the president and approved by a majority of both houses of Congress.

    c. Presidential disability may be determined by either (1) the president declaring himself or herself unable to discharge duties of office; or (2) the vice president and a majority of the heads of the executive departments (or another body designated by Congress) declare the president to be disabled. If this declaration is contested by the president, the issue is ultimately decided by Congress.

Test Tip

The Presidential Succession Act of 1947 (amended in 2006) determines who becomes president in the case of the death, resignation, disability, or removal of both the president and the vice president. This law, Article II, section 1, clause 6 of the Constitution, and the Twenty-Fifth Amendment outline the order of succession for the presidency as follows: the Vice President, the Speaker of the House of Representatives, the President Pro Tempore of the Senate, and then eligible members of the president's Cabinet beginning with the Secretary of State.

V. COMMUNICATIONS TECHNOLOGY AND THE PRESIDENCY

A. METHODS OF PRESIDENTIAL COMMUNICATION

1. State of the Union: The Constitution requires that the president "from time to time" provide Congress with information about issues facing the country. In modern times, this typically occurs annually when the president proposes his or her policy goals to a joint session of Congress. The televised event allows the president to address Congress, the nation, and the world. The president may also use the State of the Union to place pressure on Congress

about policy direction and indicate legislative action that he or she would likely support or veto.

2. Sophisticated technology has allowed for easier communication between the president and the public. During the Depression and World War II, President Roosevelt began speaking directly to the public on a regular basis using the new medium of radio, which had penetrated 90% of U.S. households. The use of radio to speak directly to citizens revolutionized presidential communications.

3. Later presidents used television to reach a broad audience about policy goals. The addition of a visual element changed Americans' perceptions of politics, as presidential appeal and effectiveness became increasingly related to physical appearance and demeanor. While earlier presidents spoke to the public on only a handful of television networks, the modern media includes a 24-hour news cycle feeding thousands of radio and television stations, as well as social media, blogs, and podcasts.

4. In the age of the Internet and the 24-hour news cycle, presidential administrations have been forced to adapt in order to effectively communicate with the nation.

   a. President Obama, in particular, took advantage of new communications technologies. He established the White House Office of Digital Strategy and used various digital avenues to exchange information with the public.

   b. Social media allows presidents to speak directly to citizens without the filter of television coverage, print media, and journalists. Social media is cheap, efficient, and instantaneous. As a result, presidents may be able to retain greater control over their messages, but the press may feel that there is diminished opportunity for examination and critical journalism.

B. THE FORMAL STRUCTURE OF WHITE HOUSE COMMUNICATIONS

1. Several offices within the White House Office coordinate and disseminate messaging for the president and his or her administration. These include the Office of White House Communications, the White House Press Office, and the Office of Digital Strategy.

2. Presidents beginning with John F. Kennedy have regularly held televised press conferences as a way of communicating with media outlets and citizens. The number of annual press conferences has steadily declined from a high of about 84 per year under FDR to

about six per year under Ronald Reagan. President Obama held about 20 press conferences per year.

3. Although members of the White House press corps look forward to opportunities to directly question the president, most press briefings are conducted by the White House Press Secretary. Traditionally, press briefings are a daily or near-daily event, but the frequency varies with the administration.

The Federal Bureaucracy

I. THE FEDERAL BUREAUCRACY

A. WHAT IS BUREAUCRACY?

1. The term *bureaucracy* is understood to refer to any administrative organization with the following characteristics:

   a. a large number of employees (bureaucrats)

   b. a hierarchical structure

   c. complex rules and procedures

   d. staffed by specialists

2. The U.S. federal bureaucracy employs 2.8 million civilians, most of whom work in the executive branch. Small segments of the bureaucracy exist under the legislative and judicial branches.

3. **Advantages of bureaucracy:**

   a. Centralized authority makes management effective.

   b. Specialized roles allow for the development of expertise.

   c. Standardized procedures make outcomes efficient and predictable.

   d. Standardization promotes equal treatment of individuals.

4. **Disadvantages of bureaucracy:**

   a. In a large bureaucracy, there can be overlapping areas of authority, creating both conflicts and repetition.

   b. Formalized procedures with especially extensive paperwork, often called *red tape*, can delay results.

c. Large, complex organizations may experience inertia, a slowness to respond to change.

d. Placing limits on individual discretion can result in unsatisfactory outcomes and stifle creativity.

B. THE STRUCTURE OF THE FEDERAL BUREAUCRACY

Funded by congress; work under pres

1. All federal government bureaucratic agencies are created and funded by Congress, but most work under the authority of the president. Article II of the Constitution states that the president "shall take Care that the Laws be faithfully executed." The president appoints the heads of the bureaucratic agencies, but full-time civil service employees do most of the work of government and are subject to laws and oversight from Congress.

2. **Executive Office of the President (EOP):** This is the group of highly influential policy-related offices and agencies in the executive branch that currently includes the White House Office, the Office of the Vice President, the Office of Management and Budget (OMB), the National Security Council, the Council of Economic Advisers, and the Office of Science and Technology Policy.

    a. EOP positions are influential in helping the president achieve his or her policy goals.

EOP doesn't require senate approval

    b. They are filled through presidential appointment and do not require Senate approval.

    c. The president can fire leaders in the executive office of the president at any time without congressional approval.

    d. The EOP is headed by the president's Chief of Staff, the highest-ranking aide to the president whose duties include overseeing White House staff, controlling access to the Oval Office, advising the president, and negotiating with other government officers in the interest of the president's policy agenda.

3. **White House Office:** This includes bureaucratic agencies within the EOP comprised of the president's most trusted and influential advisors who are appointed without Senate approval.

4. **Executive Departments:** The 15 executive departments, which comprise the bulk of the executive bureaucracy, are led by secretaries, except for the Justice Department, led by the Attorney General. These leaders are collectively referred to as the president's cabinet.

cabinets are approved by senate, can be fired

a. They are chosen by presidential appointment and confirmed by the Senate (majority vote).

b. The president can fire a department secretary at any time without congressional approval.

c. Cabinet departments are not specifically mentioned in the Constitution, but the cabinet has been in place since George Washington. The cabinet has expanded from three departments to 15 over time.

Test Tip

Be sure you understand the difference between bureaucrats in the Executive Office of the President (EOP) and Cabinet Secretaries. The president has greater latitude in selecting his or her closest advisors. White House staff, upon whom the president relies most heavily for guidance, are generally selected with greater emphasis on personal affinity and trust.

Executive Office of the President vs. Cabinet Secretaries

Executive Office of the President	Cabinet Secretaries
The EOP currently includes about 4,000 positions in the White House Office, Council of Economic Advisors, National Security Council, Office of Management and Budget, Office of National Drug Control Policy, Office of Science and Technology Policy, and the Office of the Vice President.	The heads of the 15 executive agencies that make up the president's cabinet hold the title of Secretary; the exception is the head of the Justice Department, who is the Attorney General.
likely to be strong supporters of the president alone	advise the president and manage executive departments resulting in potentially divided support
appointed by the president without senate confirmation	appointed by the president and require a majority vote by the Senate
often served on the president's election campaign	often have specialized knowledge and prior political experience
lower levels of congressional oversight	greater levels of congressional oversight

cabinet has high levels of congressional oversight

5. **Independent Agencies:** These are agencies created by Congress that are similar to Cabinet departments, but are smaller and focused on more specific policy areas.

   a. Agency heads are appointed by the president with confirmation by the Senate (majority vote).

   b. The president can remove agency heads at any time without congressional approval.

   c. Examples include the Social Security Administration and the National Foundation on the Arts and Humanities.

6. **Regulatory Commissions:** These are largely autonomous agencies that develop and enforce regulations related to public policy.

   a. Regulatory agencies are typically run by 5- to 10-member boards appointed by the president and confirmed by the Senate (by majority vote).

   b. Members of independent regulatory commission boards may not be from the same political party.

   c. The president does not have the authority to remove agency heads during their terms.

   d. Examples of regulatory commissions are the Environmental Protection Agency (EPA), which regulates and enforces safety protections for clean air and water, and the Federal Election Commission (FEC), which regulates elections and campaigns.

7. **Government Corporations:** These are government agencies that work similarly to private businesses and offer a specific service.

   a. These organizations are frequently necessary to serve markets that would not be profitable for the private sector.

   b. Unlike private businesses, government corporations keep their profits instead of distributing them to stockholders.

   c. The president does not nominate the individuals who run government corporations.

   d. Examples include the United States Postal Service and the Federal Deposit Insurance Corporation (FDIC).

IMPORTANT DEPARTMENTS AND AGENCIES OF THE FEDERAL BUREAUCRACY

Executive Departments (15)

State (1789)

Treasury (1789)

Defense (1789)

Interior (1849)

Agriculture (1862)

Justice (1870)

Commerce (1903)

Labor (1913)

Department of Veterans Affairs (1930)

Department of Education (1953)*

Department of Health and Human Services (1953)*

Housing and Urban Development (1965)

Transportation (1966)

Energy (1977)

Homeland Security (2002)

Select Independent Agencies

Social Security Administration

National Aeronautics and Space Administration

Office of Personnel Management

National Foundation on the Arts and the Humanities

Peace Corps

Select Regulatory Commissions

Federal Election Commission (FEC)

Federal Communications Commission (FCC)

Federal Trade Commission (FTC)

Environmental Protection Agency (EPA)

Securities and Exchange Commission (SEC)

Equal Employment Opportunity Commission (EEOC)

Select Government Corporations

Tennessee Valley Authority (TVA)

Federal Deposit Insurance Corporation (FDIC)

United States Postal Service

National Railroad Passenger Corporation (AMTRAK)

Corporation for Public Broadcasting

Federal National Mortgage Association (Fannie Mae)

*The Department of Health, Education and Welfare was created in 1953. In 1979, this department was split into the Department of Education and the Department of Health and Human Services.

Test Tip

Cabinet secretaries have two goals: advising the president and running their respective departments. Cabinet secretaries often have divided loyalties when the policy initiatives of the president conflict with the goals of their agency.

II. THE WORK OF THE BUREAUCRACY

A. HOW THE BUREAUCRACY FUNCTIONS

1. The implementation of most federal legislation is the job of the bureaucracy. Bear in mind that it would be impossible for Congress to legislate all of the rules that all of the players in a complex society need to follow. The nitty gritty of regulation is delegated by Congress to the hundreds of offices, bureaus, agencies, and departments that make up the bureaucracy.

2. Congress creates new units of bureaucracy by legislation and charges each with carrying out policy in a specific area. Tasks performed include distribution of funding, developing rules to carry out the agency's mandates, and enforcing compliance. Congress created the newest cabinet-level executive department, the Department of Homeland Security, in response to the terrorist attacks of September 11, 2001.

   Congress: funding, rules 4 tasks, enforcing compliance

3. Bureaucratic (administrative) discretion is the power granted to bureaucratic leadership to implement mandates within policy guidelines, which are frequently not specific and allow agencies considerable latitude. Agencies involved in national security are granted the broadest discretion.

4. *Bureaucratic rulemaking* is the process whereby government agencies formulate and implement regulations to carry congressional mandates into effect. Regulations are rules that have the force of law. The rulemaking process generally takes place according to the following steps.

   a. Enabling legislation is passed by Congress describing an agency's authority and responsibilities in a particular area.

   b. Interest groups, businesses, experts, and other stakeholders may be contacted and given the opportunity to testify to the agency regarding the potential impact of proposed rules.

c. Proposed rules are published in the *Federal Register,* and the public is given the opportunity to comment or object before rules are enacted.

d. A final rule is adopted.

e. After a 30-day waiting period, during which time Congress may take up the issue in question, the rule becomes effective.

f. The rule could become the subject of court challenges.

B. IRON TRIANGLES AND ISSUE NETWORKS

1. **Iron Triangle:** The "iron triangle" is named for the strength and long-term stability of the relationships between its three participants: interest groups, bureaucratic agencies, and congressional committees. The triangle develops mutually beneficial public policy.

   a. Interest groups act on both Congress (the legislature) and the bureaucracy (the executive branch).

      ➤ An interest group may promote its policy goals by supporting members of the congressional committee overseeing its interest area with campaign contributions and other forms of political support.

      ➤ An interest group also wants to maintain a positive relationship with the bureaucratic agency that regulates its activities. It can achieve this by using its lobbying efforts and congressional connections to influence policy made by committees to align with the desires of the agency.

   b. Bureaucratic agencies in the executive branch desire funding and support from Congress to enhance their power and promote their programs. They obtain this in two ways:

      ➤ First, they can support the goals of the congressional committee with which their work is associated.

      ➤ Second, they may influence committees through the lobbying efforts of the interest groups related to the areas they regulate. It is in the interest of agencies to maintain positive relationships with these outside groups, who often influence congressional committees on their behalf. They do so by limiting regulation and generously interpreting legislative mandates.

c. Congressional committees desire cooperation from the agencies that implement their policies.

➤ They encourage this support by providing funding and advocacy to these agencies.

➤ To maintain the backing of powerful interest groups, congressional committees offer them friendly legislation and oversight in return for political support and contributions.

d. Problems with iron triangles include:

➤ Bureaucratic organizations may prioritize the desires of powerful interest groups over their "consumers," the often marginalized and/or politically weak communities they serve.

Elitists Favored

➤ The revolving door refers to the movement of individuals between points on the iron triangle. For example, someone who has served in Congress or as a bureaucrat in a regulatory agency may be offered a lucrative job in the industry they are entrusted with regulating. They may then use their expertise and contacts on behalf of the industry. Those charged with protecting the public, therefore, may be motivated to act on behalf of special interests at the public's expense.

Iron Triangle

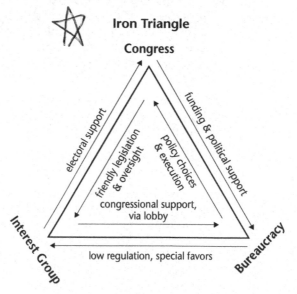

2. **Issue Network:** A connected group of individuals that may include lobbyists, experts from universities and think tanks, the media, members of Congress, and bureaucrats who regularly discuss and advocate public policies.

   a. Issue networks often form around narrower issues than iron triangles. For example, an iron triangle may exist between the House and Senate committees dealing with agriculture, the U.S. Department of Agriculture, and interest groups such as farmers and chemical producers. An issue network would be more likely to relate to a specific issue, such as the use of a particular class of pesticides in food production.

   b. Issue networks may also be seen as broader than iron triangles in that they encompass not only congressional committees, interest groups, and agencies, but all interested and active players around an issue, including activists, scholars, consultants, lawyers, lobbyists, and anyone else with expertise and concern who participates in the regulatory process.

   c. Issue networks tend to be of shorter duration, lasting only as long as necessary to resolve the issue in question.

Test Tip

Both iron triangles and issue networks exemplify the concept of pluralism. The process of regulation results in policies that reflect the participation of numerous groups. Those with the greatest political power and financial resources, however, tend to have the greatest influence on policy outcomes.

C. ENFORCEMENT

1. Federal agencies administer or enforce federal policies. That is, they collect fees, conduct testing, issue licenses, monitor compliance, issue fines, and perform related administrative tasks.

2. In some cases, federal agencies enforce the law through litigation against individuals or corporations who violate regulations. Agencies themselves may file lawsuits, but in other situations lawsuits are filed on behalf of an executive agency by the Justice Department.

3. Implementation of policy is complex, frequently involving cooperation among multiple state and federal agencies with overlapping areas of jurisdiction.

D. OTHER FUNCTIONS OF THE BUREAUCRACY

1. Agencies within the bureaucracy are frequently tasked with the distribution of funds in accordance with legislation passed by Congress. Examples include distributing social security funds and veterans' benefits.

2. The bureaucracy is a source of subject matter expertise for the government. Professionals employed in the bureaucracy frequently draw on both their subject matter expertise and their experience working within their agencies in testifying before congressional committees.

E. CIVIL SERVICE

1. The bureaucracy employs millions of civilians in a diverse range of positions, including computer programmers, diplomats, clerks, investigators of all kinds, and thousands of other jobs.

2. Before 1883, government jobs at all levels were filled largely from the ranks of those who supported the president and his party. The term *patronage* refers to the practice of filling jobs with one's political supporters. This was also known as the *spoils system*.

3. Following the assassination of President James Garfield by a disgruntled job seeker who felt he was owed a patronage job, Congress passed the Pendleton Act (1883), creating the civil service. The law created guidelines for merit-based employment and promotion for all but the highest levels of federal employment.

4. The result has been the professionalization of the federal bureaucracy. Regular federal employees may not be hired or fired for political reasons. They are hired and promoted based on standardized qualifications and procedures.

5. The civil service is overseen by the Office of Personnel Management.

6. The president appoints less than 1 percent of all federal workers, many of whom are high-level managers who develop and implement policy and work directly for the president.

7. There are benefits to a merit-based civil service system:

   a. **Professionalism:** Employees are selected based on their professional qualifications and background, so that bureaucrats are skilled and knowledgeable experts. They also hold their jobs long-term, developing both in-depth knowledge of their jobs and fields and professional networks.

   b. **Specialization:** A civil service system allows for greater expertise as professional employees pursue qualifications in more specialized roles.

    c. **Neutrality:** Because they are not hired based on partisan loyalty, civil service professionals are more likely to perform their duties with less partisan favoritism.

    d. **Continuity:** Under the spoils system, employees were regularly replaced after each new administration took over, creating inconsistencies in policy administration. A professional bureaucracy creates continuity and uniformity since professional bureaucrats are career employees who remain in their positions even as presidential administrations change.

    e. **Efficiency:** The components of professionalism, specialization, neutrality, and continuity create greater efficiency and productivity within the federal bureaucracy.

8. Federal employees are restricted in their ability to engage in certain political activities while on the job, including participation in political campaigns.

III. POWERS OF THE THREE BRANCHES OVER THE BUREAUCRACY

appt. & removal. → exec orders force implementation

A. EXECUTIVE (PRESIDENTIAL) AUTHORITY OVER THE BUREAUCRACY

1. **Appointment:** The president exercises control over the bureaucracy by appointing the heads of executive departments, independent agencies, and regulatory commissions (with majority Senate approval).

2. **Removal.** The president may remove the heads of the executive departments and the heads of independent agencies, but not the heads of the regulatory commissions.

3. **Executive Orders:** When the president issues an executive order, implementation becomes the responsibility of the relevant department or agency.

4. **Signing Statements:** These are comments, written by the president upon signing a bill, that express his or her interpretation of the legislation and provide guidance on implementation to the appropriate agency or agencies.

B. CONGRESSIONAL AUTHORITY OVER THE BUREAUCRACY

1. **Oversight:** Congress is responsible for overseeing the rulemaking and discretionary functions of the agencies of the federal bureaucracy. Congress routinely looks into the activity of executive agencies

↳ funding, committee hearings 2 review make changes 2 agencies

branch agencies but is also likely to launch an investigation in response to constituent complaints as part of casework.

   a. Committee Hearings: Congressional committees review reports from related agencies and may call individual bureaucrats in to answer questions directly. Hearings can involve testimony and questioning of both bureaucrats and other witnesses.

   b. Power of the Purse: As a result of the expressed power to spend money, Congress has control over the various agencies because it determines the levels of funding in agency budgets.

   c. The Government Accountability Office (GAO), often called the "congressional watchdog," is an independent, nonpartisan agency that works for Congress to monitor the performance of executive agencies and programs. The GAO conducts audits, writes reports, and provides reliable, objective information to Congress to ensure the effective functioning of the bureaucracy.

   d. Senate approval (by majority vote) is required for department heads and certain other executive branch officers.

2. **Legislation:** Congress has passed several key pieces of legislation that have limited the authority of the federal bureaucracy.

   a. Congress may, through legislation, create, abolish, or make changes to any bureaucratic agency. Congress may also use very precise language when writing laws in order to eliminate or reduce bureaucratic discretion.

   b. The Freedom of Information Act (1996), also known as FOIA, requires that all federal executive branch agencies release information to journalists, researchers, and the public upon request unless the material is confidential (e.g., classified military or intelligence documents).

   c. The Whistleblower Protection Acts of 1989 and 2012 and other laws protect government employees from retaliation for exposing corruption or inappropriate practices.

C. JUDICIAL AUTHORITY OVER THE BUREAUCRACY

1. **Judicial Review:** Bureaucratic actions may be challenged in the federal courts, which interpret federal law and the Constitution. An action may be invalidated if a court finds that federal law has been incorrectly implemented or if the action is found to be unconstitutional.

Judicial review

The Judicial Branch

I. IMPORTANT DOCUMENTS

A. ARTICLE III OF THE CONSTITUTION

1. Article III states that "[t]he judicial Power of the United States, shall be vested in one Supreme Court, and in such inferior Courts as the Congress may from time to time ordain and establish."

2. The Supreme Court is the only court formally created by the Constitution.

3. Congress is granted the power to create other lower federal courts as it sees fit.

4. Federal judges are appointed by the president and confirmed by a majority vote in the Senate. (Appointments Clause in Article II, Section 2)

5. Federal judges hold their positions "during good Behaviour." This means that federal Judges serve for life, unless they voluntarily retire, and can only be removed through impeachment and conviction. Also, their salaries may not be reduced while serving.

6. The Supreme Court hears cases under two types of jurisdiction (authority to hear a case).

   a. The Court has original jurisdiction (i.e., it hears a case for the first time or conducts a trial) in cases involving federal officials, international issues, and cases in which a state is named as a party.

   b. The Court has appellate jurisdiction (the authority to decide cases on appeal) in all other cases involving federal law or the Constitution.

7. Article III, Section 2 also guarantees the right to a jury trial for all crimes. Additionally, it requires that trials take place in the state in

which the crime was committed. Jury trial jurisprudence is covered more extensively in Chapter 9, Civil Liberties.

8. Article III, Section 3 defines treason ("levying war against [the United States] or in adhering to their Enemies, giving them Aid and Comfort") and requires the testimony of two witnesses for conviction. The Framers took care to define treason narrowly, so as to not inhibit political speech.

Test Tip

The term "Court" with a capital "C" is always shorthand for the Supreme Court. The Court is also frequently referred to as SCOTUS (the Supreme Court of the United States).

B. "FEDERALIST NO. 78"

1. "Federalist Paper No. 78" was written by Alexander Hamilton to describe and defend the proposed structure of the federal judiciary.

2. Hamilton argued that, of the three branches, the courts would be the weakest because they would have no way to enforce their judgments, lacking both military and financial authority. The courts would be

> the least dangerous to the political rights of the Constitution . . . The Executive not only dispenses the honors, but holds the sword of the community. The legislature not only commands the purse, but prescribes the rules by which the duties and rights of every citizen are to be regulated. The judiciary, on the contrary, does not influence either the sword or the purse. . . . It may truly be said to have neither FORCE nor WILL, but merely judgment; and must ultimately depend upon the aid of the executive arm even for the efficacy of its judgments.

3. Hamilton argued persuasively for life tenure of federal judges, pointing out that

> "[i]ndependence and permanency in office" would be necessary to compensate for the inherent weakness of the courts generally. Concerning their role as guardians of the Constitution, he pointed out that the security of life tenure would ensure their freedom and independence to defend the Constitution, which embodies the will of the people, against political forces and the power of the other branches.

If, then, the courts of justice are to be considered as the bulwarks of a limited Constitution against legislative encroachments, this consideration will afford a strong argument for the permanent tenure of judicial offices, since nothing will contribute so much as this to that independent spirit in the judges which must be essential to the faithful performance of so arduous a duty.

4. A critical power of the courts not explicitly addressed in the Constitution is that of judicial review, the power of the courts to determine the constitutionality of acts of the federal government or any state government. The objection to the courts having the power of judicial review was that it would give them too much power over the other branches by allowing them to invalidate the actions of the other branches. Hamilton made several counterarguments:

    a. The Constitution, which would be adopted through an exceptionally deliberative process, represents the will of the people more profoundly than do laws.

    b. It is the domain of the courts to determine the meaning of laws and whether a law conflicts with the Constitution.

    c. Courts must necessarily have the power in order to enforce constitutional limits on the power of the legislative and executive branches.

    d. Courts are necessary to safeguard individual liberties against the power of the legislature.

C. MARBURY v. MADISON (1803)

1. **Facts of the Case:** President John Adams, a Federalist, lost the election of 1800 to Thomas Jefferson, a Democratic-Republican. Two days before departing office, Adams appointed several dozen Federalists to newly created judicial positions in an attempt to extend the party's power. Due to the rushed nature of the appointments, several of the commissions were not delivered to the newly appointed judges before Adams left office and Jefferson took over. Jefferson saw no need to deliver the appointments, and instructed his Secretary of State, James Madison, not to do so. Marbury, one of the appointees who did not receive his appointment, sued, asking the Court to issue a *writ of mandamus* (an order from a court requiring a government official to perform a duty) instructing Madison to deliver his commission.

2. **Constitutional Issue(s):**

   a. Is Marbury entitled to his commission?

   b. Is Marbury entitled to a remedy in the courts?

   c. Should the Court grant a writ of mandamus, the remedy sought by the plaintiffs?

3. **Holding(s):**

   a. Yes, Marbury is entitled to his commission.

   b. Yes, Marbury is entitled to a judicial remedy.

   c. No, Section 13 of the Judiciary Act of 1789, giving the Supreme Court original jurisdiction to issue writs of mandamus, was unconstitutional.

4. **Reasoning:** The significance of the case is found in the third ruling, in which Chief Justice John Marshall, writing for the Court, held that Section 13 of the Judiciary Act conflicted with the Constitution, and was, therefore, void. The Constitution defines and limits the Court's original jurisdiction to those involving certain federal officials and those in which a state is a party. According to the Supremacy Clause, constitutional provisions cannot be altered by acts of Congress. The Constitution is superior to federal law, so Section 13 was unconstitutional. Marshall cleverly avoided conflict with the Jefferson administration while at the same time claiming for the Court, unquestionably, the power of judicial review.

D. JUDICIAL REVIEW

1. Judicial review is the power of the courts to determine the constitutionality of any act of government. It may be applied to any act of the legislative or executive branches.

2. Although Hamilton does not use the term *judicial review* in "Federalist No. 78," it is clearly his understanding that courts must hold this power.

3. The Constitution does not explicitly grant this power to the courts, but Chief Justice Marshall made clear in *Marbury* that the Court does hold the power of judicial review.

4. While it is broadly accepted that the Court holds this power, the decision has not gone unchallenged. The question of enforcement has been left to the executive branch.

Test Tip

Judicial review is based on the understanding that the Supreme Court is the highest authority on the Constitution. This is coupled with the Supremacy Clause (Article VI, Clause 2), stating that federal laws and treaties are superior to state and local laws. When a state or local law conflicts with a federal law, treaty, or the Constitution, it is void. The Supreme Court, using the power of judicial review, may invalidate acts of the other branches of the federal government, as well as actions of state governments.

II. THE JUDICIAL SYSTEM

A. WHAT THE COURTS DO

1. Court systems exist to resolve disputes between parties, which may be individuals, businesses, or government entities.

2. Cases begin in trial courts, where the facts of the case are presented.

    a. Cases are filed, and disputes are resolved.

    b. Evidence is presented, and witnesses testify.

    c. Juries or judges determine the outcome of cases.

3. Criminal law consists of the statutes (legislation) defining crimes as actions against the community.

    a. The parties to a criminal case are the state (or government) and the defendant. (The government is a party to every criminal case.)

    b. Crimes are punishable by serious penalties, including incarceration and, possibly, capital punishment (death penalty).

    c. Most criminal cases are resolved without going to trial through an agreement called a plea bargain, in which the defendant agrees to plead guilty to a crime, often a lesser charge, in exchange for a reduced sentence.

4. Civil law is the broad area of law encompassing non-criminal cases. It is commonly understood as the body of law relating to private rights. Examples include torts (personal injury or property damages) and contract violations.

a. The parties to a civil case are the plaintiff, or the person bringing the action (lawsuit), and the defendant. The government may be a party to a civil case.

b. The consequences for a defendant are limited to monetary payments or requirements for action.

c. Most civil cases are settled by agreement between the parties without going to trial.

B. THE COURT SYSTEM

1. The United States has a dual court system consisting of the federal court system and 50 state court systems.

2. The federal and state court systems share similar characteristics, including a pyramidal structure, with the largest number of trial courts at the base of the pyramid, a middle tier consisting of a smaller number of appellate-level courts, and a single supreme court at the top.

3. The Federal Courts

    a. The Supreme Court is the only court established by the Constitution. Congress is given the power to establish lower federal courts by legislation, and has, over the course of our history, created an extensive system of federal courts.

    b. The federal trial courts are the district courts.

        ➤ There are 94 federal districts, or geographic areas, from which the district courts hear cases.

        ➤ Each state has at least one, and district court boundaries do not cross state lines.

    c. The federal courts of appeals are called the circuit courts.

        ➤ There are 13 federal circuits, including 12 based on geographic regions and one handling certain matters of international law.

        ➤ Each circuit court hears cases from the trial courts within its geographic boundaries.

4. The Attorney General is the head of the U.S. Department of Justice and the chief legal officer of the nation, charged with enforcement of federal law.

5. The Solicitor General is the official in the Department of Justice who represents the federal government before the Supreme Court in all cases in which the United States is a party. He or she is also charged with filing *amicus curiae* briefs on behalf of the government when appropriate.

C. APPEALS

1. A party that has lost at trial may apply for review by a higher court. This procedure is called an appeal.

   a. Appeals must be based on a perceived error of law made by the judge at trial. This is often referred to as having grounds for appeal. Simply disagreeing with a verdict is not sufficient to request an appeal.

   b. Appellate cases only involve arguments about the legality of rulings made at trial. No new evidence or witnesses are introduced.

   c. A party that loses at trial has a right to appeal the decision to a higher court, with one important exception. The government may not appeal a loss in a criminal trial because the Fifth Amendment prohibits double jeopardy, or trying a defendant more than once for a crime.

   d. An appellate court may affirm or overturn a trial court's verdict, and remand (send back) the case to the trial court. (If a criminal conviction is overturned on appeal, the remedy is generally a new trial for the defendant. This is not considered a double jeopardy violation, since the defendant is the one requesting the second trial.)

2. When an appellate court makes a decision, it is creating public policy by making a rule that impacts the application of the law to citizens, which lower courts must follow in future cases.

Test Tip

*The term **jurisdiction** refers to the authority of a court to hear a particular case. Trial courts have **original jurisdiction;** they hear cases for the first time. Appellate courts have **appellate jurisdiction;** they hear appeals from lower courts. Jurisdiction may also be based on geography and subject matter. Most courts hear cases that arise in particular geographic areas, and some courts hear cases that deal with a particular subject, regardless of geography, such as the United States Tax Court.*

III. THE SUPREME COURT

A. OVERVIEW

1. The Supreme Court is the country's highest court.

2. The number of judges, called "justices," on the Court is currently nine. This number is set by Congress according to the Constitution and may be changed. It has been set at nine since 1869.

3. The Supreme Court has original jurisdiction in two specific situations (although it rarely conducts trials):

   a. cases involving ambassadors or federal officials

   b. certain cases to which a state is a party

4. Most cases reach the Supreme Court through its appellate jurisdiction. The Court hears cases from the federal appellate courts and state supreme courts in cases involving federal law or the Constitution (a federal question). A case that does not involve federal law or the Constitution may not be appealed to the Supreme Court.

B. PROCEDURES

1. The Supreme Court is not required to hear all of the cases that are appealed to it.

   a. More than 7,000 cases are appealed to the Court each year; it issues full opinions in fewer than 100.

   b. The justices decide which cases to accept according to the rule of four. That is, four of the nine justices must vote to take the case.

   c. In theory, the Court accepts only the most important cases, those involving pressing questions of national importance. These may involve any area of law. Cases frequently involve civil liberties, but most decisions involve other issues, such as business or regulatory questions.

   d. The Court will often accept cases involving an issue that has been considered by different federal courts of appeals and in which those circuit courts have reached different conclusions.

2. In order to bring suit (file a case) in a court, a party must have standing. *Standing* is a legal doctrine requiring that a party to a case must have a significant personal stake in its outcome, not a mere interest as a member of the public.

3. When the Court decides to take a case, it issues a *writ of certiorari* (Latin for "to be informed of"), a legal order to the lower court to provide the case records for review. This is commonly referred to as "granting cert." (much easier to pronounce!)

4. The case is then added to the Court's docket, a calendar of upcoming cases to be heard.

5. Parties submit briefs (summaries of facts and legal arguments) to the Court and are typically allowed thirty minutes of oral argument on the day their case is heard. During oral argument, attorneys make statements and answer questions from the nine assembled justices. Justices can sometimes be aggressive in asking questions, and often signal their opinion of a case by the questions they ask.

6. *Amicus curiae* (Latin for "friend of the court") briefs are advisory briefs submitted to the Court by individuals or groups that are not parties to the case, but who can provide expertise or insight on key issues to assist the Court in reaching a decision.

Test Tip

Amicus curiae briefs (often shortened to "amicus briefs") are frequently filed by interest groups and are one of the ways that these groups attempt to influence public policy. For example, in a Second Amendment case involving restrictions on gun purchases, amicus briefs might be filed by the National Rifle Association (NRA) and Everytown for Gun Safety. Numerous amicus briefs may be filed in important cases.

7. Following oral arguments, the justices meet, discuss, and vote on the case. The chief justice, or the senior justice in the majority, assigns one of the justices to write the majority opinion, the document announcing the Court's decision and detailing the legal reasoning behind its conclusions.

8. A justice who disagrees with the majority may write a dissenting opinion, in which he or she argues that the reasoning of the majority is in error and sets out an alternative argument.

9. A justice who agrees with the outcome of the majority opinion, but who arrives at this conclusion by following a different line of legal reasoning, may write a concurring opinion to clarify what he or she believes the correct analysis to be.

10. Given the ideological variation of the Court, one might expect most decisions to produce split opinions. In fact, the opposite is true. Although it varies by term, it is typical for a majority of

decisions to be unanimous. Reasons for this may be that many cases do not center on politically divisive issues, but on technical legal problems, and the fact that the law is generally stable and precedent is often fairly clear.

Although Supreme Court decisions may include multiple opinions, only the majority opinion is considered precedent and must be followed in subsequent cases. Concurring and dissenting opinions may be helpful in understanding the complex issues involved in a case and the arguments for the losing side, but they are not considered precedent. Dissents may also be useful in overturning precedent if it is revisited in a future case.

IV. JUDICIAL DECISION-MAKING

A. HOW COURTS MAKE LAW

1. Appellate decisions, including Supreme Court decisions, are important because they carry the weight of law. Lower courts must follow all appellate court decisions within their jurisdiction in future cases. Because the Supreme Court is the highest court, all court decisions, state and federal, must conform to Supreme Court precedent.

    a. Decisions made by appellate courts are called *precedents*. A precedent is a legal decision that must be applied in future cases involving substantially similar facts and law.

    b. *Stare decisis* (Latin for "let the decision stand") is the legal doctrine requiring courts to follow precedents in subsequent cases.

    c. Lower (inferior) courts must follow the precedent from higher courts.

Be sure you know the difference between common law and statutory law. **Common law,** *also called case law, refers to a law that is created by judicial decision, called precedent. For example, in the case of* **Baker v. Carr (1962)** *the Supreme Court's ruling led to the common law requirement that legislative districts must contain roughly equal populations.* **Statutory law** *refers to laws that are passed by legislatures, such as Congress.* **Statutes** *are laws enacted by legislatures. For example, the Voting Rights Act of 1965 outlawed literacy tests for voting.*

B. FACTORS IN JUDICIAL DECISION-MAKING

1. **The Justices**

   a. There are no constitutional requirements for qualifications of Supreme Court justices, although all have had legal training.

   b. Federal justices hold life tenure and may only be removed by impeachment proceedings.

2. **Judicial Appointments**

   a. Supreme Court justices are appointed by the president and confirmed by the Senate (by majority vote).

   b. Supreme Court vacancies give presidents opportunities to install powerful policymakers who will serve life terms. Presidents, therefore, appoint justices who share their political ideologies. Whether an appointee is more moderate or extreme in his or her views is related to the composition of the Senate. If the president's party holds a majority in the Senate, he or she has more latitude in selecting an appointee who is more ideologically pronounced. If the opposing party controls the Senate, appointees are likely to be more moderate in order to be acceptable to the opposition.

3. **How Judges Decide Cases**

   a. The interpretation of federal law and the Constitution is complex. The language of statutes (laws passed by Congress) is often unclear when applied to situations that arise in the real world. The Constitution is even more vague, frequently by design. It was written in a different era, and the Framers left many aspects of government to be defined by future leaders. Today, much of what we understand the Constitution to mean is the product of judicial decisions, and not the language of the document itself.

b. Justices, with the assistance of their law clerks, analyze the facts and arguments contained in the parties' briefs, their oral arguments, and amicus curiae briefs.

c. Justices rely on precedent.

d. As noted, justices come to the bench with political philosophies that are reflected in their decisions. Justices may be more liberal or conservative, and this is frequently evident in their opinions.

4. **Judicial Activism and Judicial Restraint**

a. Some justices may adhere to the philosophy of judicial restraint. This is the idea that the judicial branch should defer to the judgment of the elected branches of government when possible, and should use the power of judicial review to invalidate laws or executive actions only when absolutely necessary.

b. Alternatively, a justice may practice judicial activism, a philosophy that recognizes that the legislative and executive branches may not always act fairly precisely because they are elected. This philosophy holds that the judiciary should freely use the power of judicial review to protect the rights and liberties of individuals and minorities.

c. To some extent, the terms *judicial activism* and *judicial restraint* may be overly simplistic. The practice of interpreting and applying the Constitution and federal laws is complicated, and decisions will always involve some degree of innovation, or they would not be necessary. Furthermore, a judge's view of an issue may determine whether he or she takes a more restrained or more activist view of a case.

Test Tip

Don't confuse judicial restraint and judicial activism with political conservatism and liberalism. The AP® exam will require you to understand the terms liberal *and* conservative, *as well as* judicial restraint *and* judicial activism. *Students often mistakenly believe that these terms are correlated, with liberal judges being more "activist," and conservative judges being more "restrained." This is* not *the case. Judges may be politically liberal but practice judicial restraint, believing that judicial review should be sparingly used and that courts should defer to the legislature and the executive. Judges may, likewise, be politically conservative but activist, believing in the broad use of judicial power to advance their political beliefs.*

5. **Strict vs. Loose Construction**

   a. A strict constructionist believes that the federal government may only act in ways that the Constitution specifically says it can. This involves taking a close or narrow interpretation of the Constitution and is related to the idea of judicial restraint.

   b. A loose constructionist believes the federal government may take actions not specified in the Constitution as long as they are not directly forbidden. This involves taking a broad interpretation of the Constitution to adapt to a modern world and is related to the idea of judicial activism.

6. **The Court and Public Opinion**

   a. Justices of the Supreme Court are appointed for life and therefore lack the accountability to the public faced by legislators and officials in the executive branch.

   b. The justices meet and make their decisions in secret, not in public like Congress, whose proceedings are open to public observation.

   c. For these reasons, the Court has often been criticized for overreaching—using its power in ways that the Framers did not intend by contradicting the will of the people's elected representatives.

   d. Although the Court is insulated from public opinion in that justices are not elected, public opinion is a factor in how the Court decides high-profile cases. If the Court made decisions that were exceedingly counter-majoritarian, its prestige would be harmed. Its decisions would be viewed as lacking legitimacy, possibly resulting in executive or congressional action to limit the Court's power. The Court, therefore, tends to limit the scope of important decisions and avoid extreme holdings.

7. **Overturning Precedent**

   a. The Supreme Court may reverse itself, or overturn its own precedent. This is rare, but the Court has overturned precedent when it felt a previous decision was wrongly decided or circumstances have changed to make a previous result unsound under modern conditions. The best example of this is *Brown v. Board of Education of Topeka* (1954). In *Plessy v. Ferguson* (1896), the Court ruled that separate facilities for whites and African Americans were constitutional, but later reversed itself in *Brown*, ruling that segregation violated the Equal Protection Clause of the Fourteenth Amendment.

   b. The Court may overturn precedent. It most often does so under one of two circumstances (or a combination of the two): either the ideological composition of the Court has changed, or the culture of the nation has changed. An example of the latter would be the Supreme Court decision granting same-sex marriage.

V. THE COURT: CHECKS AND BALANCES

A. JUDICIAL REVIEW

1. The Court's primary check over the other two branches is judicial review.

2. The Court also exerts some control over the other branches through the interpretation of statutes and regulations.

B. CHECKS ON THE COURT

1. The executive branch has several important checks over the judicial branch, but the president's most significant check over the courts is the appointment of federal judges (subject to Senate confirmation). He or she may also grant pardons, commutations, and reprieves, and may choose to enforce case law rulings less aggressively.

2. Congress holds several important checks over the courts, including approval of judicial appointments, impeachment of judges, and passage of basic legislation.

3. Judicial implementation is the process by which judicial decisions are put into practice.

    a. The Court relies on the legislature for funding of its directives and on the executive for enforcement.

    b. Although it is generally accepted that the Court's decisions require compliance by the parties involved, several presidents have declined to enforce the Court's decisions.

    c. President Andrew Jackson, for example, refused to enforce the Court's decision in *Worcester v. Georgia* (1832), upholding certain rights of Native American tribes to sovereignty over their own lands. Lincoln also ignored a Supreme Court decision invalidating his suspension of habeas corpus rights.

    d. Overall, however, presidents have tended to use their power to enforce decisions, as when President Dwight Eisenhower used the military in 1957 to implement racial integration of schools in Little Rock, Arkansas.

Checks on the Courts

Congressional Checks on the Court	Executive Checks on the Courts
– approval of judicial appointments by Senate majority vote	– nominates Supreme Court justices and appoints all lower federal judges
– refusing or limiting funding for implementation of judicial decisions	– refusing to enforce or limiting enforcement of judicial decisions
– rewrite or revise legislation found unconstitutional	– rewrite or revise executive orders found unconstitutional
– pass new laws to limit impact of judicial decisions	– grants pardons, commutations, and reprieves
– change the (appellate) jurisdiction of the Supreme Court (*jurisdiction stripping*)	
– change number of justices on Supreme Court	
– create and define jurisdiction of lower federal courts	
– impeachment (House of Representatives majority vote) and conviction and removal from office (Senate two-thirds vote) of federal judges	
– introduce constitutional amendments to change or clarify the Constitution concerning Court decisions with a two-thirds vote of each chamber	

UNIT 3

CIVIL LIBERTIES
AND
CIVIL RIGHTS

Civil Liberties

I. THE BILL OF RIGHTS

A. WHY A BILL OF RIGHTS?

1. The Framers did not include a list of specific individual rights in the original Constitution for two primary reasons, discussed by Hamilton in "Federalist No. 84."

    a. The proposed system of government offered the best protection for individual rights.

    b. No list of rights could be drafted to cover all rights held by individuals. Any suggested list, therefore, could be used to deprive individuals of rights that were omitted from the list.

2. The lack of a specific and extensive list protecting individual rights became a primary driver of Anti-Federalist opposition to the Constitution. Ultimately, this argument did not defeat the Constitution, but resulted in the adoption of the Bill of Rights shortly after ratification.

3. The Bill of Rights is composed of the first 10 amendments to the Constitution. It protects numerous individual liberties, including rights to free speech and religion, privacy, and rights of those accused of crimes.

Test Tip

You may be asked to analyze how debates over the extent and application of the rights included in the Constitution illustrate the tension in our society between individual liberties/freedoms and the need for social order and safety. Should speech be protected if it poses a threat to order? How does protecting the rights of accused criminals impact public safety? How should one individual's right to privacy be balanced against another person's right to protection? Consider how the Court has balanced these conflicting interests as you read the cases in this chapter.

B. CIVIL LIBERTIES VS. CIVIL RIGHTS

1. Most of what we think of as "rights," such as the right to free speech and the right to bear arms, are actually *civil liberties*, those personal rights and freedoms with which the government is not allowed to arbitrarily interfere.

2. It is important to understand that civil liberties are not absolute; they all have important limits and exceptions. The government may limit specific civil liberties in many circumstances, such as limiting free speech when it poses a serious and immediate danger to the public.

3. The term *civil rights* refers to the rights of minority group members to be protected by the government against discrimination. The right to government protection is not related to the Bill of Rights, but is found in the Equal Protection Clause of the Fourteenth Amendment. (Civil rights are covered in Chapter 10.)

4. The terms *civil liberties* and *civil rights* may be confusing. This confusion is made worse by the fact that civil liberties are listed in the Bill of Rights. (It might help to think of the Bill of Rights as the Bill of Liberties.)

    a. Civil liberties are extended to apply to the states through the Fourteenth Amendment's Due Process Clause.

    b. Civil rights are protected by the Fourteenth Amendment's Equal Protection Clause.

    c. It may be helpful to remember that civil liberties prohibit government action. For example, the government may not restrict free speech or search your home without a warrant. Civil rights require the government to act. For example, the government must enforce legislation prohibiting discrimination in housing or education.

C. SELECTIVE INCORPORATION

1. *Due process* is the legal principle requiring that the government follow standardized rules and procedures and respect the rights of all persons.

2. *Selective incorporation* is the name for the legal doctrine by which the Supreme Court has interpreted most individual liberties stated in the Bill of Rights to protect citizens against state actions using the Due Process Clause of the Fourteenth Amendment. (Note that the Due Process Clause of the Fifth Amendment guarantees due process on the part of the federal government.)

Test Tip

The Bill of Rights included a due process requirement in the Fifth Amendment, which was intended to restrain the federal government. State governments, however, were not held to this standard. Following the Civil War, the Fourteenth Amendment was enacted to protect individuals against state government due process infringements. Be sure to understand the difference between these clauses. Questions on court cases about due process will almost always relate to the Due Process Clause of the Fourteenth Amendment.

3. The Bill of Rights was adopted as a means of preventing the federal government from interfering with personal liberties. Later Supreme Court decisions reinforced the idea that the Bill of Rights did not place restrictions on the actions of state governments. States' actions frequently did not comply with guarantees of individual freedoms made in the federal Constitution.

4. Following the Civil War, Congress proposed and the states ratified the Fourteenth Amendment, which made several guarantees to United States citizens, including Due Process and Equal Protection.

5. The Due Process Clause of the Fourteenth Amendment has come to be interpreted as guaranteeing that most state actions are restricted by the Bill of Rights to the same extent as federal actions.

6. The application of the Bill of Rights to the states did not happen in a single case, but piecemeal, one right at a time (selectively).

7. In *Gitlow v. New York* (1925), the Court formally extended the First Amendment's free speech protection to the states, ruling that the Fourteenth Amendment's Due Process Clause restricted state governments as well as the federal government.

8. Following *Gitlow*, the Court went on, over the next several decades, to apply most of the Bill of Rights to the states through selective incorporation. Many of the cases in this unit are incorporation cases.

9. The term *selective incorporation* refers to the process of applying the Bill of Rights piecemeal (one at a time) to the states, rather than applying these rights completely to the states all at once. The term *total incorporation* refers to the idea that *all* of the protections of the Bill of Rights apply to the states, but this doctrine has never been accepted by the Court and only appears in dissenting opinions.

Test Tip

It is important for you to be able to explain how the Supreme Court has used selective incorporation to extend the civil liberties in the Bill of Rights to apply to state and local government through the Due Process Clause of the Fourteenth Amendment. While many of the civil liberties in the Bill of Rights have been incorporated, some still do not apply to the states.

Selective Incorporation

Incorporated Rights	
First Amendment – Establishment Clause – Free Exercise Clause – Free speech – Press freedom – Right to Assemble – Right to Petition **Second Amendment** – Right to keep and bear arms **Fourth Amendment** – Freedom from unreasonable searches and seizures – Warrant requirement	**Fifth Amendment** – Right against double jeopardy – Right against self-incrimination – Right to compensation for property taken by the government (*eminent domain*) **Sixth Amendment** – Right to a speedy and public trial – Right to jury trial – Right to confront witnesses – Right to compel witnesses to testify – Right to counsel (an attorney) **Eighth Amendment** – Right against cruel and unusual punishment – Right against excessive fines
Rights Not Yet Incorporated	
Third Amendment – Right against quartering of troops in homes **Fifth Amendment** – Right to indictment by grand jury	**Seventh Amendment** – Right to jury trial in civil cases **Eighth Amendment** – Right against excessive bail.

The AP® exam may ask you to differentiate between the issues of due process and equal protection. According to the Fourteenth Amendment, a state may not "deprive any person of life, liberty, or property, without due process of law; nor deny to any person within its jurisdiction the equal protection of the laws."

> ➤ *The Due Process Clause of the Fourteenth Amendment requires that state governments may not act arbitrarily, but must follow fair and standardized procedures, and respect individual rights. This is the basis for the selective incorporation doctrine; it is used to protect civil liberties.*

> ➤ *The Equal Protection Clause of the Fourteenth Amendment requires that the law protect all people equally, and is the basis for the* **Brown v. Board of Education** *and subsequent civil rights rulings.*

D. OTHER INDIVIDUAL RIGHTS IN THE CONSTITUTION

1. The Framers were well aware of the danger of government interference in individual rights, and did include specific protections in the body of the Constitution. Article I prohibits the use of ex post facto laws and bills of attainder, and protects the right of habeas corpus.

2. *Ex post facto* (Latin for "after the fact") laws are laws passed by Congress making conduct criminal after it has taken place. Individuals cannot be charged with crimes that did not exist in law at the time the actions were committed.

3. Bills of attainder are laws passed to declare a person or group guilty of a crime and impose punishment. People may not be declared guilty of crimes by legislative acts.

4. A *writ of habeas corpus* (Latin for "produce the body") protects the right of a detained person to be brought before a judge and defend himself or herself. A writ of *habeas corpus* is issued by a judge to bring a prisoner to court for a hearing.

II. THE FIRST AMENDMENT

A. RIGHTS PROTECTED

1. Amendment I: "Congress shall make no law respecting an establishment of religion, or prohibiting the free exercise thereof; or abridging the freedom of speech, or of the press; or the right of the people peaceably to assemble, and to petition the government for a redress of grievances."

2. The First Amendment protects five specific rights:

   a. **Freedom of religion** is addressed in two parts: a prohibition of government support for or affiliation (establishment clause) with religion, and a guarantee of protection of religious practice (free exercise clause).

   b. **Freedom of speech** is broadly understood to include a wide range of expression, including symbolic speech.

   c. **Freedom of the press** is preserved and has been broadly applied, guaranteeing extensive protections to the press.

   d. **Freedom to assemble** guarantees the right of people to meet and gather in groups to peacefully protest government policies.

   e. **Freedom to petition** the government for a redress of grievances allows individuals to make complaints to or seek the assistance of their government without threat of punishment.

Test Tip

The First Amendment's protection of religious freedom includes two distinct clauses: the Establishment Clause and the Free Exercise Clause. You may be required to distinguish between these clauses.

B. ESTABLISHMENT CLAUSE

1. The Establishment Clause states: "Congress shall make no law respecting an establishment of religion." The term *separation of state and church* means that the government may not adopt or support an official religion. It has been broadly interpreted by the Court to mean that the government may not support or associate with any religion except in the most limited and necessary ways.

2. *Engel v. Vitale* (1962)

    a. **Facts of the Case:** A public school district adopted a policy of leading a daily prayer. The prayer was non-denominational (not connected with any particular religion or denomination), and non-compulsory (no student was required to participate in the prayer).

    b. **Constitutional Issue(s):** Does the classroom reading of a non-denominational, non-compulsory prayer in a public school violate the Establishment Clause of the First Amendment?

    c. **Holding(s):** Yes, the Establishment Clause prohibits the classroom reading of a non-denominational, non-compulsory prayer in public school.

    d. **Reasoning:** The Establishment Clause requires the separation of state and church. It does not allow the government to encourage or promote religion, even if students are not required to participate. The fact that the prayer was non-denominational was not significant, as it still promoted a particular type of religious thought. The Establishment Clause prohibits the government from endorsing or promoting religious activities.

3. Not all interpretations of the Establishment Clause have been quite so clear-cut.

    a. In *Lemon v. Kurtzman* (1970), the Court held that some forms of taxpayer support for private religious schools might be permissible, so long as (1) it is done for a secular (non-religious) legislative purpose; (2) it does not advance or inhibit religion; and (3) it does not create excessive government involvement with religion. These three requirements are referred to as the Lemon test.

    b. Schools may offer moments of silence, during which students may pray, but prayer may not be encouraged.

C. FREE EXERCISE CLAUSE

1. The Free Exercise Clause means that the government cannot interfere with citizens practicing their chosen religions. Citizens are allowed to pray and worship as they choose and to engage in religious rituals and practices without restriction by the government. The free exercise of religion, however, may be limited when the government has a legitimate interest in restricting it.

2. **Wisconsin v. Yoder (1972)**

   a. **Facts of the Case:** Several Amish families challenged a Wisconsin state law requiring that children attend school until the age of 16. The Amish argued that education beyond the early teen years was a violation of their religious beliefs. Their right to religious practice required that children stop receiving formal education and learn the skills and values they would need within their community.

   b. **Constitutional Issue(s):** Do laws that require school attendance violate the Free Exercise Clause of the First Amendment?

   c. **Holding(s):** Laws that require school attendance violate the Free Exercise Clause where the state cannot show an interest of "the highest order," which could not be achieved in another way.

   d. **Reasoning:** The Court balanced the interest of the state in ensuring that all citizens be reasonably well-educated against the interest of the Amish to freely practice their religion. Although the state has a legitimate interest in educated citizens, the Court concluded that the state's interest was outweighed by the need of the Amish to learn the skills and values to prepare them for life in their community. The fact that Amish children would receive two fewer years of education would not cause harm to society.

3. Other interpretations of the Free Exercise Clause.

   a. In *Reynolds v. United States* (1878), the Court upheld Reynolds' conviction for bigamy (the crime of having multiple spouses/ polygamy), even though his religion required it. The Court ruled that the Free Exercise Clause protects beliefs, not necessarily conduct. Conduct may be restricted when it interferes with the rights of others or society.

   b. Claims made under the Free Exercise Clause must be based on legitimate practices of a recognized religion. People can't invent religious reasons to justify otherwise unlawful conduct.

   c. Laws that are intended to interfere with religious practice are strictly scrutinized to ensure that restrictions are narrowly drawn and address a compelling government interest. Laws that are not intended to interfere with religious practice, but which do so inadvertently, are generally acceptable.

➤ For example, while Native Americans are allowed to use peyote in their religious ceremonies, drug use may still be used to deny unemployment benefits, according to *Employment Division v. Smith* (1990).

➤ Similarly, laws compelling vaccinations have been upheld against people who claim that their religion forbids vaccinations.

d. Religious practice may be restricted where it causes harm to others.

It may be helpful to understand how courts evaluate claims involving civil liberties, as well as those involving civil rights. Under the doctrine of strict scrutiny, government actions that infringe on a fundamental liberty or affect a "suspect classification" of people—one based on a protected status, such as race or gender—must meet three tests.

➤ *First, the government action must be based on a compelling government interest.*

➤ *Second, the government action must be narrowly constructed to achieve that interest.*

➤ *Finally, the government action must be the least restrictive method by which to protect the government's interest.*

A law that does not meet all three requirements will be found to be unconstitutional

D. FREEDOM OF SPEECH

1. *Schenck v. United States* (1919)

   a. **Facts of the Case:** Charles Schenck and Elizabeth Baer produced and distributed more than 15,000 fliers urging draft-age men to refuse conscription during World War I. Both were convicted of violating the Espionage Act of 1917. The defendants argued that their activities were protected by the First Amendment's free speech guarantee.

   b. **Constitutional Issue(s):** Is the publication and distribution of literature urging resistance to a military draft protected speech under the First Amendment?

c. **Holding(s):** The First Amendment does not protect speech promoting resistance to the draft.

d. **Reasoning:** Speech may be restricted when it poses a clear and present danger that it will cause substantial harm that the government has a right to prevent. The Court noted that the defendants' activities had been interpreted in the context of a war. During peacetime, their activities might be found to be protected.

> *The* Schenck *opinion is notable for creating the clear and present danger test and has been widely criticized for its potential to have a chilling effect on free speech. The opinion is also famous for the analogy, drawn by Supreme Court Justice Oliver Wendell Holmes, Jr., who wrote that the protection of free speech did not extend to a man "falsely shouting fire in a theatre." Such speech was unprotected, he wrote, because it would create a dangerous situation (panic) likely to result in harm to people. Today's modern analogy might be the prohibition against falsely yelling "bomb" on an airplane. The Court's decision in* Brandenburg v. Ohio *(1969) limited* Schenck *and created greater protections for political speech.*

2. *Tinker v. Des Moines Independent Community School District* (1969)

   a. **Facts of the Case:** Several students wore black armbands to school to protest the Vietnam War. The students did not make any verbal statements about the war or cause any disruption. After the students were sent home for wearing the armbands, their parents filed suit, claiming a violation of the students' free speech rights.

   b. **Constitutional Issue(s):**

      ➤ Do freedom of speech protections apply to students in public schools?

      ➤ Is the wearing of black armbands considered "speech" within the meaning of the First Amendment?

   c. **Holding(s):**

      ➤ The First Amendment protects student speech.

      ➤ Wearing armbands is a form of speech.

d.   **Reasoning:** Free speech rights apply to public schools, and students have a right to free expression, so long as it does not substantially interfere with school discipline. The armbands were symbolic speech, protected by the First Amendment.

> *The* Tinker *case recognized that wearing black armbands in protest was a form of speech. Symbolic speech is expression that is intended to convey a particular message to its viewers and is likely to be understood. Another important symbolic speech case is* Texas v. Johnson *(1989), in which the Court ruled that burning the United States flag in protest of the government is protected speech.*

3.   There are many limitations on the First Amendment's free speech guarantee.

a.   In *West Virginia State Board of Education v. Barnette* (1943), the Court found that students have a right to refuse to salute the flag and to refuse to participate in the Pledge of Allegiance. Although the refusal of the students in this case was based on religious beliefs, the Court found the right to refuse to salute or pledge to be based on free speech grounds, and applicable regardless of religious beliefs.

b.   The right of schools to limit student speech was upheld in *Morse v. Frederick* (2007). As the Olympic torch was carried through their city, several students held up a sign at the school-sponsored event that read "BONG HITS 4 JESUS" and were suspended for promoting illegal drug use. The Court held that schools may restrict student speech that substantially interferes with the school's educational mission.

c.   Defamation—falsely injuring the reputation of another—is not protected under the First Amendment freedom of speech. Defamation can take the form of libel or slander.

   ➤   *Libel* is harm caused to the reputation of another in written form.

   ➤   *Slander* is verbally harming the reputation of another.

   ➤   Public officials have less protection than private citizens concerning defamation. To prove libel or slander against himself or herself, a public official must prove that false claims were made maliciously (with evil intent), rather than simply prove that they were false. *New York Times v. Sullivan* (1964)

d. Obscenity (pornography) may be restricted. Historically, the problem for the Court has hinged on the definition of obscenity. What makes a thing "obscene"? Justice Potter Stewart noted this difficulty when he wrote that obscenity might be impossible to define, but "I know it when I see it." In *Miller v. California* (1973), the Court created a three-part test to determine whether material is obscene (the obscenity test). In order to determine that the work in question is obscene, it must be determined that it meets all three criteria.

➤ Would an average person, applying contemporary community standards, find that the work appeals to the prurient (generating lustful thoughts) interest?

➤ Does the work depict or describe sexual conduct?

➤ Does the work lack serious literary, artistic, political, or scientific value?

Note: Child pornography has no constitutional protection.

e. Attempts have been made to regulate hate speech, speech intended to offend or threaten a person or group on the basis of race, religion, sex, or another characteristic. The Court's rulings on hate speech laws have been mixed.

➤ Ordinances (local laws) that criminalize certain forms of hate speech, such as swastikas or cross-burnings have been found to be unconstitutional because they criminalize speech based on content. *R.A.V. v. City of St. Paul* (1992)

➤ Penalty enhancement laws, which create increased penalties for ordinary crimes motivated by hate, have been upheld as constitutional. *Wisconsin v. Mitchell* (1993)

➤ Many colleges and universities have rules against hate speech on campus. The Supreme Court has not ruled on this type of speech restriction.

f. Although attempts have been made to regulate Internet speech, the Court has found that online speech is entitled to full First Amendment protection. The Court struck down the Communications Decency Act, a law which attempted to regulate certain types of Internet speech, because it was too vague in its definition of obscenity. *Reno v. ACLU* (1997)

E. **FREEDOM OF THE PRESS**

   1. *New York Times Co. v. United States* **(1971)**

      a. **Facts of the Case:** The *New York Times* and the *Washington Post* newspapers obtained extensive content of a classified government report (the Pentagon Papers) detailing U.S. involvement in the Vietnam War. The *Times* began publishing a series of articles based on the classified report. The government obtained a restraining order from a federal district court requiring the *Times* to stop publishing the classified information. The case focused on the issue of **prior restraint**, the ability of the government to censor information before it is published.

      b. **Constitutional Issue(s):** May the government prevent the publication of information that may cause harm to the government, the United States, or its people?

      c. **Holding(s):** The government is not entitled to prevent newspapers from publishing classified information that may be embarrassing or cause harm to the government.

      d. **Reasoning:** By a 6–3 vote, the Court held for the newspapers in a *per curiam* opinion (an opinion with no specific author). In the opinion, the Court noted that the party seeking to restrain the press from publishing information has a heavy burden. Each of the nine justices wrote separate opinions regarding the issue. Most of the opinions agreed that the press generally has the right to publish information in its possession, even if it may cause some degree of harm to the government. Prior restraint of the press by the government is prohibited by the Constitution.

   2. Other considerations surrounding freedom of speech.

      a. Although the Framers included press freedom in the First Amendment as a specific right, freedom of the press is closely related to freedom of speech and has generally been interpreted as such. No case has recognized the press as having rights distinct from free speech.

      b. The government may not restrict publication of information critical of government officials. Officials who are criticized may, however, sue for libel. *Near v. Minnesota* (1931)

III. **SECOND AMENDMENT**

A. THE RIGHT TO KEEP AND BEAR ARMS

1. The Second Amendment reads: "A well regulated Militia, being necessary to the security of a free state, the right of the people to keep and bear Arms, shall not be infringed."

2. Because the Second Amendment refers to a "well regulated militia," it was historically interpreted as applying to militias—or, as we understand this term in modern times, the National Guard—and not to private citizens.

B. INCORPORATION OF THE SECOND AMENDMENT

1. It was not until 2008, in *District of Columbia v. Heller*, that the Court held the Second Amendment to grant a right to keep weapons to private citizens generally. Because the District of Columbia is a federal territory and not a state, however, the *Heller* decision was limited to federal law.

2. *McDonald v. Chicago* (2010)

   a. **Facts of the Case:** A Chicago ordinance banned the ownership of handguns. Otis McDonald, a city resident who lived in a dangerous neighborhood and had been the victim of crime in his home on several occasions, sued the city for violating his right to keep and bear arms.

   b. **Constitutional Issue(s):** Does the Second Amendment's guarantee of the right to keep and bear arms apply against infringement by state and local governments?

   c. **Holding(s):** The Second Amendment guarantees the right to keep and bear arms against infringement by state and local governments.

   d. **Reasoning:** The right to keep and bear arms is a fundamental constitutional guarantee, and must, therefore, be incorporated into the Due Process Clause of the Fourteenth Amendment. The right to keep and bear arms has been extended to the states under the doctrine of selective incorporation.

IV. RIGHTS OF THE ACCUSED

A. SPECIFIC RIGHTS GUARANTEED TO THE ACCUSED BY THE CONSTITUTION

1. One important function of the government is to protect citizens from criminals, and to charge and punish those who commit crimes. The Framers recognized, however, that the vast power of the government could be used to harass and punish citizens for political reasons. It was critical to ensure that government must follow the rule of law, and that it was restrained from acting arbitrarily or serving the will of those in power. In order to protect individuals against the awesome power of the government, the Bill of Rights includes several guarantees of specific rights held by those accused or suspected of crimes.

The Rights of the Accused

Fourth Amendment	Fifth Amendment	Sixth Amendment	Eighth Amendment
– prohibits unreasonable searches and seizures – requires warrant based on probable cause	– right to grand jury indictment for serious crimes – prohibits double jeopardy – right against self-incrimination – right to due process – prohibits taking of private property by government without reasonable compensation	– right to speedy and public trial – right to jury trial – right to be informed of charges – right to confront hostile witnesses – right to compel witnesses to testify – right to counsel	– prohibits excessive bail – prohibits excessive fines – prohibits cruel and unusual punishment

> *The only required case related to the rights of the accused is* Gideon v. Wainwright (1963). *However, the* Miranda *and* Mapp *precedents created important rules that you are required to understand.*

2. *Miranda v. Arizona* (1962)

> *Note:* Although the *Miranda* case is not required by the AP® course, it is important that you are familiar with the facts and holdings of this case.

    a. **Facts of the Case:** Ernesto Miranda was arrested on suspicion of rape and kidnapping, and interrogated for two hours. He confessed to the crime, and his confession was admitted as evidence at trial, where he was convicted. Miranda argued on appeal that he did not know and was not informed that he had a right to remain silent or a right to counsel (an attorney). His confession was, therefore, coerced, and could not be used against him.

    b. **Constitutional Issue(s):** Must the government guarantee that suspects in custody and subject to interrogation are aware of their constitutional rights?

    c. **Holding(s):** The government must ensure that suspects in custody are aware of their rights before questioning in what has become known as the Miranda rule.

    d. **Reasoning:** The Court found that, when an individual is in police custody, there is a significant danger that the right against self-incrimination may be violated. Based on the Fifth and Sixth Amendments, police must ensure that information is given voluntarily. Specifically, the government must ensure that a suspect is aware that he or she has the following rights:

        ➤ the right to remain silent

        ➤ anything said by the suspect may be used against him or her in a court of law

        ➤ the right to assistance of an attorney

        ➤ if the suspect cannot afford an attorney, one will be appointed to assist him or her by the court

3. The Miranda requirement is based on the custodial nature of the situation. Whether a suspect is "in custody" is dependent on circumstances. If not, the warning is not required.

4. The Court has recognized a public safety exception to the Miranda requirement. Police officers may question suspects in custody if there is a serious threat to public safety and the need for information outweighs the need for the Miranda warning. For example, police may interrogate a suspect without a Miranda warning in the case of an armed fugitive or about the location of a loaded weapon in a public place.

B. RIGHT TO COUNSEL

1. *Gideon v. Wainwright* **(1963)**

   a. **Facts of the Case:** Clarence Earl Gideon was charged with stealing a bottle of wine and money from a cash register in a pool hall in Panama City, Florida. He was too poor to hire an attorney, but requested that an attorney be appointed to represent him. Under Florida law, defendants were not entitled to have an attorney paid for by the state unless charged with a capital (death penalty) offense. Gideon was convicted of robbery and appealed his conviction on the basis that he was denied counsel in violation of the Sixth Amendment right "to have the assistance of counsel for his defense."

   b. **Constitutional Issue(s):**

      ➤ Does the Sixth Amendment right to counsel (lawyer) apply in all cases, even those not involving severe penalties?

      ➤ Does the Sixth Amendment right to counsel apply to the states?

   c. **Holding(s):**

      ➤ The Sixth Amendment right to counsel applies in all felony cases.

      ➤ The Sixth Amendment applies to the states under the Due Process Clause of the Fourteenth Amendment.

   d. **Reasoning:** The right to counsel is a fundamental right, essential to a fair trial and to due process of law. All defendants in felony cases are entitled to an attorney, regardless of ability to pay. States must provide appointed (government funded) attorneys for indigent (poor) defendants. This right had previously existed under federal law and was applied to the states in *Gideon*.

2. Additional requirements relating to the right to counsel.

   a. The right to counsel has been extended to include misdemeanor (less serious crime) cases. *Argersinger v. Hamlin* (1972)

   b. The right to counsel applies at any critical stage of a critical proceeding, such as questioning by police, in addition to trial.

   c. Counsel must be effective. That is, a defendant's attorney must be competent and helpful to their legal situation.

   d. A defendant may waive (give up) his or her right to counsel, but only if he or she does so voluntarily and with a full understanding of his or her rights.

C. SEARCH AND SEIZURE

1. The Fourth Amendment reads: "The right of the people to be secure in their persons, houses, papers, and effects, against unreasonable searches and seizures, shall not be violated, and no Warrants shall issue, but upon probable cause, supported by Oath or affirmation, and particularly describing the place to be searched, and the persons or things to be seized."

2. *Mapp v. Ohio* (1962)

> *Note:* Although the *Mapp* case is not required by the AP® course, it is important that you are familiar with the facts and holdings of this case.

   a. **Facts of the Case:** Police went to the home of Dollree Mapp, believing that she might be hiding a fugitive. When they knocked on the door and asked to search the home, Ms. Mapp asked if they had a warrant. They did not and later returned, claiming to have a warrant, which they did not have. The police forced their way in and searched the home. They did not find the suspect, but did find some obscene materials (pornographic magazines). The evidence was used against Mapp at trial, even though it had been obtained through a warrantless search. Mapp was convicted of possession of obscene materials in violation of Ohio state law. She appealed her conviction, arguing that the evidence should not have been admitted against her at trial, since it had been obtained in violation of her Fourth Amendment rights.

b.   **Constitutional Issue(s):** May evidence obtained in violation of a suspect's constitutional rights be admitted against him or her at trial?

c.   **Holding(s):** Illegally obtained evidence may not be admitted against a defendant at trial (the exclusionary rule).

d.   **Reasoning:** The Court noted that police would have little respect for the rights of suspects if any evidence they gathered would be admissible regardless of the circumstances under which it was obtained. The only way to ensure that the Fourth Amendment is meaningful is to prevent the use of evidence obtained in its violation. The exclusionary rule had been established in *Weeks v. United States* (1914) with regard to federal law. The *Mapp* decision incorporated the exclusionary rule and applied it to the states.

3.   **Other Fourth Amendment Search Issues**

a.   The Fourth Amendment prohibits unreasonable searches, but not all searches. Police searches must be based on probable cause (a reasonable belief based on facts). A warrant (an order signed by a judge based on probable cause) is required for searches in certain instances, but not in all cases.

b.   An important exception to the warrant requirement is the exigent circumstances exception, which allows the police to act without a warrant where someone's life or safety is threatened, or evidence is about to be lost or destroyed.

c.   The Court has ruled that cell phone data is entitled to Fourth Amendment protection; police need a warrant to search cell phones for data. *Riley v. California* (2014)

d.   Following the 9/11 terror attacks on the United States, Congress passed the USA PATRIOT Act in 2001. The law significantly broadened the authority of federal law enforcement to monitor communications and collect metadata on U.S. citizens without warrants. (Metadata is electronic information about computer files and digital activities. It includes things such as phone numbers called by individuals, but not the conversations themselves.) Because most service providers willingly shared user metadata, the government contended that it was not subject to Fourth Amendment protection. In other words, individual users did not have a privacy right in this type of data. In 2015 Congress passed the USA Freedom Act, which limits bulk collection of user data and requires warrants in some circumstances.

e. The Court has upheld mandatory drug testing of students participating in athletics and extracurricular activities. *Vernonia School District 47J v. Acton* (1995); *Pottawatomie v. Earls* (2002)

Test Tip

An ongoing theme in Fourth Amendment law is the constant need to adapt to changing technology. Is the use of a thermal imaging device to detect heat emanating from a house a "search"? (Yes.) Is the use of a drug-sniffing dog to detect the odor of drugs emanating from a suitcase a "search"? (No.) The law is still developing with regard to many areas of technology. For example, may police use cell phone location tracking data maintained by service providers? When applying the Fourth Amendment to a new situation, think about analogous (factually similar) cases that have already been decided.

D. CRUEL AND UNUSUAL PUNISHMENT

1. The Eighth Amendment reads: "Excessive bail shall not be required, nor excessive fines imposed, nor cruel and unusual punishments inflicted."

2. The term *cruel and unusual punishment* is generally understood to be punishment that is torturous or barbaric, or any punishment that is excessively disproportionate to the crime committed.

3. Although most countries in the world no longer allow capital punishment (the death penalty), the United States is one of a shrinking number that retains it. Most important Eighth Amendment cases relate to the death penalty and the circumstances under which it fails the test of cruel and unusual punishment.

   a. In *Furman v. Georgia* (1972), the Supreme Court struck down a Georgia statute because it failed to prescribe a logical and consistent basis for applying the death penalty. As a result, capital punishment was being applied in a disproportionate number of cases involving minority defendants.

   b. Four years later, the Court upheld a newly designed Georgia death penalty statute in *Gregg v. Georgia* (1976). The new law specified factors to be considered and procedures to be followed in applying the death penalty, theoretically resolving the problems of arbitrary application and discrimination.

   c. The death penalty has been held to be cruel and unusual when applied to defendants younger than 18 years of age at the time the crime was committed. *Roper v. Simmons* (2005)

   d. The death penalty has been held to be cruel and unusual when applied to defendants with an intellectual disability. *Atkins v. Virginia* (2002)

V. PRIVACY

A. SUBSTANTIVE DUE PROCESS

1. The Fourteenth Amendment states that no state may "deprive any person of life, liberty, or property, without due process of law."

   a. The Due Process Clause was initially interpreted to apply only to the procedures followed by the government in regulating private activities. In other words, the Court would not evaluate the content, or substance, of a law, so long as the government followed appropriate procedures.

   b. Later, the Court began to rely on the principle of "liberty" contained in the Fourteenth Amendment to strike down laws that, although they followed acceptable procedures, were unfair in their content.

   c The term *substantive due process* refers to the idea that the law must be fair and reasonable in content and in application. This idea has been used by the Court to protect the fundamental rights of the individual against government interference.

2. *Griswold v. Connecticut* (1965)

Note: Although the *Griswold* case is not required by the AP® course, it is important that you are familiar with the facts and holdings of this case.

   a. **Facts of the Case:** Estelle Griswold, the Executive Director of the Planned Parenthood League of Connecticut, and Dr. C. Lee Buxton, medical director of the League, opened a birth control clinic in violation of a Connecticut law that prohibited the use of any drug or device to prevent conception. (It outlawed birth control.) They were convicted of providing birth control information to married persons.

b. **Constitutional Issue(s):** Does the Connecticut statute outlawing birth control use violate a fundamental right protected by the Constitution?

c. **Holding(s):** The Connecticut law violated the right of marital privacy and was, therefore, unconstitutional.

d. **Reasoning:** The Court faced a problem in the *Griswold* case: although a law invading the contraceptive practices of married couples was unreasonable and seemed outrageous to many, the state of Connecticut argued there was nothing in the Constitution to prevent it from enforcing the law. There is no "right to privacy" in the Bill of Rights. The Court disagreed. Although the Constitution does not specifically list a right to privacy, the Ninth Amendment reads: "The enumeration in the Constitution, of certain rights, shall not be construed to deny or disparage others retained by the people." The Framers made clear in the Ninth Amendment that the people held unspecified fundamental rights. The Court pointed to several rights, such as freedom of religion and speech, the right to be free from unreasonable searches and seizures, and the right to remain silent, to justify its finding of a right to privacy by calling these zones of privacy. When taken together, these rights include within their sphere a right to privacy in marriage. The Court applied the substantive due process doctrine to strike down the Connecticut law as violating marital privacy.

B. EXTENDING PRIVACY RIGHTS

1. *Roe v. Wade* (1973)

   a. **Facts of the Case:** Norma McCorvey, a 21-year-old woman, challenged a Texas law prohibiting abortion. (McCorvey used the pseudonym Jane Roe to protect her identity.)

   b. **Constitutional Issue(s):** Did the Texas law prohibiting abortion violate women's constitutional right to privacy?

   c. **Holding(s):** Under the Ninth and Fourteenth Amendments, the constitutional right to privacy protects a woman's right to an abortion but may be regulated or restricted by the government in the second and third trimesters.

   d. **Reasoning:** *Roe* extended the right to privacy established in *Griswold* to include a woman's right to make reproductive decisions, including whether to continue or terminate a pregnancy. The Court, however, balanced the right of the woman in making reproductive decisions against the interest of society in protecting the health of both the mother and the fetus. The result was the trimester test, under which:

➤ abortion may not be restricted in the first trimester of pregnancy.

➤ beginning in the second trimester, abortion may be regulated to protect the health of the woman.

➤ after the beginning of the third trimester, the state's interest becomes sufficient to restrict abortion to protect the developing fetus.

Many important cases involve the conflict of rights, situations in which the rights of an individual conflict with those of another individual or with society generally. In Roe, the Court balanced the privacy right of pregnant women against the interest of society in "potential life." There are many other examples of the Court balancing rights. Debates over the right to bear arms are frequently framed in terms of the individual's right to self-protection versus society's need to maintain order and public safety. Government surveillance cases consider the extent of the government's right to monitor and collect data on its citizens against the right of citizens to privacy in their data and communications.

2. **Post-Roe Cases**

a. The trend since *Roe v. Wade* has been for states to place increasing burdens on abortion access.

b. *Planned Parenthood v. Casey* (1992) upheld a fundamental right to abortion from the *Roe v. Wade* decision but allowed states to regulate abortion at any point in pregnancy as it does not pose an "undue burden" on the woman. The Court has ruled that after the point of viability (the point at which a fetus can survive outside of the womb), the state may restrict or prohibit abortion. The *Casey* decision also struck down a husband-notification requirement for women seeking an abortion.

c. In recent years, the membership of the Supreme Court has changed. Recognizing the Court's changing ideological composition, some states have enacted increasingly restrictive abortion laws in anticipation of the Court possibly revisiting the issue. Other states, however, have enacted laws explicitly recognizing and protecting abortion rights. The Court may consider various state positions relating to the regulation of abortion in coming years.

d.   The right to die has also been argued in the context of a right to privacy. A competent person may have a protected interest in refusing life-sustaining medical procedures. (*Cruzan v. Missouri Department of Health* (1990)) There is, however, no constitutionally protected right to commit suicide, or to have others assist in suicide. (*Washington v. Glucksberg* (1997))

Test Tip

Although the term privacy *is not directly mentioned in the Constitution, other rights such as those found in the First, Third, Fourth, and Fifth Amendments imply that people have a right to privacy. For example, the Third Amendment's right to not have soldiers quartered in the home and the Fourth Amendment's protection from unreasonable searches and seizures imply a right to privacy in the home.*

Civil Rights

I. THE FOURTEENTH AMENDMENT AND CIVIL RIGHTS MOVEMENTS

A. THE FOURTEENTH AMENDMENT

1. Prior to the Civil War, in the *Dred Scott v. Sandford* decision (1857), the Supreme Court declared that slaves, former slaves, and their descendants were not citizens of the United States, and therefore not entitled to the rights of citizenship.

2. Following the Civil War, the Southern states resisted the social and economic integration of freed slaves by enacting Black Codes to preserve white supremacy. In response, three amendments were added to the Constitution:

   a. The Thirteenth Amendment abolished slavery.

   b. The Fourteenth Amendment defined citizenship to include "[a]ll persons born or naturalized in the United States," and outlined protections for individuals against state government actions.

   c. The Fifteenth Amendment guaranteed voting rights regardless of "race, color, or previous condition of servitude."

3. Section 1 of the Fourteenth Amendment reads:

   All persons born or naturalized in the United States, and subject to the jurisdiction thereof, are citizens of the United States and of the State wherein they reside. No State shall make or enforce any law which shall abridge the privileges or immunities of citizens of the United States; nor shall any State deprive any person of life, liberty, or property, without due process of law; nor deny to any person within its jurisdiction the equal protection of the laws.

4. The final clause of this section, the Equal Protection Clause, has formed the basis for civil rights claims for many groups, beginning with African Americans. The Equal Protection Clause has been interpreted to require the federal government to address and prevent discriminatory practices.

5. Civil rights are those rights to equal treatment that all persons are guaranteed. The government must protect people from being discriminated against based on group membership and personal characteristics, including race, national origin, religion, and sex. The government has a positive obligation (must take action) to prevent and address discrimination against members of minority groups.

B. THE FIGHT AGAINST SEGREGATION

1. Adding the Fourteenth Amendment to the Constitution did not automatically change the culture of the nation. Many states resisted equality for African Americans. The Civil Rights Movement was born out of the struggle of former slaves and their descendants for equal treatment under the law.

2. In the late decades of the nineteenth century, the former Confederate states passed laws that segregated African Americans. These Black Codes, or Jim Crow laws, required African Americans to use separate facilities, such as bathrooms and water fountains, and separated them from whites in public spaces, such as theaters and railroad cars.

3. Legal segregation (laws requiring the separation of the races) was challenged in *Plessy v. Ferguson* (1896). In that case, the Supreme Court upheld a Louisiana state law requiring that African Americans ride in separate railroad cars. The Court ruled that, as long as the accommodations provided to African Americans were substantially the same as those provided to whites, legal segregation was constitutional. This separate but equal doctrine remained law throughout the first half of the twentieth century.

4. The National Association for the Advancement of Colored People (NAACP), was founded in 1909 to advocate for social justice and equal treatment for African Americans. Led by Thurgood Marshall, who would go on to become the first African American Supreme Court justice, the NAACP Legal Defense Fund brought *Brown v. Board of Education* and other important civil rights cases to the Court.

5. *Brown v. Board of Education of Topeka* (1954)

    a. **Facts of the Case:** Segregation laws in Topeka forbade Linda Brown, a third grader, to enroll in the public school closest to her house. Instead, she was forced to walk several blocks and then ride a bus to the segregated Black school, which was much farther away than the local "white" public school. Linda's father and several other plaintiffs sued, arguing that African American children could not receive an equal education in segregated schools and that the Equal Protection Clause required the Court to strike down state laws requiring segregation.

    b. **Constitutional Issue(s):** Does the Equal Protection Clause of the Fourteenth Amendment prohibit segregation based on race?

    c. **Holding(s):** The Equal Protection Clause prohibits segregation based on race because separation creates inherent inequality.

    d. **Reasoning:** Of critical importance to the plaintiffs (the people bringing the case to court) and the African American community was the idea that segregation is inherently (naturally) unequal. That is, that African American students who attended separate schools by law were being denied educational opportunities and benefits that they would be given in an integrated setting, even if their school facilities and teachers were roughly equal. Furthermore, the negative message of segregation toward African American students was harmful to their education and self-worth. The Court agreed and unconditionally overturned *Plessy*, stating

> Segregation of white and colored children in public schools has a detrimental effect upon the colored children. The effect is greater when it has the sanction of the law, for the policy of separating the races is usually interpreted as denoting the inferiority of the negro group. A sense of inferiority affects the motivation of a child to learn. Segregation with the sanction of law, therefore, has a tendency to [retard] the educational and mental development of negro children and to deprive them of some of the benefits they would receive in a racial[ly] integrated school system.

The Court concluded that "separate educational facilities are inherently unequal" under the Fourteenth Amendment.

6. The following year, in *Brown v. Board of Education II* (1955), the Court ordered that school systems desegregate with "all deliberate speed." Especially in the South, however, compliance was slow and frequently not implemented for many years.

Test Tip

> Remember that the Supreme Court is influenced by many factors that change over time. Citizen-state interactions, which are driven by cultural changes, influence the Court's decision-making. Also, as the composition of the Court changes (via turnover in the nine justices serving at any given time), the ideological makeup of the Court changes. In Brown, these changes led the Court to overrule the precedent set by Plessy after almost 60 years.

C. THE CIVIL RIGHTS MOVEMENT

1. The mid-1950s marked a turning point in American society. African Americans, who had long been subjected to discrimination and mistreatment, including violence and murder, began to push for change with renewed energy, and the Civil Rights Movement began.

2. The African American community organized—that is, they took collective action to persuade state and local governments to change their policies. An important leader in the movement was Dr. Martin Luther King, Jr., who advocated nonviolent resistance to government oppression. In addition to legal challenges and lobbying for legislation, the methods they used to bring about reform included boycotts, sit-ins, marches, and freedom rides, which were bus trips through the South to protest segregated buses.

    a. African Americans and others who supported the movement engaged in acts of civil disobedience, or preplanned organized actions in which individuals refuse to follow unjust laws. Notably, Rosa Parks refused to give up her seat on a Montgomery, Alabama, city bus to a white rider and was arrested.

    b. Following Parks' arrest, King led a boycott of the Montgomery city buses by African Americans. The Black community organized carpools and walked rather than ride buses, causing a massive loss of revenue to the city.

3. King led numerous protest marches during the 1950s and 1960s. In 1963, he was arrested for leading a march in Birmingham, Alabama, and held in solitary confinement.

4. While in jail in Birmingham, a supporter smuggled King a newspaper that had published an opinion piece by several white Alabama clergy members opposing the marches. King composed a response during his time in jail in which he addressed the religious leaders' statement, poignantly describing the experience of African Americans in the South and defending the protesters' actions.

   a. King first responds to the assertion that he was an "outsider" who should not be stirring up trouble in Birmingham. He argues that he had been invited as head of the Southern Christian Leadership Conference (SCLC). Moreover, he argues that people have a duty to fight injustice wherever it exists, emphasizing that communities are interrelated.

   b. King goes on to point out that Birmingham, at the time, was probably the most segregated city in the country, with a brutal record of abuse and oppression of African Americans.

   c. King makes the point that "direct action," or nonviolent resistance, is sometimes necessary to drive negotiation and reach resolution when attempts at cooperation have been refused.

      You may well ask: 'Why direct action? Why sit-ins, marches and so forth? Isn't negotiation a better path?' You are quite right in calling for negotiation. Indeed, this is the very purpose of direct action. Nonviolent direct action seeks to create such a crisis and foster such a tension that a community which has constantly refused to negotiate is forced to confront the issue. It seeks so to dramatize the issue that it can no longer be ignored. My citing the creation of tension as part of the work of the nonviolent resister may sound rather shocking. But I must confess that I am not afraid of the word 'tension.' I have earnestly opposed violent tension, but there is a type of constructive, nonviolent tension which is necessary for growth.

   d. King points out that "[h]istory is the long and tragic story of the fact that privileged groups seldom give up their privileges voluntarily."

e. He passionately defends nonviolent direct action as a middle ground between despair and violence.

f. King distinguishes between just and unjust laws and argues that it is one's moral duty to uphold just laws and to disobey unjust laws.

> How does one determine whether a law is just or unjust? A just law is a man-made code that squares with the moral law or the law of God. An unjust law is a code that is out of harmony with the moral law. To put it in the terms of St. Thomas Aquinas: An unjust law is a human law that is not rooted in eternal law and natural law. Any law that uplifts human personality is just. Any law that degrades human personality is unjust.

g. King expresses disappointment in the white religious establishment for failing to stand against the injustice of racism, and in the inaction of white moderates, referring to the "appalling silence of good people."

h. He closes by pointing out that the clergy members' praise of the "nonviolent" police response to protests is misplaced. Instead, he praises the actions of the protesters, who refrained from violence in the face of attacks and humiliation.

D. THE CIVIL RIGHTS MOVEMENT RESULTED IN IMPORTANT LEGISLATION

1. **Civil Rights Act of 1964:** This sweeping law was introduced under John F. Kennedy and signed into law by Lyndon Johnson. It protected civil rights in several regards, including:

   a. Outlawing discrimination in public accommodations or any place "open to the public" such as restaurants, hotels, and theaters.

   b. Prohibiting discrimination in employment based on race, color, religion, sex, or national origin. This section is notable for including "sex" as a basis for civil rights protection.

2. **The Twenty-fourth Amendment:** Ratified in 1964, this amendment outlaws the requirement of a tax in order to vote (poll tax). Because the process of creating constitutional amendments is extremely difficult, the civil rights movement focused more on achieving goals through litigation (law suits) and advocating for legislation.

3. **Voting Rights Act of 1965**: This landmark law prohibits discrimination in voting procedures throughout the United States. Although the Civil Rights Act of 1964 had prohibited discriminatory voting requirements, the Voting Rights Act significantly clarified and expanded voting protections for African Americans. Significant provisions include:

   a.   The Voting Rights Act outlaws literacy tests and similar mechanisms for disenfranchising (disallowing voting rights) minorities.

   b.   The law placed special restrictions on particular jurisdictions (states or areas) with a history of voter discrimination against minorities.

      ➤ These jurisdictions were required to obtain *preclearance*, or prior approval, from the Justice Department before implementing any changes to voting procedures.

      ➤ Whether a jurisdiction could be regulated was dependent on a coverage formula, but the formula was struck down in *Shelby County v. Holder* (2013) as being out of date and not appropriate for addressing modern conditions.

      ➤ The holding in *Shelby* effectively made preclearance unenforceable. As a result, numerous states and jurisdictions that had previously been subject to preclearance requirements have passed laws that place increased restrictions on voting rights.

   c.   The Voting Rights Act led to a significant increase in the election of African American legislators in southern states.

Test Tip

The government may respond to social movements through judicial decisions, such as **Brown v. Board of Education,** *or its response may be legislative, as when Congress passed the Civil Rights Act of 1964 or the Voting Rights Act of 1965. As you continue reading, note the various governmental responses to the civil rights demands of particular groups.*

E. OTHER ISSUES IN SEGREGATION

1. One problem the courts have grappled with is how to deal with situations in which segregation is not the result of laws requiring

it (de jure segregation, Latin for "by law"), but a consequence of individual choices (de facto segregation, Latin for "in fact").

    a. Schools may be segregated due to citizens' choices and preferences as to where they live. This is de facto segregation—segregation in fact, rather than by law.

    b. In *Swann v. Charlotte-Mecklenburg Board of Education* (1971), the Court held that busing students to integrate schools was constitutionally acceptable, even though students might need to be transported to schools farther away than their local schools.

    c. Generally, the Court has held that the government is not required to act to desegregate in situations of de facto segregation.

2. An area of significant controversy has been the use of affirmative action policies in hiring and education, particularly in the college admissions process.

    a. Affirmative action refers to policies intended to prevent discrimination and to correct the lasting effects of historical discrimination by ensuring that minority groups are appropriately represented in employment and higher education environments. This is typically achieved by allocating a minimum percentage of places to minorities.

    b. In *Regents of University of California v. Bakke* (1978), Bakke, a white student who was denied admission to medical school while less qualified minority students were admitted, claimed that the university's admissions policy resulted in illegal discrimination against white applicants (sometimes referred to as reverse discrimination). The Court held that race-based quotas (concrete percentages or numbers of seats) were a violation of the Equal Protection Clause, but that race could be considered as a factor in admissions decisions.

    c. Recently, the Court has struck down admission systems that seem to make race too significant a factor in college admissions, but has continued to hold that race may be taken into consideration.

Remember that the courts use the standard of strict scrutiny to evaluate both civil rights and civil liberties claims. Regarding civil rights, government actions that impact a minority group must be

(1) based on a compelling government interest;

(2) narrowly tailored to address that interest; and

(3) the least restrictive way to do so.

3. Following changes to the Voting Rights Act in 1982, some states redrew congressional districts to allow African Americans the opportunity to elect representatives to Congress. The districts were the result of an effort to draw the boundaries to create majority-minority districts, in which a racial minority (African Americans) made up the majority of the voters in a district. These districts were essentially racial gerrymanders, but the gerrymandering was done to create an advantage, rather than a disadvantage, for the minority group. In *Shaw v. Reno* (1993), the Court struck down this type of plan as a violation of the Equal Protection Clause of the Fourteenth Amendment, holding that racial gerrymandering is unconstitutional regardless of its intent.

II. THE WOMEN'S MOVEMENT

A. THE STRUGGLE FOR WOMEN'S EQUALITY

1. Ratified in 1920, the Nineteenth Amendment culminated the first wave of the women's rights movement, which had mainly focused on acquiring the right to vote.

2. In the 1960s, the second wave of the women's movement focused on equality. It grew out of increasing awareness of the inequities faced by women in American society.

3. In 1963, *The Feminine Mystique* by Betty Friedan was published. The book critiqued popular ideas surrounding women's place in society and argued that women were entitled to self-fulfillment including educational and professional opportunities.

4. The National Organization for Women (NOW) was co-founded in 1966 by Betty Friedan "to bring women into full participation in the mainstream of American society now, exercising all the privileges and responsibilities thereof in truly equal partnership

with men." NOW advocates for many feminist policy goals, including:

   a.   equal rights under the law

   b.   reproductive choice

   c.   workplace equality

   d.   ending sexual harassment and violence against women

   e.   global feminist issues

B. KEY OUTCOMES OF THE WOMEN'S MOVEMENT

1. The Equal Pay Act of 1963 required equal compensation for substantially equivalent work regardless of gender, race, religion, or national origin.

2. Title VII of the Civil Rights Act of 1964 included "sex" as a prohibited basis for discrimination, forming the basis for legal action to enforce equal treatment for women in the workplace.

   a.   Women are protected against discrimination in hiring and employment conditions, generally, and may not be treated differently from men if the difference is unreasonable.

   b.   Women also have a right to be free from sexual harassment in the workplace.

      ➤ *Quid pro quo* sexual harassment describes situations in which demands for sex are made on an employee in exchange for continued employment or advancement.

      ➤ Hostile environment sexual harassment is behavior that creates a workplace that is intimidating or abusive such that a reasonable person would find it difficult or impossible to do his or her job.

3. Title IX of the Education Amendments Act of 1972 (amending the Higher Education Act of 1965) prohibits discrimination on the basis of sex in federally funded educational activities.

   a.   Although the law prohibits discrimination in all educational activities, it is best known for increasing women's access to athletic activities.

   b.   Title IX also prohibits sexual harassment in educational environments.

4. An Equal Rights Amendment, guaranteeing equal rights for women, was proposed by two-thirds of each chamber of Congress

in 1972. Ratification failed, however, with only 35 of the necessary 38 states passing the amendment in the 10-year ratification period.

Test Tip

It is sometimes confusing to think of women as a legally protected minority group, since there are actually more women than men in the United States. Although not a numerical minority, women are a legal minority, or a group that is designated as having legal protection against discrimination. Most legal minorities are also numerical minorities. However, women are a legal minority with a (slight) numerical majority.

III. OTHER SOCIAL MOVEMENTS

A. PERSONS WITH DISABILITIES

1. Because individuals with disabilities have unique physical needs concerning access, they have historically faced systemic discrimination. The disability rights movement began in the 1960s.

2. Under the Rehabilitation Act of 1973, Section 504:

   a. Employers must provide reasonable accommodations to disabled applicants and employees, so long as they can otherwise perform the essential functions of their jobs.

   b. Schools must evaluate the needs of students with disabilities and create an educational plan accommodating his or her educational requirements (a 504 plan for a student).

3. The Americans with Disabilities Act (ADA) was passed in 1990. The ADA frames the need for accommodations of disabled persons as a civil rights issue, rather than as a medical issue. The ADA clarifies and builds on the previous law by

   a. broadly defining the term *disability* to include both physical and mental conditions.

   b. prohibiting discrimination by all employers with more than 15 employees. The ADA applies not only to entities receiving federal funds, but to private businesses as well.

   c. requiring places open to the public to ensure physical access to facilities, including wheelchair access.

    d. requiring access to public accommodations. Like Title VII of the Civil Rights Act of 1964, the ADA requires private businesses to take steps to ensure accessibility if the cost is not prohibitive.

    e. guaranteeing access for service animals, with limited exceptions.

*Keep in mind that most civil rights laws, including the Civil Rights Act of 1964, the Voting Rights Act of 1965, and the Americans with Disabilities Act (ADA) are **unfunded mandates**—laws passed by the federal government that do not provide federal funding to cover the costs of implementation. These laws are frequently criticized for requiring states to pay for their implementation. The ADA, because it legally required government entities and private businesses to physically modify buildings and public places to allow access to the disabled, created a particularly steep financial burden and faced considerable opposition.*

B. LGBTQ RIGHTS

1. Members of the LGBTQ community have a long history of experiencing discrimination and are a more recent group to seek legal protections in the areas of marriage, military service, and personal freedoms. Until 1973, homosexuality (a term then used by the medical community) was considered a mental disorder by the American Psychiatric Association.

2. There is no federal law protecting individuals based on sexual orientation or gender identity. However, many states have passed laws prohibiting this type of discrimination in various situations.

3. The right to marry had long been a priority of LGBTQ activists. Legal marriage, generally taken for granted by heterosexual couples, grants spouses a series of rights that LGBTQ couples were denied, including rights to inheritance, insurance benefits, and medical decision-making.

    a. Same-sex marriage was illegal in all 50 states until 2003, when the Massachusetts Supreme Court struck down the state's same-sex marriage prohibition, making Massachusetts the first state to allow same-sex marriage.

b. Vermont became the first state to legalize same-sex marriage by legislative action in 2009.

c. The Defense of Marriage Act (DOMA), passed by Congress in 1996, limited marriage to heterosexual couples for federal purposes, including access to insurance benefits for federal employees, social security survivorship (the right to collect a spouse's social security benefits after his or her death).

d. In *United States v. Windsor* (2013), the Court struck down DOMA, ruling that the federal government's differential treatment of same-sex couples served no legitimate purpose and violated the Due Process Clause of the Fifth Amendment. (The Due Process Clause of the Fifth Amendment applied here because DOMA was a federal law. The Fifth Amendment applies to the federal government, while the Fourteenth Amendment applies to state actions.)

e. By 2015, 37 states had fully legalized same-sex marriage. In that year, the Supreme Court heard the case of *Obergefell v. Hodges* (2015), which challenged state laws restricting marriage licenses to heterosexual couples. The Court struck down such laws under both the Due Process and Equal Protection Clauses of the Fourteenth Amendment, and ruled that all states must grant marriage licenses to same-sex couples and must recognize same-sex marriages made in other states.

Test Tip

Students are sometimes confused by the term marriage, because it has both religious and legal meanings. Civil rights court cases relate only to marriage as a legal status, a group of rights based on a license issued by the government. Religious organizations are not required by the government to perform or recognize same-sex marriage.

4. Members of the LGBTQ community have served in the military since the Revolutionary War, but have only recently gained some level of legal protection.

a. LGBTQ service members have been allowed to serve openly since 2011.

b. The right of transgender individuals to serve in the military was established in 2016. However, the Trump administration reversed the policy in 2018 to prohibit most transgender persons from serving in the military. The new policy was the subject of several appellate cases and was reversed by President Biden shortly after taking office. The new policy allows transgender people to serve openly and prohibits discrimination.

C. OTHER ETHNIC AND RACIAL MINORITIES

1. Hispanic and Latino Americans, Native Americans, Asian Americans and other ethnic minority groups have organized and waged civil rights campaigns in the United States.

2. The Civil Rights Act of 1964 prohibits discrimination based on race, color, religion, and national origin. (It prohibits employment discrimination based on sex, as well.) The Act, therefore, offers protection for all of these minority groups.

D. THE PRO-LIFE MOVEMENT

1. The pro-life movement has sometimes framed the abortion issue as a question of civil rights for the unborn fetus.

2. Several Human Life Amendments have been proposed in Congress since *Roe v. Wade* was decided in 1973. None of these have passed Congress and been sent to the states for ratification.

Important Civil Rights Amendments and Laws

Name of Law	Important Provisions
The Civil War Amendments	– Thirteenth Amendment: outlaws slavery – Fourteenth Amendment: defines citizenship, guarantees due process and equal protection – Fifteenth Amendment: guarantees the right to vote regardless of race, color, or previous condition of servitude.
Nineteenth Amendment	– guarantees the right to vote regardless of sex
Civil Rights Act of 1964	– prohibits discrimination in public accommodations, government services, programs receiving federal funds, education and employment based on race, color, religion, and national origin – prohibits discrimination in employment based on sex
Twenty-fourth Amendment	– outlaws poll taxes

Name of Law	Important Provisions
Voting Rights Act of 1965	– prohibits discrimination in voting rights, including literacy tests – requires preclearance for changing voting procedures in jurisdictions with a history of discrimination (currently unenforceable as a result of a Supreme Court decision)
Title IX of the Education Amendments Act of 1972	– prohibits discrimination in educational programs and activities on the basis of sex
Americans with Disabilities Act (1990)	– prohibits discrimination in employment, public accommodations, and government programs – requires reasonable accommodations for individuals with disabilities

UNIT 4

AMERICAN POLITICAL IDEOLOGIES AND BELIEFS

American Political Ideologies and Beliefs

I. AMERICAN POLITICAL CULTURE

The term *political culture* refers to the values and patterns of thinking that a country's citizens share regarding politics. The core values of American political culture are found in the Constitution, the writings of the founders, and the laws and court rulings that have evolved throughout the country's history. While there is overall agreement among Americans regarding the shared values that make up the political culture, interpretations of these values and how they should be implemented in public policy vary. Various interpretations have led to divergent ideas about the role of government.

A. INDIVIDUALISM

1. The American ideal of protecting personal freedoms from government interference is evident in the way the Bill of Rights safeguards civil liberties.

2. The values of individualism and sanctity of personal rights must be balanced with the responsibility of government to ensure order and stability. What limits on personal freedom are acceptable in the pursuit of security?

3. The Declaration of Independence stresses that the purpose of government is to ensure individual (natural) rights and that governments that fail to protect these rights may be abolished.

B. EQUALITY OF OPPORTUNITY

1. Americans share a belief in equality of opportunity that all individuals should have the ability to compete on a level playing field where success is determined by hard work and talent.

2. Equality of opportunity is present in the Constitution and key pieces of legislation, including the Civil Rights Act (1964) and the Americans with Disabilities Act (1990).

Test Tip

Be prepared to differentiate between the ideas of equality of opportunity and equality of outcome. Equality of opportunity *means that all persons have the same ability to compete and succeed; whereas* equality of outcome *refers to the idea that all persons should be assured basic minimums for human existence and society should strive to reduce gross inequalities.*

C. FREE ENTERPRISE

1. An important American political belief in free enterprise, an economic system in which private business operates for the most part independently of government control and involves the private ownership of property, is often associated with laissez-faire economics.

2. Although Americans broadly support the idea of a free enterprise system, ours is a mixed economy. Americans differ in their opinions about how much government regulation is needed. The federal government uses regulation to force companies to obey standards for the protection of citizens, but its control of business and industry is limited.

3. The right of citizens to own property free of government interference is most clearly seen in the Due Process Clauses of the Fifth and Fourteenth Amendments, which prohibit the taking of life, liberty, or property without due process of law. Property rights may also be affected by the government power of eminent domain, described in the Fifth Amendment, which allows the government to take private property for public use, so long as fair compensation is paid.

D. RULE OF LAW

1. Rule of law is the American political value requiring that all individuals, including leaders, be held accountable to the same laws. It also stands for the idea that laws are applied the same regardless of an individual's position.

2. The rule of law includes the value that all individuals are treated the same in the eyes of the courts. This is seen in the various aspects of the Bill of Rights that protect the rights of the accused, including the Fifth, Sixth, and Eighth Amendments. Americans

expect that all individuals accused of a crime are granted due process and equal protection under the law.

3. The Constitution provides for a method in which government officials, including the president and federal judges, may be impeached and removed from office for violating the rule of law.

4. In "Federalist No. 51," Madison stated that the rule of law is the ultimate aim of government:

    > Justice is the end (goal) of government. It is the end (goal) of civil society. It ever has been, and ever will be, pursued, until it be obtained.

E. LIMITED GOVERNMENT

1. The American political value of limited government is expressed in the Constitution, which restricts both the government and its leaders by carefully enumerating the powers of government, the powers denied to the government, and the rights of the people.

2. In "Federalist No. 51," Madison argued that the system of checks and balances created by the Constitution prevented any one branch of government from becoming too powerful, thus limiting the authority of the government. "It may be a reflection on human nature, that such devices [checks and balances] should be necessary to control the abuses of government."

3. In "Federalist No. 78," Hamilton argued that the independent courts created by the Constitution restrict the power of the other branches and safeguard individual rights.

    > The complete independence of the courts of justice is peculiarly essential in a limited constitution . . . which contains certain specified expectations to the legislative authority; such, for instance, is that it shall pass no bills of attainder, no ex post facto laws, and the like.

II. POLITICAL SOCIALIZATION

A. SHAPING POLITICAL ATTITUDES AND VALUES

1. The complicated manner in which an individual's sense of political identity, political party affiliation, and values related to government are shaped by the broader culture, is known as political socialization.

B. FAMILY AND PEER INFLUENCES

1. The family is the factor that most affects an individual's political socialization, including the development of a liberal or conservative ideology and political party preference.

2. The family is particularly influential because children are repeatedly exposed to their parents' views through discussions and media choices.

3. Peers and friends also influence the development of political ideas, in both children and adults. The time that people spend with peers and friends often impacts attitude development. Also, to the degree that individuals associate with like-minded friends, their shared attitudes may be amplified. However, friends are usually not as strong an influence in political socialization as family.

C. EDUCATIONAL INFLUENCES

1. American schools influence political socialization by teaching basic government, democratic values, and patriotism, as well as by promoting political participation.

2. There is a strong correlation between education level and political participation because education increases political efficacy, or the belief that an individual can have an impact on political outcomes.

3. Educational level is positively correlated with voter turnout; individuals who have higher levels of education are more likely to vote.

D. SOCIAL ENVIRONMENTS/ORGANIZATIONAL MEMBERSHIP

1. Membership in organizations is often based on shared values and goals (e.g., interest groups, labor unions, professional organizations). Social interaction within these groups influences members' political party affiliations and views on policy issues. Occupational groups may be dominated by a particular ideology, which may influence political attitudes and values.

2. Religious organizations influence the political beliefs and voting behaviors of their membership through the positions or stances the groups take on specific policy issues. Religious leaders can serve as agents of political socialization when they speak directly to members about specific public policy issues.

3. Social environment also encompasses geographic factors. Persons from specific regions tend to share certain perspectives. Likewise,

rural residents and urban dwellers each have unique shared interests.

E. GLOBALIZATION

1. The world has become increasingly interconnected economically, socially, and politically. As a consequence, American political values have impacted, and been impacted by, other nations.

2   The passage of the Affordable Care Act in 2010, which expanded healthcare for Americans, reflects the influence of other countries, many of which guarantee healthcare for all or most citizens.

3. Social media platforms developed in the United States now bridge cultures and nations throughout the world.

F. GENERATIONAL, LIFE-CYCLE, and MAJOR POLITICAL EVENTS

1. The shared experiences of individuals born in the same time period or generation can impact political attitudes and behavior. Different generations—such as the Millennials, Generation X, the Baby Boomers, and the Silent Generation—have shared experiences that shape long-lasting attitudes toward domestic and foreign policy.

    a. Americans who grew up during the Great Depression (Silent Generation) shared certain traits, including financial responsibility and frugality. They also largely developed a strong and lasting loyalty to the Democratic Party.

    b. Today's young Americans (Generation Z) have come of age in an era of gun violence and school shootings, influencing their attitudes toward gun control.

2. Life-cycle effects—changing personal circumstances that occur across the life span—are a factor in political socialization. Each stage of life has known and predictable effects on citizens' political attitudes and behaviors that correlate with the physical, social, and psychological changes of the life cycle. For example, college-age students, as a group, may be more concerned with student debt; those with children more concerned with education; and older persons who have accumulated greater wealth may be more concerned with taxation.

3. Major political events differ from generational influences in that significant events, such as the Kennedy assassination or 9/11, affect all persons who experience them across the generational spectrum.

Test Tip

On the AP® exam you will not be asked to identify the specific years for each generational cohort (e.g., Baby Boomers), but you should be prepared to analyze charts and graphs to discern voting trends and policy stands within these groups.

G. MEDIA INFLUENCES

1. Since the advent of radio and, later, television, media has had a significant impact on the process of political socialization and on public opinion related to policy and overall trust in government.

2. The media, through entertainment, news, and informational programming, provides people with background knowledge and shapes their attitudes about the functions and value of government institutions.

3. The expansion of political coverage in the media to include cable news networks, Internet news outlets, and social media have allowed individuals to selectively choose to receive information from sources that share their own political perspective, thereby reinforcing their pre-existing perceptions and limiting new information. This is sometimes referred to as an "echo chamber."

4. Social media users tend to interact most with others who have similar political viewpoints and share information that reinforces those attitudes.

III. POLITICAL IDEOLOGY

A. A WIDE SPECTRUM OF BELIEFS

1. A political ideology represents a collection of beliefs about morality, economics, efficiency, how society should function, and the proper role of government.

2. Political ideology can be measured and represented in various ways, including grids and graphic representations. Traditionally, the liberal-conservative spectrum has been represented as a line, with liberalism on the left and conservatism on the right. (Hence the terms *left* and *right*.)

3. Although ideological belief systems are generally consistent, they may at times seem to lack internal consistency.

    a.   Liberal and conservative ideologies are closely tied to the Democratic and Republican parties in the United States.

    b.   Party constituencies change over time, and changing constituencies may influence ideological systems.

  4. A party's platform is a compilation of the policy positions the party favors, which reflect its ideology.

B. LIBERAL IDEOLOGY

  1. Liberal ideology encompasses the following beliefs:

    a.   Government has an important role to play in society.

    b.   The government should regulate the economy in order to ensure that efficiency is maximized and noneconomic interests are protected.

    c.   Government should refrain from regulating moral issues in most cases. Issues such as abortion, same-sex marriage, marijuana, and other private matters should be left up to individuals.

    d.   Government should spend money to assist citizens with social services, such as housing, food, and healthcare.

  2. The Democratic Party is closely aligned with liberal ideology.

C. CONSERVATIVE IDEOLOGY

  1. Conservative ideology encompasses the following beliefs:

    a.   Government should play only a minimal role in society.

    b.   The government should engage in minimal regulation of the economy; market forces maximize efficiency and solve most problems.

    c.   Government has an important role to play in regulating moral issues. The government should regulate moral issues in order to uphold traditional moral beliefs.

    d.   Government funding of social goods should be limited. Citizens should not be restrained and should be expected to provide for themselves.

  2. The Republican Party is closely aligned with conservative ideology.

D. COMPARING IDEOLOGIES

1. The following chart shows the general liberal (Democratic) and conservative (Republican) positions on common issues.

Liberal Position	Public Policy Issue	Conservative Position
– increased government regulation of business to protect workers and the environment – markets need regulation to function efficiently – favors taxation of businesses and the wealthy to support spending on public goods	Economy	– government should minimally regulate the economy – market forces operate to produce efficiency and productivity in markets – favors reduced taxation of businesses and the wealthy in order to stimulate the economy
– favors federal power	Federalism	– favors states' rights
– favors reducing military spending – supports involvement in global affairs, diplomacy, and foreign aid	National Security	– favors increasing military spending – supports limitations on foreign aid, limited involvement with foreign nations, and military strength
– increased funding of social welfare programs	Social Welfare Programs	– reduced funding of social welfare programs
– increased funding of public education	Education	– vouchers and support for private and religious education
– supports legal immigration and citizenship path for certain groups of undocumented immigrants	Immigration	– reduced legal immigration and opposes citizenship path for undocumented immigrants
– favors abortion rights (pro-choice)	Abortion Rights	– opposes abortion rights (pro-life)
– favors expanded civil rights protections – favors affirmative action	Civil Rights	– favors limited civil rights protections – opposes affirmative action

Liberal Position	Public Policy Issue	Conservative Position
– favors regulations to protect the environment and combat climate change	**Environmental Protection**	– opposes government action to regulate business – views climate change as an insignificant problem
– favors restrictions on gun purchases and ownership	**Gun Control**	– opposes restrictions on gun purchases and ownership
– supports expanded access and government involvement in healthcare	**Healthcare**	– favors private sector, free-market healthcare system with minimal government involvement

Test Tip

Be sure you understand the difference between the similar-sounding and interrelated concepts of political culture, political socialization, and political ideology.

➤ *Political culture is the broadly shared set of political values, beliefs, and norms held within a society.*

➤ *Political socialization is the process by which individuals within a society acquire their political values and opinions. Agents of socialization include family, education, and the media.*

➤ *Political ideology is a coherent set of political ideas held by an individual or organization. Note that party affiliation is related to, but different from, political ideology. Members of political parties may not share the party's ideology in its entirety.*

E. LIBERTARIAN IDEOLOGY

1. Libertarian ideology shares beliefs with both liberal and conservative ideologies.

2. Libertarian ideology opposes government regulation of both economic activity and personal choices. For libertarians, individual liberty is the highest value, and government should exist only to protect private property rights.

3. Libertarians are consistent in their view of the proper role of government in society, believing:

   a. The government should not regulate the economy, but allow the market to function freely according to the decisions of its participants.

   b. The government should not involve itself in people's personal decisions. Government interference in choices involving marriage, sex, drugs, gambling, and other issues is a violation of personal liberty.

   c. For example, a libertarian would favor policies legalizing the commercial sale of marijuana and reducing government spending on prisons.

IV. POLITICAL CULTURE AND PUBLIC POLICY

A. LIBERTY VS. ORDER

1. The debate between conservatism and liberalism reflects the tension between liberty and order, which must be balanced in order for society to function optimally.

   a. Excessive personal liberty will lead to chaos.

   b. Excessive social order will stifle personal liberty and creativity.

2. Historically, policy outcomes reflect the preferences of whichever position is dominant among voters and policymakers at any given time.

3. The changing power of various groups is often reflected in policy changes, as when alcohol prohibition was enacted and then repealed fourteen years later.

B. THE CULTURE WAR

1. The term *culture war* is used to describe the deep division and increasing polarization between those Americans who wish to return to an idealized culture based on traditional values (conservatism) and those who favor change (liberalism).

2. Differing belief systems are both exploited and exacerbated by political organizations, interest groups, and media outlets to drive enthusiasm and support for parties and causes.

3. United States politics may at times reflect polarization, or the tendency for citizens to adopt more extreme positions.

4. The polarization characteristic of the culture war creates political gridlock as fewer voters and politicians inhabit the middle of the political field.

V. IDEOLOGICAL DIFFERENCES: THE ROLE OF GOVERNMENT IN THE ECONOMY

A. THE POLITICS OF THE ECONOMY

1. The health of the economy has historically been one of the most significant predictors of voter attitudes toward the party in the White House.

2. Maintaining a strong economy is a top priority for politicians of both political parties.

   a. Politicians desire to keep unemployment rates low. When unemployment is low, citizens have money to spend, which stimulates business activity and creates more jobs. It also reduces the cost of government unemployment and social welfare programs.

   b. Politicians also attempt to control inflation, which is the rate at which the cost of goods and services in an economy increases. Economists generally agree that a low inflation rate is necessary for healthy economic growth. A high inflation rate can negatively affect workers' standard of living. If growth in wages does not exceed inflation, standards of living remain flat or decline.

B. FISCAL POLICY

1. Fiscal policy refers to the taxing and spending methodology followed by the government in order to foster economic health.

2. Keynesian theory (developed by economist John Maynard Keynes) is based on supply and demand in an economy.

   a. When consumer demand for goods and services drops, businesses sell fewer goods and services, and workers lose jobs.

   b. When jobs are lost, spending contracts further, and an economic recession may result.

   c. Keynes believed that the government should actively intervene to maintain or restore economic health.

d. To stimulate consumer spending and business activity, the government should put money into the economy when necessary by reducing taxes or implementing more government programs that put money into the hands of consumers by creating jobs or providing benefits in order to drive demand.

e. Keynesian economics formed the basis for FDR's New Deal legislation, which was enacted in response to the Great Depression, as well as the American Recovery and Reinvestment Act of 2009, passed in response to the Great Recession.

f. These types of policies are often referred to as stimulus policies, because they are intended to stimulate the economy to sustain independent growth.

3. Supply-side economic theory, popularized by economist Arthur Laffer, advocates the reduction of taxes, primarily on businesses and wealthy individuals, in order to stimulate business investment, which will stimulate job creation and economic growth.

a. Supply-side theory is sometimes called trickle-down economics, because the theory proposes that leaving more wealth in the hands of those at the top of the economy will result in more wealth making its way down to the middle and working classes.

b. Supply-side economics advocates reducing taxation and limiting government spending as a way to stimulate economic activity.

c. Supply-siders theorize that because taxes on economic transactions stimulate government revenues, tax cuts will generate more revenue than is lost by reducing taxes.

Test Tip

Keynesian economic theory is favored by liberals and is associated with Democratic presidents, notably Franklin Roosevelt, Barack Obama, and Joseph Biden. Supply-side economic theory is favored by conservatives and is associated with Republican presidents, notably Ronald Reagan, George W. Bush, and Donald Trump. Supply-side theory is, in fact, sometimes called Reaganomics.

C. MONETARY POLICY

1. Another tool at the disposal of the government for maintaining the health of the economy is monetary policy, which is the ability to regulate the amount of money available in the economy.

2. The prices of goods and services are heavily influenced by how much money is available within a society. The more dollars floating around in the economy, the easier they are to come by, and the less each one will buy.

3. The Federal Reserve System is the central banking system of the United States and the vehicle through which the government controls the supply of money in circulation.

    a. The Federal Reserve System consists of 12 regional Federal Reserve Banks through which money is distributed to financial institutions, and a Federal Reserve Board (the Fed) of seven members appointed by the president (with Senate confirmation) to staggered terms.

    b. The Fed controls the money supply by:

        ➤ setting interest rates for government bonds.

        ➤ buying and selling government bonds and other financial instruments with member banks. Bond purchases from banks put money into the economy; bond sales to banks reduce the amount of money banks have available to lend.

        ➤ setting the federal funds rate, which requires banks to keep a minimum percentage of deposits on hand in cash. Increasing the reserve rate reduces the money available to lend, while reducing the rate increases the money supply.

        ➤ setting the rates at which banks may borrow directly from the government and may charge each other for funds.

4. The money supply affects the economy in two primary ways.

    a. Increasing the amount of money available to banks to sell as loans puts more money into the economy, which stimulates spending and growth.

    b. Reducing the money supply slows the economy and checks inflation.

5. The Fed is charged with modulating the supply of money in the economy and regulating banks in order to maintain economic stability and sustainable economic growth.

The economic health of the country requires constant attention and fine-tuning. The ability to adjust both fiscal and monetary policy provides the government with tools for maintaining a stable and growing economy. Be sure you understand the differences between these two areas of policy.

Fiscal Policy	Monetary Policy
– impacts economy through adjustments in taxation and spending	– impacts economy through adjustments in interest rates and the money supply
– initiated by Congress	– implemented by the Federal Reserve Board

Political Data and Polling

I. POLITICAL RESEARCH

A. PUBLIC OPINION POLLS

Political scientists collect data using a variety of polling, or mass survey methods, to assess the opinions, policy preferences, and voting patterns of citizens. Data from polling is used by policymakers, politicians, and the media, which ultimately impacts policy debates and elections.

1. Opinion polls are used to determine the beliefs that citizens have regarding policy issues, government institutions, elected officials, or candidates running for office.

2. Benchmark polls, surveys used at the beginning of a campaign, used to reveal the attitudes citizens have about a particular candidate or issue that can be later used as a basis for comparison.

3. Tracking polls are surveys that involve asking individuals the same questions at different time intervals as a method of measuring data over time (trends).

4. Entrance polls are surveys given to individuals just before voting takes place to predict the outcome of an election and determine voter reasoning.

5. Exit polls (surveys taken directly outside of a polling location) are used to predict the winners of elections and collect data about how voters made their decisions, as well as which groups support which parties and candidates.

   a. Media outlets may use exit poll data to predict or "call" the winners of elections, or, in the case of presidential elections, the winner of the popular vote within states. Such reporting may, in turn, affect voter turnout and impact election results.

b. To avoid interfering in the election process, most media outlets follow careful guidelines and refrain from reporting election results until polls have closed.

6. A push poll is not a true poll or survey, but a propaganda technique designed to manipulate voter opinion through the use of such devices as biased question wording or by spreading false information.

7. A straw poll is a nonscientific survey method of gauging opinion based on a nonrandom sample. It has no scientific or predictive value.

B. COMPONENTS OF SCIENTIFIC POLLS

1. **Sampling:** It is not possible to give a survey to every member of a large population, such as the voting-eligible population of the United States. For this reason, political scientists choose a small group, or sample, to study to make predictions about the larger population. *Sampling error* and *margin of error* are terms describing the potential discrepancy between poll results and the opinions of the larger population being measured. To reduce sampling error, samples should be large enough to make inferences about the population, as well as being random and representative.

   a. A mass survey is a poll given to a larger sample size in order to reduce the margin of error, increasing the chances that data can be applied to the larger population. Mass surveys for large populations typically involve 1,000 to 2,000 respondents.

   b. The term *random sample* refers to the individuals chosen by chance to be in the study. To ensure the randomness of the sample, each member of a population must have an equal probability of selection or an equal chance of being chosen to participate. It is difficult to obtain a random sample of the population being studied—for example, the voting-eligible population of the United States. Political scientists have developed various methods to achieve a random sample.

   ➤ Random-digit dialing is a polling method that involves having computers call listed and unlisted landline phone numbers by chance to reach survey respondents.

➤ Because landline usage is declining, and federal law prevents automated calling of cell phones for survey purposes, pollsters must supplement the use of random-digit dialing with human volunteers calling cell phone numbers.

➤ Modern communications technology, such as cellular phones with caller identification, has decreased response rates to polling attempts and made random samples more difficult to generate.

c. Researchers use a variety of methods to create a *representative sample* or one that accurately and proportionally mirrors the diversity of the population being surveyed.

➤ One such method involves the process of weighting, in which the sample data is mathematically manipulated to match the demographic characteristics of the population. For example, in a poll measuring voter attitudes where the population of the state is 54% urban dwellers, the number of urban dwellers in the sample data could be adjusted (weighted) to match the population being measured.

➤ This process can be applied to other demographics, including age, education level, and ethnicity.

Test Tip

The goal of all polls is to obtain a large enough random sample that is also representative of the population. If the sample is random and representative, it is possible to make generalizations that apply to the entire population.

d. All scientific polls have a margin of error or sampling error, terms quantifying the potential mathematical difference between the survey's results and the opinion of the larger population. Polling organizations strive to reduce the margin of error through several methods:

➤ One of the main factors influencing the size of the sampling error is the size of the sample. In general, the larger the sample, the lower the sampling error.

➤ Most public opinion polls for large populations have between 1,000 and 2,000 respondents, resulting in reduced sampling error. Interestingly, sample sizes larger than 2,000 result in negligible increases in poll accuracy, regardless of the size of the population being studied.

➤ Given an adequate sample size, a margin of error is quantified using percentage points. A sampling error of plus or minus 3 percentage points, for example, indicates that 95% of the time the poll results from the sample are accurate to within 3 percent of what the larger population believes.

➤ It is important to consider the size of the sampling error when evaluating claims made by polls (large sampling errors make the results unreliable as an indicator of the population), and polls that do not report a sampling error are considered unscientific and unreliable.

➤ The margin of error may negate a lead in a poll where, for example, candidate X is leading candidate Y by 47% to 45% and the margin of error is 3%.

➤ Note that the margin of error applies to both results, so that if candidate X is leading candidate Y by 47% to 43%, the actual level of support for candidate X is somewhere between 44%–50%, while the actual level of support for candidate Y is somewhere between 40%–47%, placing the poll within the margin of error, or too close to call.

Test Tip

Margin of error *and* sampling error *describe potential discrepancies in generalizing poll results to larger populations. Although there are technical differences between these terms, you should be aware that they may be used interchangeably.*

2. **Question Design:** Polling questions may be written in several ways, affecting the quality of the information the poll will produce.

a. Question types include:

➤ Forced-choice, also called selective-response, questions, that require respondents to choose from among given options or rate themselves on a scale, produce more accurate results. Multiple choice or yes/no questions are effective because they simplify data calculation and analysis.

➤ Open-ended questions, those that allow respondents to answer outside of a preselected framework, generate data that is difficult to quantify or generalize.

b. How questions are worded can impact poll results.

➤ Questions should be concise and worded in neutral, careful language to avoid influencing responses. Leading questions, those which suggest a particular response, should be avoided.

➤ Vocabulary should be simple and straightforward; biased or emotionally charged language may influence responses.

➤ As an example, the statement "America is not spending enough money helping the poor," is likely to produce different responses from the statement "America is not spending enough on welfare."

c. Question order can impact responses when a question creates an impression that may influence a later response.

d. Polling questions must be administered according to standardized procedures.

➤ Printed surveys eliminate variables associated with human questioners, who may not read questions in a standardized way, for example, by explaining terms. Questions should be read as written, without elaboration, to maximize the accuracy of results.

➤ A questioner's personal characteristics, such as age, race, or gender, may influence respondents, who may be concerned with the impression they are making on the questioner.

e. Some polls force respondents to select an opinion in cases where they may lack the information or interest to form an opinion. Offering an "I don't know" (or similar) response improves accuracy because respondents are not forced to respond to questions about which they lack information or opinions.

Test Tip

Be prepared to critically evaluate polling data presented in both multiple-choice and free-response questions. A scientific poll would have each of the following components:

➤ *A large sample size, typically between 1,000 and 2,000 respondents.*

➤ *A random and representative sample that allows for inferences to be made about the larger population.*

➤ *A small reported sampling error.*

➤ *Clearly worded questions that are neutral in tone.*

C. FOCUS GROUPS

1. Focus groups are another method by which information about public opinion can be obtained. A focus group involves a small group of people who participate in a structured discussion to discover insight into public opinion.

2. Focus groups are usually led by a moderator, who leads the discussion and attempts to elicit participants' opinions.

3. Focus groups are often limited to specific policy issues.

4. Focus groups can provide qualitative data and insights into voter perceptions of political issues, but do not generate statistically significant quantitative data and cannot be generalized to a broader population.

D. POLLING AND ELECTIONS

1. Data from public opinion polls and focus groups collected during elections impact candidate messaging in advertising and preparation for public debates. Candidates are interested in tailoring their responses to policy stances that align with voter opinions and priorities.

2. Candidates who have high polling ratings are at an advantage because they are more likely to:

   a. be invited to participate in publicized debates, where participation in a large field of candidates may be limited to a minimum polling threshold.

      b.   receive more (free) media coverage.

      c.   have an easier time raising campaign donations.

  3. The results of national polls leading up to elections can also create a bandwagon effect. According to this principle, the more people adopt a particular opinion or position, the more others are influenced to adopt it. In other words, gains in support for a candidate lead to further gains in support.

E. POLLING AND PUBLIC POLICY

  1. Politicians use polling data to understand how the public feels about proposed or existing public policies, and how strongly those opinions are held.

  2. Polling data helps public officials to understand what problems are important to the public and what solutions are favored.

  3. Public opinion influences politicians because they are concerned with reelection. The length of an official's term and the time until he or she must run for reelection may impact his or her sensitivity to polling data.

  4. Polling is only one factor that influences the legislative process. Politicians may disregard public opinion if they disagree with it, or they may be influenced by interest groups or other factors.

  5. Politicians do not always act according to the results of opinion polls.

      a. Policy issues may be complex and difficult for the average citizen to fully understand. Politicians may take this into account in policymaking.

      b. Polling data may be helpful to officials in explaining their decisions to their constituents.

      c. Officials may vote against public opinion.

        ➤ They may believe that policy outcomes may influence voter opinions over time. For example, elected officials know that sometimes polices that are not initially popular gain support over time as the benefits become more clear.

        ➤ They may attempt to use their influence to change public opinion.

F. POLLING RELIABILITY AND VERACITY (VALIDITY)

The credibility of conclusions based on data from public opinion polls is dependent upon the reliability and validity of the survey materials. (The terms *validity* and *veracity* are synonymous.) As a result, mass surveys are carefully evaluated to ensure that results are consistent and accurate.

1. Reliability refers to the consistency or repeatability of a survey and can be measured in a variety of ways. A common way to measure reliability in a survey is to look for internal consistency by including several questions about the same idea spread throughout the survey. Responses may also be compared over time or between two similar versions of a survey. Reliability, by itself, however, does not necessarily ensure that the data is correct.

2. Veracity (validity) describes data accuracy. Beyond making certain that mass surveys provide consistent (reliable) results, political scientists want to be certain that the data is accurate, which is called validity. There are several types of validity for which surveys are examined, including predictive and content validity.

   a. Predictive validity describes how accurate a poll is at forecasting (predicting) future behaviors. It can be used to evaluate benchmark and tracking polls. If an election poll during the campaign accurately identifies the eventual outcome of an election, the poll would be said to have predictive validity.

   b. Polling accuracy also involves content validity, which means that the poll accurately measures the full topic area being studied and that important aspects are not excluded.

Test Tip

Expect to encounter the terms reliability *and* veracity (validity) *on questions related to scientific polling. Simply stated,* reliability *refers to the consistency of the poll and* veracity *refers to the accuracy of the poll. Think of a scientific poll as a measuring device such as a bathroom scale that you want to be both reliable (consistent) and valid (accurate). It is possible that a poll, like a scale, could be reliable, but not valid. For example if a scale were to indicate that you weighed 15 pounds every time you stepped on it, the scale would be reliable, but not valid.*

UNIT 5
POLITICAL PARTICIPATION

Political Parties, Interest Groups, and Campaign Finance

I. LINKAGE INSTITUTIONS

A. FUNCTION OF LINKAGE INSTITUTIONS

1. Linkage institutions are organizations or systems through which people connect and interact with the government.

2. Linkage institutions provide legitimate channels for the flow of information between the government and citizens, allowing for peaceful interaction in policy development.

B. TYPES OF LINKAGE INSTITUTIONS

1. **Political Parties:** These are organizations of people who share similar political ideologies which attempt to gain political power and implement a policy agenda by getting candidates elected.

2. **Interest Groups:** These are organizations of people who share similar causes or concerns which attempt to influence the government to address specific problems and public policies.

3. **Elections:** The primary method of participation in a democracy is the election, a contest in which citizens vote to select political representatives.

4. **Media:** The news media includes all those sources through which information is published including Internet, print, and broadcast news sources.

II. POLITICAL PARTIES

A. THE THREE ROLES OF POLITICAL PARTIES

1. **Party in the Organization.** Political parties exist to promote a political agenda. They accomplish this goal by recruiting and

running candidates for office, raising money, and maintaining an administrative structure to carry out party functions.

2. **Party in the Electorate.** Political parties reach out to voters, work to develop stable coalitions, and function as shorthand, or a label that conveys information about candidates and politicians to voters.

3. **Party in Government.** Members of a political party who are currently serving in government positions work to achieve the party's policy goals. Many aspects of government, notably Congress, are organized by political party. Party affiliation determines leadership positions and committee memberships.

B. FUNCTIONS OF POLITICAL PARTIES

1. Political parties educate and mobilize voters to participate in elections.

   a. Parties sponsor and organize activities to inform and motivate voters.

   b. Parties recruit and train volunteers.

   c. Party names are understood by voters to correspond to core sets of values. A candidate's party affiliation is reliable shorthand for his or her policy views.

2. Political parties develop platforms, which are statements of principles explaining the party's policy goals.

3. Political parties recruit candidates to run for office.

   a. Party organizations are often able to influence qualified and talented candidates to run.

   b. Parties serve a seal-of-approval function. The endorsement of the party is understood to provide assurance that the candidate is a good citizen and qualified for the office that he or she is seeking.

4. Political parties provide campaign support for their nominees.

   a. During the primary stage of an election, the party's role is to moderate the contest among its own member candidates for the party's nomination to each office on each ballot.

   b. During the general election campaign, parties provide several types of assistance to candidates, including:

      ➤ campaign management expertise

      ➤ media strategy

> ➤ voter information databases

> ➤ scientific polling

> ➤ canvassing and get-out-the-vote events

> ➤ direct campaign contributions or financial support (within legal limits)

c. Political parties are becoming increasingly sophisticated in their efforts to target and influence voters.

> ➤ Parties maintain and continuously update detailed databases of voter profiles using information from scientific polling, census records, and other data sources.

> ➤ Parties use sophisticated software and computer models to tailor messages and advertising strategies based on the psychological and demographic characteristics of specific voter groups they are targeting.

> ➤ Parties use social media to efficiently spread targeted messaging.

5. Parties organize and manage many of the operations of government.

a. Although political parties are not mentioned in the Constitution, they play a major role in the operation of government.

b. The majority party in Congress holds the key leadership positions and committee chair roles, effectively determining Congress's agenda.

c. The majority parties in state legislatures hold similar positions and control the redistricting process, which may confer a significant electoral advantage in future congressional elections.

d. The party out of power, or the minority party, plays a vital role as a watchdog, actively scrutinizing and criticizing the party in power to ensure against abuses of power.

C. THE TWO-PARTY SYSTEM

1. The United States has a two-party system.

a. Political parties are not discussed in the Constitution.

b. Nothing in U.S. law requires the two-party system or prohibits other parties from competing.

  c. Due to the structure of our electoral system, the vast majority of political offices are held by members of the two major parties.

 2. The two major parties have changed over time. Since 1860, the Democratic and Republican parties have dominated American politics.

 3. In order to achieve and maintain major party status, a party must create a party coalition, a collection of voting groups that support the party's policies and candidates. Examples of important voting groups include African Americans, women, blue-collar workers, the LGBTQ community, Christian evangelicals, and others.

  a. Coalitions are generally stable, but they may change over time.

  b. Group connections to political parties may change. This happened during the Great Depression when large numbers of traditionally Republican voters, including African Americans, began voting Democratic in large numbers, in a process known as realignment.

  c. Parties may modify their positions and messaging to appeal to specific groups.

  d. Conversely, a new constituency (group of loyal voters) may influence changes in a party's policy positions.

  e. Critical elections are those in which a major and lasting realignment of group loyalties is seen. These occur in times marked by national crisis or major social movements, as when several important voting groups left the Republican Party and united behind FDR.

  f. Realignments may also be regional, as when conservative white southerners began to switch in the late 1960s from the Democratic Party to the Republican Party.

Test Tip

Realignment, dealignment, and critical elections are terms that can be confusing, but they are important to understand.

➤ **Realignment** *refers to the switching of party loyalty by important voting groups.*

➤ **Critical elections** *are those in which a major realignment of important voting groups takes place, so that the party that had been weaker becomes dominant.*

➤ **Dealignment** *describes the process of voters detaching from political parties and becoming independent.*

4. Recent decades have seen a decrease in the power of the major parties.

   a. Beginning in the 1960s, voters' party loyalties began to weaken (dealignment). Increasingly, voters identified as independent, rather than as Democrats or Republicans.

   b. Generally, national party organizations have a loose relationship with state and local party organizations. National parties do not hold authority over state and local parties, and, in fact, influence often runs in the other direction.

   c. Campaign finance restrictions have reduced the power of political parties by limiting party donations to candidates ($5,000 per federal candidate per election cycle, combined $10,000 for primary and general elections).

   d. Campaigns have become more candidate-centered and less focused on parties.

      ➤ In many other democracies, candidates for offices are chosen by party leaders rather than voters. In the U.S. system, candidates for office are chosen by party members and highly engaged voters in primary elections.

      ➤ Traditionally, candidates have relied heavily on party support in the form of financial and campaign assistance, ensuring their loyalty.

      ➤ More recently, individuals interested in running for office frequently solicit donations and hire their own professional campaign staffs, allowing them to be more independent.

      ➤ The influence of political parties in determining voters' choices has declined. Voters are less loyal to parties in general (dealignment) and more likely to vote with a split-ticket.

      ➤ Political party leadership generally prefers candidates who are more centrist, making them more likely to appeal to moderate voters.

      ➤ Political party members are more ideologically driven than the general public, making them more prone to select candidates who are more ideologically pronounced.

      ➤ Candidates have access to television and other forms of media. They can appeal directly to voters and spread their messages without the support of party structures.

➤ Voters are now more likely to be influenced by individual candidates' messages and to vote for candidates of different parties.

Test Tip

It is easy to assume that the national party organizations control the state and local party organizations, but this is not true. Remember that parties in the United States are decentralized (state and local political party organizations are not controlled by the national party). This weak organizational system means that local parties choose their own candidates for office and are not obligated to follow party platform positions, allowing for candidate selection based on local preferences.

D. MINOR (THIRD) PARTIES

1. The United States has evolved a political system in which two parties dominate, but numerous minor parties (also called third parties) exist and compete.

   a. The two-party system is not required by law; however, the way U.S. elections are held makes it difficult for minor parties to compete.

   b. Some countries have proportional representation systems in which citizens vote for parties rather than individual candidates, and each party receives a number of legislative seats in proportion to its share of the popular vote. Proportional representation systems allow multiple parties to hold political power.

   c. In U.S. congressional elections, each voter has one vote, and the candidate who wins the most votes is the winner, even if that candidate received less than a majority of the votes cast (a plurality). This is called a single-member plurality system. It is also called the first-past-the-post (FPTP) electoral system.

   d. The one-voter-one-vote system leads invariably to a two-party system by influencing voters to vote for a stronger party that is more likely to win an election, rather than a smaller party that has almost no chance of winning the most votes in a district, thus allowing the two major parties to remain dominant.

   e. In presidential elections, all but two states (Maine and Nebraska) allocate all of their electoral votes to the popular vote winner. Because this winner-take-all method is used in most states, it is almost impossible for a minor party candidate to win a plurality of votes within a state, and the state's electoral votes.

   f.   The two major parties also actively work to prevent minor parties from achieving equal status.

   ➤ Minor party candidates are required to achieve 15% support in order to qualify for participation in televised presidential debates. ·

   ➤ Candidates are required to collect minimum numbers of signatures in order to appear on a ballot. This is a greater challenge for minor party candidates who have fewer resources.

   g.   The two major parties are extremely well-funded and highly organized, making it difficult for smaller parties to compete.

2. Despite the challenges, minor parties occasionally win elections. Minor parties, especially the Socialist, Green, and Libertarian parties, have often won local and state elections, as well as federal seats.

3. Minor parties serve several functions in the United States.

   a.   Minor parties can be agents of innovation. Because they generally focus on smaller, more ideological groups, they are free to adopt positions that are more outside the mainstream and bring innovative ideas to the public.

   b.   Minor parties can motivate voters who are unhappy with their major party choices.

   c.   Minor parties can influence the political agenda.

   ➤ When a minor party receives support, the major parties take notice, and may adopt the minor party's positions. For example, the Democratic Party has been influenced by the Green Party's focus on the environment.

   ➤ This process of major parties co-opting minor party issues further diminishes minor parties' electoral prospects.

   d.   Minor party candidates may have a spoiler effect; that is, they may draw a significant portion of the vote from other candidates. If a minor party candidate draws enough votes from a major party candidate, he or she may hand the election to the other major party. For example, in the presidential election of 1992, George H.W. Bush ran for the Republicans, and Bill Clinton ran for the Democrats. H. (Henry) Ross Perot, a businessman and billionaire, ran as an independent. The results were as follows:

1992 Presidential Election	Popular Vote	Electoral Votes
Bill Clinton (D)	43%	370
George H.W. Bush (R)	37.4%	168
H. Ross Perot (I)	18.9%	0

➤ Perot, a conservative, drew votes primarily from Bush. Had he not run, most of those who voted for him would have voted for Bush, altering the outcome of the election (the spoiler effect).

➤ Even though Perot made a very strong run, drawing nearly 20% of the popular vote, he failed to win any electoral votes, illustrating the challenge that the winner-take-all system presents for minor parties.

Test Tip

Understand the barriers to minor party success.

➤ *single-member plurality (FPTP) electoral election system for Congress*

➤ *winner-take-all Electoral College system for presidential elections*

➤ *incorporation of minor party issues/positions by major parties*

➤ *lack of funding and party infrastructure make it difficult to compete with major parties*

➤ *signature requirements for ballots*

➤ *minimum polling thresholds for debate participation*

III. INTEREST GROUPS

A. TYPES OF INTEREST GROUPS

1. Interest groups are organizations of people who come together to advance a common cause.

2. Freedom of association is the right of individuals to unite with others for expressive or political purposes. Although not specifically listed in the First Amendment, is has been recognized by the Court as a protected right related to the freedom of speech.

3. Interest groups form around different types of issues, including economics, group welfare, professional membership, recreational interests, single issues, and areas of public concern. Some groups fall into multiple categories.

   a. Labor unions formed to address the conditions of working people, including safety, hours, and compensation. Examples of labor unions include the American Federation of Labor (AFL) and the Congress of Industrial Organizations (CIO), which merged in 1955 to form the AFL-CIO.

   b. Business organizations exist to promote the collective interest of businesses and generally oppose regulation and legislation promoting workers' rights. The United States Chamber of Commerce has more than three million member businesses and promotes a wide variety of business interests. Other groups, such as the National Association of Manufacturers, represent smaller segments of the economy.

   c. Professionals form interest groups for economic and other professional reasons. These include the American Bar Association (ABA) and the American Medical Association (AMA).

   d. Agriculture has traditionally been recognized as a unique economic interest, and there are many agricultural interest groups, such as the American Farm Bureau Federation. In recent years, changes in this economic sector have created conflicts between the interests of traditional small and mid-sized farms and large-scale agribusiness.

   e. Environmental groups advance environmental protections. Examples include the Sierra Club, Greenpeace, and the Environmental Defense Fund.

   f. Consumer groups advocate for the interests of consumers generally. Examples include Consumers Union, which provides product information and publishes *Consumer Reports*; and the Center for Science in the Public Interest (CSPI), which advocates for food safety.

   g. Interest groups also form to protect and advance group welfare on a societal level or for ideological reasons. Such groups include the National Organization for Women (NOW), formed in 1966 to advance women's rights; the National Association for the Advancement of Colored People (NAACP), established to promote the civil rights of African Americans; and the American Association of Retired Persons (AARP), which promotes the interests of older Americans.

   h. Single-issue groups focus on one specific concern. Examples include the National Rifle Association (NRA) and Mothers Against Drunk Driving (MADD).

   i. Government interest groups are composed of representatives of state and local government organizations. An example is the National Governors Association (NGA).

  4. Interest groups can form around very narrow issues, such as the protection of a particular species; or around broad issues, such as environmental protection generally.

Test Tip

Recall that Madison, in "Federalist No. 10," addressed the commonly held concern that factions were both dangerous and inevitable. Madison argued that in a large republic multiple factions would compete, ensuring that none would be dominant. He also believed that the negative effects of factions would be mitigated through the decisions of a sophisticated group of elected representatives, the separation of power among the three branches, and the system of federalism, which allowed for issues to be addressed at the appropriate level of government (multiple access points).

B. LOBBYING: HOW INTEREST GROUPS INFLUENCE GOVERNMENT

  1. *Lobbying* describes the various activities in which interest groups engage in order to influence government officials.

  2. Interest groups offer financial support to candidates' campaigns.

   a. Interest groups form political action committees, or PACs. Through their PACs, interest groups offer financial contributions to politicians' campaigns. These types of contributions are limited by law to $5,000 per candidate per election cycle (combined $10,000 for primary and general elections).

   b. In addition to direct contributions, interest groups frequently offer indirect financial support to politicians. They may do this by donating to political parties or by sponsoring political advertising, so long as they do not coordinate their messaging with the candidate or campaign.

3. Interest groups may offer to endorse a candidate, encouraging their members to vote for the candidate.

4. Interest groups educate politicians by conducting research, providing data and information.

5. Interest groups frequently write legislation and provide draft legislation for politicians to propose.

6. Interest groups educate and motivate the public to vote and become involved in political activities.

7. Interest groups may put grassroots pressure on politicians by calling on their members to contact politicians and agitate for their political goals.

8. Interest groups attempt to influence judicial outcomes by filing lawsuits or amicus curiae briefs.

9. Interest groups *do not*:

    a. run candidates for office.

    b. concern themselves with political issues outside of their area(s) of interest.

C. INTEREST GROUPS VS. POLITICAL PARTIES

1. Most interest groups' policy goals are more closely aligned with one party than another. For example, the concerns of environmental groups are reflected in the Democratic platform. Most interest groups form associations with and support members of one of the political parties. The parties support the policy goals of their interest group constituencies. For instance, the NRA is overwhelmingly supportive of the Republican Party, and the Republican Party opposes gun regulation.

2. Interest groups may contribute financially to both candidates in an election to ensure a favorable relationship with the winner.

3. Interest groups are more likely to support the incumbent than the challenger during an election. This is because the incumbency advantage makes it more likely that the current officeholder will win re-election.

4. Both interest groups and political parties work to promote the agenda of their membership, but there are important differences.

Interest Groups vs. Political Parties

Interest Groups	Political Parties
– attempt to influence the government through lobbying, donations, grassroots efforts, and other methods – do not run candidates for office – limit policy concerns to one or a small group of related areas	– attempt to control the government by running candidates for office/winning elections – have a comprehensive platform addressing a wide variety of political issues

D. IRON TRIANGLES AND ISSUE NETWORKS

1. As components of iron triangles and issue networks, interest groups work to influence members of Congress and bureaucratic agencies.

2. Interest groups offer support to members of Congress who serve on committees related to their policy areas. In return, members take their agendas into consideration.

3. Interest groups offer to promote congressional support for bureaucratic agencies and priorities. In return, bureaucratic agencies offer favorable implementation of legislative policies and friendly regulation.

4. Politicians and bureaucrats are frequently offered jobs working for interest groups. Additionally, interest group employees may take jobs within the government bureaucracy regulating the group's area of concern. The movement of personnel between government and lobbying positions is described as the revolving door.

E. INTEREST GROUP FUNDING AND MEMBERSHIP

1. The power of interest groups is determined by funding and membership, with the best-funded groups having the most power.

   a. Some groups are very well-funded and may offer politicians donations to their campaigns or various forms of indirect contributions.

   b. Some groups offer less financial support, but have large memberships. These groups offer the support of their members in the form of voting and campaign assistance. For example, AARP, an interest group representing older Americans claims a membership of nearly 40 million.

    c. Causes that lack financial resources and large or influential membership groups will not be as effective in advocating their policies, even though they might be worthy and important.

    d. While campaign contributions may succeed in securing access to politicians, they do not necessarily translate into policy support from those politicians.

  2. The free rider problem is a funding challenge faced by interest groups whose work often benefits many people outside the group who are not members and are not motivated to contribute money or effort. A classic example of the free rider problem is union membership. If (as in some states) workers in a particular industry or workplace are not required to pay union dues, many will not but will still benefit from the union's negotiating power.

  3. Interest groups encourage support and membership through three primary methods.

    a. Purposive incentives are the rewards of ethical or moral behavior. People feel satisfaction when contributing to a greater social good.

    b. Solidarity incentives offer social rewards. Joining an interest group may allow people to spend time with other like-minded citizens.

    c. Material incentives are tangible benefits, such as discounts offered to members, magazine subscriptions, and tote bags.

IV. SOCIAL MOVEMENTS

A. SOCIAL MOVEMENTS IN HISTORY

  1. Social movements are broad-based coalitions of groups and individuals advocating for social change.

    a. Social movements have a moral component, and their goals involve challenging and changing norms and values.

    b. Social movements advocate for a variety of reasons:

      ➤ social change and group rights, such as the Civil Rights, Women's Rights, and LGBTQ Rights movements

      ➤ current issues, such as environmental protection or consumer rights

2. Social movements often include numerous interest groups advocating for policy in the same field. For example, the Civil Rights Movement was supported by the National Association for the Advancement of Colored People (NAACP), the Urban League, and other interest groups.

3. Recently, several social movements have arisen in the United States.

    a. Black Lives Matter formed in 2013. The movement's goals include organizing protests, promoting Black leadership, and opposing state-sanctioned and vigilante violence against Black communities.

    b. The #MeToo movement developed when the #MeToo hashtag trended virally on social media when victims of sexual harassment and assault began to share their stories in order to call attention to the prevalence of these problems.

    c. March for Our Lives is a social movement that began as a student demonstration for increased government action to reduce gun violence in schools. It has expanded to become a larger movement focused on specific goals, including increasing youth voting.

B. DISTINCTION BETWEEN INTEREST GROUPS AND SOCIAL MOVEMENTS

1. Interest groups generally concern themselves with specific issues, while social movements champion broader causes.

2. Multiple interest groups may agitate for change as part of a broader social movement.

3. Interest groups are generally smaller, better organized, and more cohesive. They have clear memberships and funding mechanisms. They rely primarily on lobbying to achieve their goals.

4. Social movements are generally more dispersed and lack an administrative structure and clear membership. They generally rely on protest activities and demonstrations to call attention to their causes.

C. SOCIAL MOVEMENT METHODS

1. Social movements employ protests and public demonstrations in order to create change within a social and political system.

2. Civil disobedience is the intentional breaking of laws or rules in order to call attention to injustice.

The roles of political parties, interest groups, and social movements in the U.S. political system provide numerous examples of participatory democracy (majoritarianism), pluralist democracy, and elite democracy (elitism) theories.

➤ *Candidates and parties win when they are supported by the largest number of voters in elections (participatory).*

➤ *The thousands of interest groups in our society represent a vast array of organizations and concerns, so that no single group or small minority of groups is dominant (pluralist).*

➤ *Powerful and wealthy elites support and participate in certain groups that are highly effective in advancing their interests. Money gains access to political power and a primary role in setting the political agenda. Also, wealthy, connected candidates who can significantly finance their own political campaigns have an advantage in the candidate selection process and in elections (elitist).*

V. CAMPAIGN FINANCE

A. HISTORY AND LIMITS ON CAMPAIGN EXPENDITURES

1. **Campaigns are expensive.**

   a. Presidential campaign spending runs into the billions of dollars.

   b. The danger of money in politics and the need for regulation of campaign donations and expenditures has long been recognized.

   c. The history of campaign finance law in the United States is also the history of efforts to challenge and exploit loopholes in these regulations.

   d. The first comprehensive law to effectively limit and regulate campaign finance was the Federal Election Campaign Act (FECA), passed in 1971 and amended in 1974.

2. **The Federal Election Campaign Act (FECA) of 1971**

   a. placed limits on individual and political action committee (PAC) contributions.

   b. placed limits on campaign spending.

   c. required reporting of campaign contributions and expenditures.

   d. established a system for public financing of presidential campaigns, which became effective in 1976. (Presidential candidates generally no longer accept public monies available for their campaigns because they can raise almost unlimited money and prefer not to be subject to the restrictions attached to public funding.)

   e. created the Federal Election Commission (FEC), a bipartisan commission charged with enforcing campaign contribution and spending limits and monitoring disclosure compliance.

   f. In 1976, in *Buckley v. Valeo*, the Court struck down limits on campaign spending (but not necessarily contributions), ruling that spending money to influence elections is a form of constitutionally protected free speech.

3. **The Bipartisan Campaign Reform Act (BCRA), also called the McCain-Feingold Act, was passed in 2002.**

   a. Prior to BCRA, unlimited monetary contributions to political parties were allowed, so long as these funds were spent on "party-building purposes," such as get-out-the-vote (GOTV) drives and issue advertisements (ads that provide information about a political issue but do not advocate voting for a specific candidate). These funds, which are donations to political parties, are referred to as *soft money*.

   b. When BCRA was passed, it

   ➤ prohibited national parties from soliciting or spending soft money.

   ➤ placed specific limits on contributions to candidates, parties, and PACs.

   ➤ prohibited issue advertisements on television or radio that used a candidate's name, were paid for by corporations or unions, and were broadcast within thirty days of a primary election or within 60 days of a general election.

➤ required candidates and any group running political advertisements to disclose who paid for the ad. This is known as the *stand-by-your-ad provision*.

c. BCRA did not regulate spending by 527 committees, which are not-for-profit groups organized under Section 527 of the Internal Revenue Code for the purpose of influencing elections. They do not, however, advocate for specific candidates and may not coordinate with campaigns. The 527s primarily engage in issue advertising, or provide information about specific issues to the public. The 527 groups are required to report donors and donations to the IRS.

Test Tip

Campaign finance regulation is technical and involves its own vocabulary. Remembering a few key terms can help make it clear.

➤ **Hard money:** *money donated directly to candidates*

➤ **Soft money:** *money donated to political parties for general "party-building" activities*

➤ **Dark money:** *money donated anonymously to certain nonprofit (501 groups) organizations and used for political purposes*

➤ **Outside spending/independent expenditures:** *spending by unaffiliated groups to promote a candidate*

➤ **Issue advocacy:** *advertisements that are intended to educate the public regarding a particular issue, rather than to promote a particular candidate*

B. CAMPAIGN FINANCE REGULATIONS TODAY

1. *Citizens United v. Federal Election Commission* (2010)

   a. **Facts of the Case:** Citizens United, a conservative nonprofit organization, was restrained by BCRA from promoting a film called *Hillary: The Movie*, which negatively portrayed Hillary Clinton.

   b. **Constitutional Issue(s):** Does the BCRA ban on election advertising violate the First Amendment right to free speech? Does Citizens United, a nonprofit corporation, have this First Amendment right?

   c. **Holding(s):** The BCRA ban on election advertising does violate the First Amendment right to free speech and is unconstitutional. Citizens United, a corporation, does have a free speech right.

   d. **Reasoning:** Because Citizens United is a nonprofit corporation, a central question for the Court was whether corporations have a First Amendment right to freedom of speech. The Court held that corporations do have this right and viewed the ban on political advertising by corporations as a prior restraint on political speech. This ban would be acceptable if the corporate spending was likely to lead to corruption. To prevent corruption, the organization may not communicate or coordinate with a candidate. Be aware that the decision is broadly written and applies to spending by unions, as well as corporations.

2. *Citizens United* did not impact the limits on direct contributions to candidates and campaigns (hard money), or the ban on soft money contributions, which remain enforceable. As a practical matter, the removal of limits on outside spending makes candidates less reliant on direct donations (hard money).

3. The removal of limits on organizational spending to influence campaign outcomes has led to the growth of other types of political organizations, including:

   a. **Super PACs.** These organizations are also known as independent-expenditure-only committees because they engage only in outside spending and do not contribute to parties or candidates. Unlike traditional PACs, they are not limited in how much money they can raise and spend, but must not directly coordinate with campaigns.

   b. **501 organizations.** These nonprofit organizations, which include social welfare groups (charities), unions, and trade associations, are named for the part of the Internal Revenue Code under which they are organized, and are not subject to FEC regulation.

      ➤ 501(c)4 organizations are defined by the IRS as "social welfare organizations," or charities.

      ➤ Unlike Super PACs, 501 groups are not required to disclose their donors. For this reason, the money they raise and spend is commonly referred to as *dark money.*

➤ 501 organizations frequently contribute to Super PACs, allowing Super PACs to indirectly collect large sums of money anonymously.

Type of Organization	Function and Regulations
PAC	– political action committee – collects funds from members and distributes funds to candidates and political causes – federal law places limits on contributions to PACs – federal law places limits on donations made by PACs to parties and candidates – required to disclose donors
Super PAC	– collects and spends unlimited amounts – may not coordinate with candidates or campaigns – required to disclose donors
501 (nonprofit) groups	– receives and spends unlimited amounts – not required to disclose donors (dark money)

Test Tip

Questions relating to campaign finance regulation are likely to relate to a few important concepts. Be sure you understand:

➤ *the tension between free speech and the need to prevent corruption in elections*

➤ *the effect of two key pieces of legislation—FECA and BCRA*

➤ *the relationship between money and speech*

➤ *the argument that groups with more money can purchase "more speech," and concerns about the impact of virtually unlimited fundraising and spending on the fairness of elections*

➤ *the impact of* Citizens United *on electoral politics*

Voter Behavior and Elections

I. VOTER BEHAVIOR

A. AMENDMENTS AND LEGISLATION AFFECTING VOTING

1. Voting requirements are set by states but are subject to constitutional requirements and federal law.

2. **The Constitution**

   a. **Fifteenth Amendment:** prohibits states from restricting voting rights on the basis of race

   b. **Seventeenth Amendment:** requires direct election of senators by the voters of each state, replacing the method of election of senators by state legislatures

   c. **Nineteenth Amendment:** prohibits states from restricting voting rights based on sex

   d. **Twenty-fourth Amendment:** prohibits states from charging a poll tax to vote

   e. **Twenty-sixth Amendment:** guarantees voting rights to persons over 18 years old

3. **Federal Law**

   a. **Civil Rights Act of 1964:** prohibited racial discrimination in voter qualification requirements

   b. **Voting Rights Act of 1965:** outlawed literacy testing and all forms of voter qualification that result in racial discrimination. This law also required preclearance for changing voting procedures for certain jurisdictions. *Preclearance* is the term for the legal requirement that jurisdictions with a significant history of racially discriminatory voting laws obtain approval from the Department of Justice before making changes to voting and election procedures. This provision was struck down in *Shelby County v. Holder* (2013).

c. **National Voter Registration Act of 1993 (Motor Voter Act):** required states to provide individuals with the opportunity to register to vote at the same time that they apply for a driver's license or seek to renew a driver's license

Test Tip

Remember that the trend in U.S. history and the goal of most legislative efforts has been to expand the franchise, also called suffrage, which is the right to vote.

B. FACTORS AFFECTING VOTER TURNOUT

1. Voter turnout is widely studied as an important metric on the health of a democracy.

2. Voter turnout can be calculated in different ways, including as a percentage of:

    a. the voting-age population—that is, all persons old enough to vote;

    b. the voting-eligible population—that is, all persons who meet all legal qualifications for voting, not just age; or

    c. registered voters.

3. In the United States, numerous personal characteristics have been shown to correlate with the likelihood of an individual voting. It is important to recognize that these factors are associated with voter participation, but they do not necessarily cause it.

    a. **Socioeconomic status (SES).** This is a measure of education, occupation, income, and wealth. Persons with higher socioeconomic status are more likely to vote and more likely to participate in politics generally.

        ➤ Higher education level is the factor most strongly associated with voting participation. Highly educated people may be less intimidated by the voting process and more likely to feel a sense of political efficacy—the sense that their vote matters.

        ➤ Education, income, and occupation are strongly correlated. For example, persons with a higher level of education are more likely to have higher prestige occupations and higher incomes.

    ➤ Persons with greater wealth are more likely to bear the cost of belonging to interest groups, which may motivate voter participation.

  b. **Political efficacy.** This is one's belief that voting is an effective way to influence the world. Persons with a strong sense of political efficacy feel that their vote will make an impact and are therefore more likely to vote.

  c. **Age.** There is a strong correlation between age and voting participation. Older people have the highest turnout, and young people have the lowest turnout.

    ➤ Older people often have escalating concerns about mortgages, children, retirement, social security, and Medicare, and therefore may perceive public policy as having a greater impact on their lives.

    ➤ Younger people may not have developed strong political views or may not perceive that they have a significant personal stake in public policy outcomes.

  d. **Gender.** Men and women vote at similar rates, although in recent decades women have voted at a rate just slightly higher than men.

  e. **Race.** Historically, race correlates significantly with voter turnout.

    ➤ Whites have the highest turnout rates.

    ➤ African American voter turnout rates were historically significantly lower than those of whites, but in recent decades the African American turnout rate has risen to within 2 to 3 percentage points of the white turnout rate.

    ➤ Hispanic Americans' and Asian Americans' voting rates are significantly lower than those of whites and African Americans.

4. Many structural barriers affect voter turnout rates. *Structural* in this context is a term used to describe the characteristics of elections themselves.

  a. **Expansion of the franchise.** Historically, voting rights in the United States have expanded as marginalized groups gain access to the ballot. Because these groups face structural and social challenges to voting and have historically voted at lower rates than more privileged groups, the expansion of the franchise has resulted in lower overall voting rates.

b. **Negative campaigning.** Attacking the political opposition, and even the government itself, are effective in influencing voter choices. They also discourage voting by creating negative feelings toward politics in general.

c. **Declining trust in government.** Political corruption contributes to voter apathy.

d. **Registration process.** Voting rates are reduced in states with more restrictive registration laws. Voting rates are increased by registration laws that allow:

> ➤ opportunities for registration when applying for or renewing a driver's license (now required by federal law)

> ➤ online registration

> ➤ registration at the polls on election day

> ➤ automatic voter registration, in which voters are automatically registered by the state

e. **Voter identification requirements.** In recent years, a growing number of states have passed laws requiring voters to prove their identity at the polls.

> ➤ The type of identification acceptable (for example, college ID cards or a Medicare card) varies by state.

> ➤ Stricter voter identification laws reduce voter turnout. Less restrictive requirements are associated with higher voter turnouts.

> ➤ The groups most likely to be impacted by voter identification requirements are the elderly, low-income, and less-educated populations.

f. **Tuesday elections.** In most democracies, elections take place on weekends. In some countries, election day is a national holiday.

> ➤ Tuesday elections in the United States create barriers to voting by making it more difficult for working people to go to the polls.

> ➤ Expanded early voting and absentee voting options may help to mitigate the burden of in-person, weekday elections.

g. **Felony disenfranchisement.** States have different rules regarding the eligibility of convicted felons to vote. These rules affect a significant proportion of the population.

> ➤ Some states reinstate the right to vote when a felon has finished serving his or her parole, or a fixed period of time thereafter.

> ➤ A small number of states have laws requiring mandatory lifetime disenfranchisement for all felons.

> ➤ A small number of states allow felons, including current prisoners, to vote.

h. **Federal vs. state elections.** Voter turnout is higher in federal than in state-level elections, and higher in state than in local elections. In general, the more local the election, the lower the turnout rate.

i. **Presidential vs. midterm elections.** Turnout rates are highest in presidential elections and lower in midterm elections.

Test Tip

Understand how personal characteristics influence voter turnout.

Factors Associated with Increased Voting Participation	Factors Associated with Decreased Voting Participation
more education	less education
greater income/wealth	lower income/wealth
higher occupational status	lower occupational status
older age	younger age
race: white or African American	race: Hispanic or Asian
union membership	non-union member
more religious	less religious
more community involvement	less community involvement
female (slight)	male (slight)

C. FACTORS AFFECTING VOTER PREFERENCES

1. Like turnout, voter preferences correlate with certain demographic characteristics.

   a. Religious beliefs strongly correlate with voter preferences.

      ➤ Christian Protestants, the largest religious group in the United States, generally support Republicans. This is especially true of its Evangelical Christian subgroup.

      ➤ Catholics, the second-largest religious group, historically favored Democrats, but now appear to split their support evenly between Democrats and Republicans.

      ➤ Jews, who comprise a small percentage of the electorate, have historically favored Democrats by a wide margin.

   b. There is a gender gap in voting preferences, with women generally preferring Democrats, and men generally preferring Republicans.

   c. Voter preferences also diverge along racial lines.

      ➤ Whites generally prefer Republicans by a small margin.

      ➤ African Americans prefer Democrats by a large margin.

      ➤ Hispanic and Asian Americans also prefer Democrats by wide margins.

   d. The gap in voting preferences between non-college-educated voters and those with higher levels of education has increased in recent elections. Beyond college, the tendency to favor Democratic candidates increases as levels of education increase.

   e. Voter preferences are strongly correlated with rural or urban residence. Urban voters tend to favor Democrats, while rural voters tend to favor Republicans.

   f. Some voters feel strongly attached to a political party. This is known as party identification. The extent to which voters identify with one party or the other is strongly influenced by one's family, as well as other factors such as education and region of residence.

2. Voter preferences may also be affected by factors specific to candidates and elections.

   a. Different voters and voting groups may be attracted to a party based on a critical issue in an election, such as immigration or women's rights.

   b. Voter preferences are significantly affected by candidate characteristics. For this reason, parties attempt to promote candidates who are attractive, pleasant, and appealing.

   ➤ A candidate's personal characteristics may resonate with certain groups of voters. John F. Kennedy overwhelmingly won Catholic voters, and Barack Obama overwhelmingly won African American voters.

   ➤ Voters may be drawn to a candidate based on personal charisma or attractiveness.

   c. Some states have ballots that offer voters the option of straight-ticket voting, or marking only one box that automatically casts their votes for all candidates running on a party's ticket.

   ➤ Voters with a strong sense of party identification are more likely to vote straight-ticket.

   ➤ Although the percentage of split-ticket voting (in which voters choose certain candidates from one party and certain candidates from the other party) varies from election to election, it is always a significant number of voters.

Factors Influencing Political Preferences

Voter Demographics Favoring Democrats	Voter Demographics Favoring Republicans
minority	white
female	male
Jewish, Muslim, Hindu, Buddhist, unaffiliated with a religion	Protestant/evangelical, Church of Jesus Christ of Latter-day Saints
urban	rural
Northwest and coastal regions	South and Midwest regions

Note: Catholics historically favored Democrats but recently are split between Republicans and Democrats.

Understand the distinction between voter turnout (whether people vote) and voter preferences (who people vote for) and how these are affected by the structural and personal factors described in the text. Also, be aware that correlations between voter characteristics and voter behavior are generalizations and do not necessarily apply to individual group members.

D. THEORIES OF VOTER BEHAVIOR

1. Voting is the primary method by which citizens direct the activities of government.

2. Political scientists have suggested several theories of how citizens in democracies make voting decisions. Each of the following theories attempts to explain the process through which citizens decide which candidates to vote for in an election.

   a. **Rational-Choice Voting.** Voters seek out information about candidates and issues and vote for the person they believe will advance their policy preferences.

   b. **Retrospective Voting.** Voters consider the track record of each candidate and party to determine how effectively that party or candidate has governed.

   c. **Prospective Voting.** Voters evaluate promises and proposals made by candidates and predict how their own priorities will be affected.

   d. **Party-Line Voting.** Partisans (voters with a strong sense of party identification) are likely to make voting decisions based on the party affiliation of the candidates.

II. ELECTIONS

A. ELECTIONS GENERALLY

1. Elections (along with political parties, interest groups, and the media) are an important linkage institution through which voters interact with government officials to produce public policy.

2. Federal elections are held on the first Tuesday after the first Monday in November in even-numbered years.

3. Presidential elections are held every four years.

4. Americans also regularly elect members of state governments, including governors, state legislatures, and state judges. (Judges in the federal system are appointed for life terms.)

5. Additionally, elections encompass the selection of officials at the local level, including county, city, and school board offices, among others.

6. As a result of democratic reforms at the state level, state and local elections feature several types of ballot questions not found in federal elections. These reforms reflect a trend toward placing greater political power in the hands of voters.

   a. An initiative is a procedure that allows voters to bypass their legislatures to propose laws or (state) constitutional amendments that may be placed on the ballot.

   b. A referendum is a policy question placed on a ballot by a state legislature for voters to accept or reject, thus allowing voters to make policy choices directly.

   c. A recall allows voters to hold an election to remove and replace an elected official before his or her term in office is finished.

Test Tip *Initiatives and referenda are often difficult to distinguish. Initiatives are laws proposed by citizens using petitions. These proposed laws may be placed on the ballot or submitted to the legislature, depending on state law. Referenda (plural of referendum) are placed on the ballot by the state legislature.*

B. NOMINATING CANDIDATES FOR OFFICE

1. Most candidates for political office at the state and federal levels are nominated by political parties.

2. Nominees were historically selected by party leaders, but reforms have granted this power to the regular party members.

   a. Voters now select nominees through direct primaries.

   b. The direct primary resulted in

   ➤ a loss of power by the party leadership and increased influence for voters.

> ➤ increased responsibility on candidates for fundraising and managing campaigns.

> ➤ a focus on candidate characteristics and qualities.

3. Parties select a nominee from among declared candidates for each office within the party.

4. Each party then supports and promotes its nominees in the general election.

5. Some candidates run as independents in the general election.

Test Tip

Keep in mind that candidates who are most popular with a party's base of core voters are often ideologically pure or extreme. This is generally the type of candidate who will resonate with politically engaged partisans early on in the election process. In the general election, however, moderate candidates will draw more support from nonpartisan, middle-of-the-road voters. For this reason, moderates have historically been more electable. The choice of nominees for office demonstrates the tension between a more partisan candidate who will motivate the party's voter base in a general election, versus a moderate candidate who will draw votes from the middle.

C. PRIMARIES

1. Most states hold primary elections in which voters choose each party's nominees for each office on the ballot.

   a. In an open primary, voters may choose at their polling places to vote in either the Democratic or Republican contest.

   b. In a closed primary, voters must be registered as Republicans or Democrats in order to receive their party's ballot.

2. In presidential primaries, held every four years, parties select their presidential and vice presidential nominees.

   a. The parties have systems for choosing a candidate on the national level.

   b. In the presidential primaries, the voters are selecting delegates who will vote for the chosen nominee at the party's nominating convention.

The term caucus *has two distinct political meanings. In the discussion below,* caucus *refers to a meeting of party members within a state to participate in the presidential nomination process.* Caucus *can also refer to voting blocks of legislators who are associated based on party membership, demographics, or ideology, such as the Congressional Hispanic Caucus and the Bipartisan Disabilities Caucus.*

D. CAUCUSES

1. About one-fifth of the states hold caucuses, rather than primary elections, to select delegates to the presidential nominating conventions.

2. Caucuses are local meetings of party members held in precincts across the state.

3. Voters discuss and debate the merits of their party's candidates for the presidential nomination and vote publicly by grouping themselves according to candidate.

4. The process is complicated and time-consuming and results in delegate selection by only the most committed voters in a state.

E. OPEN PRIMARIES, CLOSED PRIMARIES, AND CAUCUSES

1. The differences among primaries and caucuses are significant because they involve different sets of participants and result in different candidate selection patterns.

2. Primary turnout runs low overall, at about half that of the general election. Caucus turnout is even lower.

3. The more limited the nominating procedure, the more partisan and motivated the voters are, and the more ideologically intense the nominee is likely to be. This can be a problem in the general election when the more moderate elements of the electorate are more likely to participate.

4. Closed primaries and caucuses tend to produce more extreme candidates than open primaries because participation is limited to the most dedicated partisans.

5. Although open primaries encourage the most participation, they also allow the opportunity for voters to use their votes to strategically impact the other party's nomination. In other words, voters may vote as members of the party they oppose to support a candidate who would be a weak challenger in the general election.

F. DELEGATES

1. The selection of a state's delegates to the presidential nominating convention is determined by the primary or convention process in the state.

2. A state's delegates may be awarded in proportion to the outcome of the election or caucus, or on a winner-take-all basis. The method depends on state and party rules.

3. Delegates that are awarded through primary elections or caucuses are called pledged delegates because they are committed to voting for a particular candidate.

4. Both parties' systems also include delegates who are unpledged.

5. The Republican process includes three unpledged delegates from each state, usually the top officials in the state party leadership.

6. The Democratic system includes hundreds of superdelegates, including members of Congress and party leaders, who are free to vote for any candidate.

G. FRONT-LOADING

1. The practice of front-loading, or holding a primary or caucus early in the election cycle, confers political and economic advantages on a state.

2. States with early candidate selection processes have a disproportionate impact on the selection of the nominee and are the focus of attention by candidates and the media.

3. Early primaries and caucuses bring attention, advertising dollars, and media coverage to the state. For this reason, states may engage in front-loading, which involves moving up their primary contests to be among the first.

4. Both major parties have implemented guidelines and sanctions to discourage front-loading by states.

5. Iowa holds the first caucuses, and New Hampshire holds the first primary.

H. NATIONAL NOMINATING CONVENTIONS

1. Following the primary contests, in the summer of presidential election years, each of the major political parties holds a national convention, also called a nominating convention.

2. Party conventions serve several functions:

   a. Conventions include the formal adoption of the party platform, which is a statement of the party's positions on political issues.

   b. Formal selection of the presidential nominee takes place at the convention as the delegates cast their votes.

   c. The vice-presidential nominee is selected.

   d. Parties attempt to unify behind the platform and the nominee. This is important, as the supporters of losing candidates may be dissatisfied and must be encouraged to support the party nominee.

   e. Modern conventions are glamorous, staged, and televised events. They serve as advertising spectacles, promoting the party's message and candidate to the general public.

3. Although the nominee is generally known long before the convention, it is possible that no single candidate wins a majority of the delegates, resulting in a brokered, or contested, convention. Multiple rounds of votes may be taken until a winner is determined.

III. THE GENERAL ELECTION: CONGRESS

A. CONGRESSIONAL ELECTIONS

1. Congressional elections are held every two years.

2. Winners are determined using the single-member plurality system, also called the first-past-the-post system. This means that the candidate with the most votes wins the election, even if no candidate wins a majority of votes.

3. In each congressional election, voters in the states select all (435) members of the House of Representatives and one-third of the Senate seats.

4. In presidential election years, the politics of the presidential election impact congressional candidates.

a. Both the popularity of the presidential nominees and the level of opposition to them may impact voter turnout.

b. An extremely unpopular presidential candidate of the opposite party may help a congressional candidate's performance at the polls.

c. Likewise, a popular presidential candidate may boost votes for other "down-ballot" candidates from his or her party in what is called the *coattail effect*.

5. Congressional elections that do not coincide with presidential elections are called midterm or off-year elections.

a. Voter turnout rates are normally significantly lower in midterm than in presidential elections.

b. Another notable phenomenon associated with midterm elections is that the president's party tends to lose seats in Congress.

➤ This loss of seats occurs regardless of which party holds the White House and has been remarkably consistent since the first election of FDR. In only two elections since then has the incumbent president's party gained seats in a midterm election.

➤ The reasons for seat loss appear to be structural, in part because the opposition base (set of core voters) is more likely to be motivated and energized in off-year elections.

➤ Losing seats can weaken the president's ability to enact his or her agenda in the second two years of the presidential term.

6. In addition to presidential and congressional races, ballots in federal election years include state and local races.

a. Voters who vote exclusively for one party's candidates are said to be voting straight-ticket. A few states' ballots still allow voters to efficiently vote straight-ticket by marking a single box, but the practice has been eliminated in most states.

b. Voters may vote for candidates of both parties for different offices. For example, a voter may vote for the Democratic candidate for president, the Republican candidate for the Senate, and so on. The practice of voting for candidates of both parties is called split-ticket voting.

c. In most elections, about half of voters split their votes, and about half vote straight-ticket.

B. CAMPAIGNING FOR CONGRESS

1. As party power has receded, campaigns have become more candidate-centered, creating both advantages and disadvantages for candidates.

    a. Candidates must raise more of their own funds.

        ➤ The fundraising aspect of campaigns creates pressure for all candidates, but is more acute for members of the House, who must campaign every two years to hold their seats.

        ➤ Senators, with a longer interval between elections, spend more per campaign than members of the House, but have to run for re-election only once every six years.

    b. Candidates hire professional campaign management staff who create advertising campaigns, speak to the press, conduct polls, and develop strategy independent of party preferences.

    c. Individual campaigns must efficiently use funds and target voters for messaging.

    d. Candidates are more independent of political party control.

2. A candidate may be running for office for the first time or re-election. The person currently holding an office is called the incumbent. (Remember: **in**cumbent = **in** office.)

3. The incumbent holds a number of strategic advantages called *the incumbency advantage.*

    a. **Name recognition.** Incumbents receive free publicity, both through the media and as a function of their role in government. Voters have heard incumbents' names many times, while the names of challengers may be unfamiliar. Research shows that recognition of a candidate's name, by itself, is likely to positively affect voters.

    b. **Casework.** Members of Congress provide personal assistance to constituents (voters in their states or districts) with problems involving the federal government. Members have staff dedicated to providing this type of assistance, which produces a favorable impression on voters and increases voter support. Examples of casework types include:

        ➤ assistance in applying for Social Security, veterans' benefits, and educational benefits; or in tracking lost payments

> ➤ assistance in immigration matters or passport applications

> ➤ applying to a military academy

c. **Franking privilege.** The franking privilege allows lawmakers to send materials to citizens within their states or districts at taxpayer expense (no cost to Congress members). Challengers must fund their own mailings.

> ➤ This privilege is intended to facilitate legislators' communication with constituents. Informative materials, however, generally include the incumbent's smiling face and plenty of information about all that he or she has done for the district or state.

> ➤ The effect of the franking privilege may be somewhat reduced with the proliferation of electronic communications. It still provides a unique advantage, however, as it may be more difficult to dispose of paper found in a mailbox without glancing at the content, than it is to delete or ignore electronic messages.

d. **Committee assignments.** All members of Congress serve on one or more committees, allowing them to develop relationships with specific, often powerful constituencies.

e. **Interest group support.** Interest groups favor incumbents in terms of donations and support.

> ➤ These groups have often developed relationships with incumbents with whom they have worked on issues. (This may relate to committee assignments.)

> ➤ Interest groups recognize that incumbents are likely to win re-election and often direct their support toward current members to ensure access to those legislators. Supporting incumbents is perceived as a safer investment.

> ➤ Note that groups often support both candidates for a single office in order to ensure that they will have access to and the goodwill of the office holder.

f. **Gerrymandering.** Gerrymandered districts have created hundreds of safe seats for particular parties, which translates to strongly advantaged elections for individual office holders.

g. **Paid budgets.** Incumbents have staffing, administrative, and travel budgets paid for by taxpayers. These may technically not be used for campaign purposes, but they support a candidate's ability to travel and function in ways that challengers lack.

h. **Staff support.** Party leaders, popular politicians, and party structures help incumbents campaign and win elections.

i. **Donor support.** Those currently in office have a significant fundraising advantage because individual and institutional donors seeking access are more likely to contribute to incumbents, who are more likely to win than challengers.

4. Although most congressional elections involve an incumbent facing off against a challenger, candidates sometimes find themselves competing for an open seat.

a. An open seat happens when the incumbent does not seek re-election. This may occur when the incumbent dies, retires, faces criminal or ethical allegations, or seeks a higher office.

b. In an open election, the popularity of the outgoing incumbent may be a factor, but it is not as substantial as the incumbency advantage.

IV. THE GENERAL ELECTION: THE PRESIDENCY

A. CAMPAIGNING IN THE GENERAL ELECTION

1. The convention is over. The delegates have cast their votes, and a presidential nominee has been selected. As the party turns toward the general election, decisions must be made and a course charted to win the general election.

2. The candidate at this point must devise a strategy to address his or her change in audience. He or she must appeal to moderate voters in addition to the party base. These voters are less likely to be strongly partisan or to vote in primary elections or caucuses.

a. At this point, candidates often "pivot" on issues or soften their views to appeal to moderate voters.

b. The challenge for candidates during the general election is to maintain the enthusiasm of base voters while moving toward the middle in terms of policy.

3. The likelihood of one of the presidential candidates being an incumbent is lower than in congressional races. This is due to the fact that presidents are limited by the Twenty-second Amendment to two four-year terms, or, in the case of having succeeded to the

presidency (due to the death or disability of the president), a total of 10 years. (Remember: 22 is 2 terms or 10 years.)

    a. Presidential races are often for open seats due to term limits.

    b. For incumbent presidents, the election is a judgment by the public of their first-term performance.

4. An early decision that must be made by the candidate is the selection of a running mate.

    a. A flaw in the original Constitution created an electoral balloting system that chose the president and vice president separately, so that the candidate with the most votes became president, and the candidate with the second-most votes became vice president.

    b. This system resulted in two problems: First, it could result in the election of a president and vice president of different parties. Second, because electors each cast two ballots, which did not specify whether the ballot was being cast for president or vice president, it could result in a tied electoral vote between the presidential and vice presidential candidates of the same party. This happened when presidential candidate Thomas Jefferson and vice presidential candidate Aaron Burr received the same number of electoral votes. (Burr then unsuccessfully lobbied the House of Representatives to elect him president.)

    c. The Twelfth Amendment provides for presidential and vice presidential candidates to run together on a ticket.

5. The choice of a running mate is a strategic decision made by the presidential candidate and his or her leadership team. The selection involves several important considerations, most importantly, how to add support or compensate for weaknesses of the presidential candidate.

    a. A running mate may be selected to draw support from a populous state with a large number of electoral votes.

    b. A presidential candidate from one geographic area, for example, the Northeast, may draw support from another geographic area, such as the South or West, by selecting a popular politician from that region as a running mate.

    c. Candidates may choose running mates to broaden their appeal to minority groups, such as African Americans, Hispanics, or women.

    d. A running mate may also be chosen to balance the ticket ideologically, as when a more partisan candidate chooses a more moderate running mate, or with other political considerations in mind.

6. Finally, an important part of general election strategy involves how to allocate time and resources among states. In presidential politics, all states are definitely not equal.

    a. Certain categories of states receive disproportionate amounts of time and money from presidential campaigns.

> ➤ States with early primary elections or caucuses are often frequent campaign stops for candidates because an early lead or disadvantage in delegates may impact the trajectory of the campaign.

> ➤ Candidates generally focus on swing states, states in which both parties have a strong base and history of winning elections, and battleground states where polls show close races.

> ➤ All other things being equal, states with more electoral votes are likely to draw more attention from candidates.

    b. Certain categories of states are likely to receive less attention from candidates.

> ➤ Safe states are those in which one party has a lock on presidential elections. Illinois, for example, is reliably won by the Democratic candidate, while Alabama is reliably won by the Republican candidate. Because campaigning in these states will not affect the outcome of that state's vote, safe states are generally ignored by both candidates.

> ➤ States with smaller populations and fewer electoral votes are less important in the scheme of presidential campaign strategies.

B. THE ELECTORAL COLLEGE

1. The United States chooses its presidents not by direct popular election, but according to a system known as the Electoral College. Although the system of electors is described in Article II, Section 1, the term *Electoral College* is not found in the Constitution.

2. The Electoral College system is best understood as 51 separate contests, each with a different-sized prize.

a. Each state has a total number of electoral votes equal to its number of seats in Congress (Senate seats + House seats). The number of Senate seats is always two, but the number of House seats varies by state population. (Recall that House seats are reapportioned every 10 years based on the decennial census.)

b. In 1961, ratification of the Twenty-third Amendment granted Washington, D.C., a number of electoral votes equal to that of the least populous state (currently 3, as the smallest states have only one House seat). (Remember: 23 is 3 for DC.)

c. The winner of each contest receives all of that state's electoral votes (the winner-take-all system), except in Maine and Nebraska. Maine and Nebraska are unique because in those states, the popular vote winner within the state wins the two electoral votes associated with Senate seats, and each of the remaining electoral votes are divided according to the popular vote winner in of each of the states' congressional districts.

d. Winning a state means that the winning candidate's electors will be eligible to cast their votes for president.

   ➤ Electors are dedicated party members chosen to fill this honorary roll who have pledged, or promised, to vote for their party's nominee should that person win the popular vote within their state.

   ➤ Although electors almost always vote as promised, they may occasionally vote for someone other than the candidate they have promised to vote for. Cases of faithless electors are infrequent and have never affected the outcome of a presidential election, although this is certainly possible.

e. There are 538 electors in total (435 total House seats + 100 total Senate seats + 3 votes for the District of Columbia = 538).

   ➤ A majority of 270 votes or more is required to win the presidency. (A plurality is not sufficient.)

   ➤ If no candidate captures a majority of electoral votes, the winner of the presidential election is chosen by the House of Representatives, with each state having one vote. The vice president is chosen by the Senate following a similar procedure.

3. Proponents of the Electoral College have made several arguments in its support.

   a. The founders disliked the idea of direct popular election, primarily because they feared the ascent of a tyrant who might win the presidency by misinforming and inflaming the passions of the common people. Hamilton wrote in "Federalist No. 68" (not a required document):

      > It was equally desirable, that the immediate election should be made by men most capable of analyzing the qualities adapted to the station, and acting under circumstances favorable to deliberation, and to a judicious combination of all the reasons and inducements which were proper to govern their choice. A small number of persons, selected by their fellow-citizens from the general mass, will be most likely to possess the information and discernment requisite to such complicated investigations. It was also peculiarly desirable to afford as little opportunity as possible to tumult and disorder.

   b. Hamilton's quotation also reflects a confidence in elites, whom he and others felt could be better trusted than less educated, unsophisticated common people to elect the president. Common people at the time were also frequently rural dwellers with limited means of obtaining political information. It is important to keep in mind that the Electoral College has evolved from a system of largely independent electors to one in which parties choose electors who reliably vote for the party's nominee.

   c. The Electoral College is often defended because it protects the interests of less populous, more rural states, which would have little political influence under a system of direct popular election. In such a system, the argument goes, politicians would concern themselves primarily with urban states to the detriment of rural areas.

4. There are also numerous criticisms of the Electoral College, some of which have been highlighted by the failures of recent elections. These assessments point out that the Electoral College is undemocratic in various ways including the following:

   a. The popular vote winner may not win the presidency.

      ➤ This can occur because state populations are not proportionate to their voting power in the Electoral College. The combined effect of disproportionate electoral voting strength and the winner-take-all system of vote allocation sometimes leads to the popular vote winner failing to win the presidency.

➤ The popular vote winner failed to win the presidential election five times in American history, notably in 2000 and 2016.

➤ Winning the popular vote but losing the election has occurred more often as population differences between more and less populous states have increased.

b. Because the votes of minority party voters in safe states have negligible impact, the Electoral College system negates the value of these votes and depresses turnout.

c. Finally, it has been argued that the Electoral College is a vestige of the slave system that gave disproportionate power to slave states as a way to incentivize ratification of the Constitution.

Test Tip

The argument for direct popular election of the president reflects a preference for majoritarian democracy, whereas the Electoral College system reflects the concept of elite democracy. Pluralist democracy can be most easily seen in multi-party parliamentary systems that rely on government by coalition.

The Media

I. HISTORY, TYPES, AND STRUCTURE OF MODERN MEDIA

A. THE MEDIA AS A LINKAGE INSTITUTION

1. *Linkage institutions* (political parties, interest groups, elections, and the media) are formal organizations in society that connect people with the government and government with the people. Linkage institutions, including the media, create access points that allow people to connect with government.

   a. The news media provides citizens with information about policy issues and government activities.

   b. The media also provides the government with information about citizen attitudes and preferences that may impact policy issues on the government's agenda.

2. The press is sometimes called the fourth estate, a reference to the fact that the press is one of the most powerful and important institutions in society, tasked with advocating for the citizenry and influencing the political agenda.

3. In the Western democratic tradition, the independence of the press is vital.

   a. It is not affiliated with the government, and its role as a linkage institution is considered essential to democracy.

   b. In other political systems, the press may be an arm of the government and may serve primarily to disseminate official propaganda.

B. HISTORY OF MEDIA

1. The role of the media in American politics began in the Colonial Era when printing presses were used to publish newspapers that presented political news and events.

2. During the ratification debates, the *Federalist Papers* and *Brutus* essays were shared with the public through newspapers, making the competing views public.

3. From the beginning, a press with the freedom to publish information has been viewed as vital to democracy.

4. The First Amendment, which is understood as protecting the most important rights in a free society, explicitly protects both freedom of speech and freedom of the press.

5. As the media has evolved from print to broadcast to cable to Internet, it has played an increasing role in American political life.

   a. Radio and television broadcasts during the twentieth century reached the vast majority of Americans and were dominated by a small number of news networks.

      ➤ Market pressures to accurately report the news without offending a portion of the audience by taking partisan positions supported the practice of politically neutral, fact-based reporting.

      ➤ News reports were overwhelmingly developed by professional journalists who adhered to accepted standards for accuracy and professional norms.

      ➤ As a result, citizens received largely uniform information about news and politics.

   b. In the late twentieth century, talk radio, which was losing market share to new forms of media, became more partisan and emotionally charged, influencing political discourse.

   c. With the advent of cable news and the birth of the Internet, the news is now generated by a broader variety of outlets.

      ➤ Recently created news networks, foreign news sources, social media platforms, and Internet news sources have vastly expanded the marketplace for news.

      ➤ Some cable news channels present a strongly partisan view of the news in order to compete for viewership and advertising.

      ➤ Partisan news sites style their coverage to appeal to consumers with particular ideologies and political beliefs.

C. THE MODERN MEDIA

1. The modern media includes various forms of information outlets, including newspapers and magazines, radio, television, Internet sources, and others, that provide information and programming content to a broad segment of society. The media provides not only news, but entertainment and information too.

2. The term *mainstream media* refers collectively to broad-based, influential news outlets that reach large numbers of people.

3. Social media, which includes such platforms as Twitter, Facebook, Snapchat, Instagram, YouTube, and weblogs (blogs), is a form of media that allows users to create online communities and share information. Social media has transformed political information in the twenty-first century.

D. REGULATION OF MEDIA

1. Americans have always recognized the crucial role played by the press in society and have regulated the content of print and broadcast media and the structure of media organizations.

2. The Federal Communications Commission (FCC) was created by Congress in 1934 to regulate broadcast media on the premise that "the airwaves belong to the people."

    a. In order to broadcast, radio and television stations are required to maintain federal licensure, serve the public interest, and follow certain rules.

    b. Broadcast media may be regulated to ensure that content is suitable for minors.

    c. Broadcast media must follow the equal-time rule, which requires a broadcast outlet that gives or sells time to a political candidate to provide that candidate's opponent the same amount of time at the same cost. Although the rule is still in effect, it is rarely enforced as Americans receive information from many more sources than they did in the mid-twentieth century, when only a small number of networks provided news.

3. The Supreme Court has broadly interpreted the First Amendment's press and speech protections, upholding the right of news outlets to publish political information and prohibiting prior restraint. (See the required case of *New York Times Co. v. United States* (1971), covered in Chapter 9.)

4. In addition to regulating media content, the FCC historically enacted regulations to prevent the concentration of corporate ownership of media outlets. The concern has been to protect press independence and foster the presence of diverse viewpoints in the information marketplace.

    a. Beginning in the 1980s, restrictions on corporate ownership of media outlets were relaxed.

    b. Since that time, the trend has been toward the deregulation of media outlet ownership, and media consolidation has accelerated.

    c. Most news outlets today are owned by a handful of massive media companies, including Comcast, Time Warner, Disney, Viacom, and News Corp. Each of these has numerous subsidiary labels, making it difficult to recognize the corporate affiliations.

    d. The consequences of corporate consolidation of media outlets include:

        ➤ content is profit-driven; the presentation of information has a significant marketing function.

        ➤ the important role of the media in setting the policy agenda may be dominated by a small number of powerful corporate leaders with limited interests.

5. The FCC regulates the activities of Internet Service Providers (ISPs), the massive telecommunications companies that sell Internet access to consumers and businesses.

    a. Net neutrality is the principle that all ISPs must treat information equally and may not discriminate against any content provider, typically done by throttling, or slowing down, specific information streams. The idea is to create an Internet playing field on which the same rules apply equally to all content providers and prohibit powerful telecom companies from effectively censoring information from some sources, thereby controlling access to information by consumers.

    b. The net neutrality rule is a subject of controversy.

II. THE MEDIA IN MODERN POLITICS

A. ROLES OF THE MEDIA

1. Over the course of U.S. history, the news media has evolved from simple reporting of political speeches and developments to investigative journalism in which reporters serve as watchdogs, scrutinizing and exposing the motives and activities of politicians and powerful organizations.

    a. The earliest investigative journalists were the muckrakers, who exposed corruption in politics and spotlighted corporate greed and human rights.

    b. Scrutinizing government activities on behalf of the citizenry is an important function of the press.

    c. The exposure of corruption associated with investigative journalism, however, has resulted in the disillusionment of voters and an increasingly negative view of politics and politicians.

    d. The Freedom of Information Act (FOIA) is a 1967 law that requires executive branch federal agencies to provide information about the government that is not already published in the *Federal Register* when requested by journalists, researchers, or the public in the name of an open and transparent government in a democracy.

        ➤ FOIA is an important law for protecting the First Amendment freedom of the press because it forced the government to be more transparent.

        ➤ The act can require the full or partial release of records, although there are some exceptions, including personal privacy, privileged communication, trade secrets, and law enforcement or national security concerns.

        ➤ The law has been amended over the years to address changes in technology.

2. Another important function of the media is its role in agenda-setting. The media serves as a gatekeeper, selecting which issues and stories become part of the public perception. Those issues that the media covers frequently and prominently are perceived as being the most significant by voters.

3. Related to agenda-setting is framing. In general, media promotes the news that journalists believe should concern Americans. Additionally, however, its presentations structure how consumers view issues and promotes particular ideas about what questions should be asked. For example, are groups of immigrants approaching the U.S. border with Mexico roving bands of dangerous criminals seeking to enter the United States illegally? Or are they desperate refugees seeking asylum? Different media outlets frame issues differently to appeal to or influence viewers.

4. So, how do media outlets make coverage choices? The American press is independent and primarily for-profit. A profit-driven media implements various strategies for gaining consumers' attention, many of which are problematic.

   a. Some outlets attract market share by maintaining high standards of journalistic integrity.

   b. Media outlets may attract market share by catering to the belief system of certain consumers.

      ➤ This bias, or ideological tendency to view and present information from a particular political point of view, may be more or less pronounced.

      ➤ Some outlets incorporate a subtle bias, while others may be obviously or extremely biased.

      ➤ Bias may reflect the ideology or business interests of a corporation's leadership, as well as a marketing strategy.

   c. During election years, media outlets frequently engage in horse race journalism. This form of reporting entails reporting poll results tracking voter preferences in upcoming elections.

      ➤ The focus by media on polls attracts larger audiences by focusing on the competitive aspect of the race, making political news more exciting.

      ➤ An important criticism of horse race journalism is that it lacks substance. The media focuses on polling to the exclusion of substantive policy issues and differences between candidates, failing in its duty to educate the public.

5. In recent decades, massive growth of technology infrastructure and the media culture has led to the proliferation of fake news or information that lacks credibility.

   a. Fake news may be understood as a type of propaganda intended to spread false information or cast doubt on legitimate journalism.

b. Fake news may be difficult for even sophisticated viewers to detect. For example, YouTube videos that appear to be clips from legitimate news sources have been seamlessly edited in a sophisticated manner to be misleading or divisive.

c. Individual citizens may lack the sophistication to distinguish reliable, unbiased news sources from unreliable or biased news, causing many to distrust and tune out the news media.

d. Fake news may promote negative attitudes toward both the media and government, decreasing voter turnout and political participation generally.

e. Characterizing news stories as fake news may cause confusion about the reliability of media outlets and erode trust in journalism.

> ➤ Utilizing nonpartisan online fact checkers such as Snopes, Washington Post Fact Checker, PolitiFact, and FactCheck.org is also helpful in identifying reliable information.

Evaluating the Credibility of Information

Question to Ask	If it's real:	If it's fake:
Evaluate the publisher or news outlet.	– respected news outlet – named author – websites should end in .com or another legitimate domain extension	– not a known or respected outlet – author is not named or not reliable – websites end in unusual domain extensions
Question the source.	– claims are supported with citations and/or reliable sources	– claims are not supported
Evaluate the quality of the writing.	– does not contain grammatical errors – date is current	– may contain grammatical errors – may be out of date
Verify the information.	– other legitimate outlets have also reported the information	– no respected outlets are reporting the same information
Evaluate the presentation and emotional appeal.	– style, tone, and image choices are appropriate and not sensationalized	– sensational style, tone, and/or image choices

B. SOCIAL MEDIA

1. One of the most significant developments in twenty-first-century democracy has been the proliferation of social media platforms.

2. Social media allows communication in both directions between political figures and citizens. Politicians can speak directly to constituents, and voters can communicate feedback to politicians.

3. The explosion of social media has drastically altered the role of the mass media as an intermediary, or filter, between politicians and the public. While the role of the traditional media is still important in questioning and eliciting information from politicians, it is no longer necessary as a medium of communication.

4. Social media also provides a platform for citizen journalism.

   a. Citizen journalists are private citizens who collect, report, and analyze news and political events.

   b. Reporting on social media may not be as well-resourced or have the same responsibility as professional journalism.

   c. Social media and citizen journalism increase diversity and choice in news sources.

   d. Increasing media choices may contribute to political polarization as more options allow consumers to choose news sources that reinforce their existing views.

5. Social media platforms may be effectively used by various political actors to spread misinformation and influence public opinion and elections.

C. MEDIA CHOICE AND ECHO CHAMBERS

1. The proliferation of news sources in the twenty-first century would intuitively seem likely to produce a more informed public. This does not, however, appear to be the case.

2. Media outlets are profit-driven; readership and viewership determine advertising revenue, which drives content.

3. Increasing numbers of easily accessible information sources go hand in hand with increasing choices for consumers.

4. Increasing competition has promoted new, more ideological models of journalism in order to attract audiences and sell advertising.

5. Rather than creating broader exposure to a variety of news sources, consumers choose content that appeals to their worldviews.

6. Social media exacerbates this phenomenon by incentivizing users to create and share biased content within social groups, creating bubbles or echo chambers rarely penetrated by extraneous information. The vast majority of content encountered by Internet users is largely in line with and reinforces their existing beliefs.

7. The Internet thus creates a kind of insularity, as opposed to exposure.

PART III

KEY DOCUMENTS, COURT CASES, AND LAWS

Required Foundational Documents

The AP® U.S. Government and Politics exam requires you to be familiar with nine foundational documents that will be represented on both the multiple-choice and free-response questions.

1. **The Declaration of Independence**
Separation from Great Britain

   ➤ Describes the philosophical basis that justifies the separation of the colonies from Great Britain based on the social contract theory of John Locke.

   ➤ The Declaration is a kind of "breakup letter," describing in a detailed list the colonies' grievances against the British government.

   ➤ Outlines key democratic ideals including popular sovereignty, natural rights, and the social contract.

   ➤ Announces that the United States is an independent and sovereign state.

2. **The Articles of Confederation**
A Loose Alliance

   ➤ Created a confederate-style government that granted most of the authority of government to independent states and only limited authority to a weak national government.

   ➤ Unicameral national legislature that did not have the power to tax, regulate commerce, or raise an army, leading to an ineffective national government and economic instability.

   ➤ The national government lacked an executive branch to enforce laws and had no national courts to settle issues that arose between the states.

3. **Brutus No. 1**
   Power Should Remain with the States: Small Republics Are Best

   ➤ Anti-Federalist essay opposing ratification of the Constitution because the proposed federal government would threaten liberty and state sovereignty.

   ➤ Claims that the Necessary and Proper (Elastic) Clause creates a federal government with limitless power.

   ➤ Argues that the Supremacy Clause creates a federal government with authority to cancel out any state law and reduces the importance of state government.

   ➤ The Constitution creates a Congress with essentially unlimited authority to tax through potentially broad interpretations of the provision for the government to provide for the common defense and promote the general welfare.

   ➤ The ability of the national legislature to keep a standing army, even during times of peace, is a threat to liberty.

   ➤ The large size and diverse population of the United States would make it impossible for a federal government to accurately represent the will of the people.

   ➤ Democracy works best if there are only a few competing factions. The large republic proposed in the Constitution would have too many competing groups, resulting in a threat to the interests of individual citizens.

4. **Federalist No. 10**
   The Constitution: A Solution to the Problem of Factions

   ➤ Madison provides a counterargument to *Brutus No. 1* presenting how the Constitution will control factions.

   ➤ Factions are undesirable, but inevitable, because the only way to eliminate factions is to destroy liberty or give everyone the same opinions.

   ➤ A large republic addresses the problem of factions by creating a climate in which many groups compete for influence. Under such a system, no single group would be able to dominate the others.

   ➤ The principle of the popular vote would prevent any group (faction) from dominating if it held less than majority support.

➤ A republic (representative democracy) is superior to a democracy (direct or pure democracy) because educated and thoughtful people would be elected to make policy.

5. **Federalist No. 51**
   Checks and Balances: Ambition Must Counteract Ambition

   ➤ Madison argues that Montesquieu's ideas of separation of powers and checks and balances, which are present in the federal government created by the Constitution, prevent the abuse of power by the government.

   ➤ Separation of powers that is built into the government by the Constitution prevents the concentration of power in one person, group, or government institution.

   ➤ Three distinct branches, each with different areas of authority and combined with the natural personal ambition of members of the government, will prevent any one branch from dominating the government.

   ➤ Acknowledges that the legislative branch will be the most powerful, but argues that it is checked by the other branches (such as the executive use of the veto) and by the inter-branch check of the bicameral legislature.

6. **Federalist No. 70**
   Power to the President

   ➤ Hamilton's argument for the single, powerful executive created by the Constitution (as opposed to an executive committee).

   ➤ A single executive will be able to operate with more energy and efficiency in executing the law and responding in the case of a crisis.

   ➤ A single president will not become a tyrant because one individual will be easier to control.

7. **Federalist No. 78**
   An Independent Judiciary

   ➤ Hamilton's essay about the need for a strong federal judiciary, including the theory of judicial review and the importance of life terms of justices.

   ➤ The judicial branch is the least dangerous because (1) it must rely on the other branches to carry out its rulings; and (2) it lacks the power of the purse and the power of the sword held by the other branches.

8. **The Constitution of the United States**
   A Strong Union

   ➤ **Preamble:** Introduction to the Constitution setting forth the purposes for which the new government is formed.

   ➤ **Article I: The Legislative Branch**

   – creates a bicameral legislature

   – sets terms and qualifications for members in both houses of Congress

   – lists the powers of Congress

   – includes the Necessary and Proper Clause (Elastic Clause) that creates implied powers

   ➤ **Article II: The Executive Branch**

   – describes the office, qualifications, term, and powers of the president

   – establishes a system of presidential electors to choose the president

   – the Vesting Clause grants executive authority to the president

   – the president is granted the responsibility of enforcing the law and the role of commander in chief

   ➤ **Article III: The Judicial Branch**

   – creates one Supreme Court

   – grants Congress the power to create and structure additional federal courts

   – federal judges serve for life and can only be removed by impeachment

   ➤ **Article IV: Relations Among States**

   – Full Faith and Credit Clause: states must respect the official actions and records of other states

   – Privileges and Immunities Clause: states may not discriminate unreasonably against the citizens of other states

   – grants Congress the power to regulate the admission of new states to the union

   – guarantees to each state a republican form of government

➤ **Article V: Amendment Procedure**

– establishes a procedure for amending the Constitution that reflects federalism because both the national government and the states are needed to change the Constitution

– proposal requires two-thirds vote of both houses of Congress or a two-thirds vote in a national convention called by the states

– ratification requires the approval of three-quarters of the states

➤ **Article VI: Debt, Supremacy, and Oath**

– the new federal government accepted responsibility for existing debt

– the Supremacy Clause: the Constitution, federal laws, and treaties are the supreme law of the land and take precedence over any state rulings

– sets forth oath to support the Constitution for state and federal officers and prohibits a religious test for office

➤ **Article VII: Ratification**

– creates procedure for ratification of the Constitution (approval by three-quarters of the states, which was nine of the 13 original states)

➤ **Amendments 1–10: Bill of Rights**

– protections for personal liberties

– places limits on federal power

➤ **Amendments 11–27**

– amendments addressing problems with and changes to the original Constitution, civil rights, and the expansion of suffrage

9. **Letter from a Birmingham Jail**
   Appealing to the Conscience of the Nation

➤ Written by Martin Luther King, Jr., after his arrest for participating in a nonviolent march against segregation. He wrote it as a response to white clergy members who opposed the protests.

➤ Makes a case for nonviolent protest and the need to demonstrate in order to call attention to discriminatory laws.

➤ Presents support for an end to segregation as a moral imperative; distinguishes between just and unjust laws.

Required Supreme Court Cases

This course requires you to thoroughly understand 15 Supreme Court cases. Each case represents an important principle of law.

 I. **THE COURT**

1. Supreme Court cases make law. The law established by Court rulings (precedent) must be followed in subsequent cases that present the same legal question. This is the principle of *stare decisis*. Precedent must be followed in subsequent cases unless there is a compelling reason to break with previous case law.

2. Additionally, remember the following important terms relating to court cases.

   ➤ *Judicial review* is the power of the courts to determine if any law or action of government is inconsistent with the Constitution and, if so, to invalidate that law or action.

   ➤ *Writ of certiorari* is an order from an appellate court requiring that a lower court provide the record of a case for review. When the Supreme Court "grants cert," it agrees to take an appeal.

   ➤ *Civil liberties* are personal rights and freedoms held by individuals with which the government may not interfere.

   ➤ *Civil rights* are those rights that the government must enforce, to be free from discrimination or unequal treatment based on membership in a minority group or class under the Equal Protection Clause of the Fourteenth Amendment.

   ➤ *Selective incorporation* is the piecemeal application of the civil liberties in the Bill of Rights to the states based on the Due Process Clause of the Fourteenth Amendment.

   ➤ *Majority opinion* is the written document containing the decision or ruling of the Court.

3. Each case may be understood in terms of four elements:

➤ facts of the case (What happened?)

➤ constitutional issue presented (What is the legal question that must be answered?)

➤ holding (How did the Court answer the legal question?)

➤ reasoning (What logic and law did the Court follow in drawing its conclusion?)

Test Tip

The AP® U.S. Government and Politics exam requires students to analyze a real-world scenario based on a Supreme Court decision, or compare a non-required case to one of the required cases.

Note: Each of the required cases is explained at length in the relevant chapter of this book, which is indicated next to the case name in the list below.

1. Judicial Review

An early question that had to be answered was whether the Court had the power to apply the Constitution to invalidate the actions of the other branches of government.

***Marbury v. Madison* (1803)** (see chapter 8)
The Supreme Court claims the power of judicial review.

➤ In *Marbury*, the Supreme Court established its power of judicial review (the power to nullify acts of the legislative or executive branches or state governments as unconstitutional), which greatly strengthened the federal judicial branch.

➤ The Constitution does not explicitly grant the courts the power of judicial review, but Alexander Hamilton's essay "Federalist No. 78" indicates that this was the Framers' intention.

➤ In *Marbury*, Chief Justice John Marshall famously struck down a federal statute for the first time—the Judiciary Act of 1789—that had given the Court the power to hear a case under original jurisdiction (which means to hear a case for the first time).

> The Court held that the Judiciary Act was unconstitutional because Congress could not give the Court original jurisdiction beyond that granted by the Constitution.

> Because Chief Justice John Marshall effectively sided with Jefferson, the new president, the executive branch did not challenge the Court's proclamation that it held the power of judicial review.

2. Federalism

The division of powers created by the Constitution has led to an ongoing tension between the states and the federal government.

McCulloch v. Maryland **(1819)** (see chapter 4)
The Necessary and Proper Clause is elastic, and the Federal Government is supreme.

> The state of Maryland imposed a tax on a branch of the Second Bank of the United States that operated in that state.

> The Supreme Court held that, although the Constitution does not specifically grant Congress the power to establish a bank, that power is implied by the Necessary and Proper Clause of Article 1. In other words, *Congress has implied powers.*

> Under the Supremacy Clause, federal laws are more powerful than state laws. Federal law and the U.S. Constitution are supreme over state law.

United States v. Lopez **(1995)** (see chapter 4)
The Court limits the power of Congress.

> Before *Lopez*, the Court had greatly expanded Congress's implied powers based on the Commerce Clause.

> In *Lopez*, a student was charged with carrying a gun into a school in violation of federal law.

> The Court held that Congress may not use the commerce power to criminalize carrying a gun in a school, because the federal government could not show that there was any connection between this behavior and interstate commerce.

> *Lopez* reversed a long trend of Supreme Court rulings expansively interpreting the Commerce Clause to enhance federal power.

3. Civil Liberties

Civil liberties are personal freedoms with which the government may not interfere (except in limited circumstances).

➤ In the Bill of Rights, the Due Process Clause of the Fifth Amendment prohibited the federal government from infringing on individual liberties. The states were not restrained by the Fifth Amendment.

➤ The Due Process Clause of the Fourteenth Amendment, added to the Constitution in 1868, has been held by the Supreme Court to make most of the Bill of Rights applicable to state governments.

➤ The Court did not find all civil liberties to be protected from state action at once, but piecemeal, or one at a time. The Supreme Court's pattern of applying civil liberties protections against state governments one-by-one is called *selective incorporation*.

➤ Most, but not all, of the civil liberties protected in the Bill of Rights, have been applied to the states.

Note: The required civil liberties cases follow. Some, but not all, are cases that incorporated a right against the states for the first time.

Engel v. Vitale (1962) (see chapter 9)
School prayer in public schools violates the Establishment Clause.

➤ The Establishment Clause of the First Amendment prohibits government sponsorship of or affiliation with religion.

➤ Public schools may not sponsor prayers, even if the prayer is non-denominational and non-compulsory.

➤ *Engel* is understood as prohibiting any school-sponsored/sanctioned religious activity in public schools.

Wisconsin v. Yoder (1972) (see chapter 9)
Compulsory school attendance laws violate the Free Exercise Clause.

➤ The Free Exercise Clause of the First Amendment protects the right of individuals to engage in their religious rituals and practices.

➤ In *Yoder*, the Court held that compulsory secondary education violated the religious practice of the Amish, which prohibits education past the eighth grade.

➤ The government may not enforce laws against individuals when such enforcement interferes with the free exercise of an individual's religious practices.

Tinker v. Des Moines Independent Community School District (1969)
(see chapter 9)
The First Amendment protects students' free speech in schools, including symbolic speech.

➤ Students wore black armbands to school in protest of the Vietnam War.

➤ The protest was purely symbolic; the students did not speak or disrupt the school.

➤ The Court held that students' First Amendment right to free speech is protected in schools, so long as the speech does not interfere with discipline or the operation of the school.

➤ Wearing black armbands is a form of symbolic speech protected by the First Amendment.

Schenck v. United States (1919) (see chapter 9)
The "Clear and Present Danger" test is established for speech protection.

➤ During World War I, the defendants in *Schenck* distributed literature urging young men to defy the draft and were charged with violating the Espionage Act of 1917.

➤ The defendants argued that the charges violated their First Amendment right to free speech.

➤ The Court held that the First Amendment does not protect speech that presents a "clear and present danger" of causing serious harm that Congress has a right to prevent.

New York Times Co. v. United States (1971) (see chapter 9)
No prior restraint of the press is allowed to the government.

➤ The Nixon administration obtained a restraining order preventing *The New York Times* and *The Washington Post* from publishing classified information (the Pentagon Papers) relating to the war in Vietnam that had been leaked to the press.

➤ The Pentagon Papers contained information that might be embarrassing to the government, but not harmful to military operations.

➤ The Court held that, under the First Amendment, the government could not restrain the press from publishing information unless the government could meet a very high burden, which the Court did not clearly define.

***McDonald v. Chicago* (2010)** (see chapter 9)
The right to keep and bear arms applies to states.

➤ A Chicago ordinance prohibited the possession of handguns. Otis McDonald, a city resident who lived in a dangerous neighborhood, argued that the Second Amendment guarantees an individual the right to keep and bear arms.

➤ The Supreme Court incorporated the Second Amendment against the states and struck down the Chicago handgun ordinance.

Gideon v. Wainwright (1963) (see chapter 9)
The right to counsel

➤ Clarence Earl Gideon was charged with breaking into a pool hall and stealing cash, a felony.

➤ Although Gideon was indigent (too poor to pay for an attorney), he was not entitled to a public defender under Florida law because he was not charged with a capital (death penalty) crime.

➤ The Supreme Court incorporated the Sixth Amendment's right to counsel, holding that all felony defendants are entitled to an attorney paid by the state if they fall below a minimum financial threshold.

***Roe v. Wade* (1973)** (see chapter 9)
The right to abortion

➤ Norma McCorvey (pseudonym "Jane Roe") was denied an abortion in Texas and challenged the constitutionality of Texas's restrictive abortion law.

➤ The Supreme Court held that the right to privacy (not explicitly stated in the Constitution, but established in a previous case) protects a woman's right to access an abortion.

Test Tip

Note that civil liberties cases always involve balancing the rights of the individual against the rights of others or society at large. The individual freedoms guaranteed in the Bill of Rights are not absolute. Civil liberties do not allow individuals to violate the rights of others. Keep in mind that one person's rights end where another's begin.

4. Civil Rights

Civil rights claims are based on the Equal Protection Clause of the Fourteenth Amendment and require the government to protect members of certain minority groups against discrimination.

***Brown v. Board of Education of Topeka* (1954)** (see chapter 10)
Separate is not equal: No legal segregation of public education.

➤ African American children were required under Kansas law to attend racially segregated schools.

➤ The Court overturned the separate but equal doctrine, established in *Plessy v. Ferguson* (1896), which allowed segregation in public accommodations so long as the facilities offered to Blacks and whites were roughly equal.

➤ In *Brown*, the Court held that separate is inherently unequal and unconstitutional under the Equal Protection Clause of the Fourteenth Amendment.

5. Redistricting

Redistricting involves creating new district boundaries for legislative representation.

The Court has heard several cases related to creating both congressional districts and districts for state legislatures. The Court has ruled, over a series of cases, that, based on the Equal Protection Clause of the Fourteenth Amendment, legislative districts must be roughly equal in population or the "one person, one vote" principle.

In terms of legislative districts, the Court has ruled that districts must be drawn so that they are roughly equal in population, are contiguous and connected, and do not dilute minority voting strength. However, district lines cannot be drawn solely based upon race *(Shaw v. Reno)*.

***Baker v. Carr* (1962)** (see chapter 5)
Courts have the power to evaluate the constitutionality of redistricting schemes.

➤ *Baker* is important because the Court held that redistricting may be a justiciable question (something the courts can decide) and not merely a political question (something for the legislature or executive). That is, courts have the authority to decide redistricting decisions. (Partisan gerrymandering claims are considered nonjusticiable under *Rucho v. Common Cause*, 2019.)

> In a series of cases based on the *Baker* decision, the Court went on to establish the principle that legislative districts must be approximately equal in population, so that each citizen's vote is equally weighted. (The "one person, one vote" principle.)

Shaw v. Reno (1993) (see chapter 5)
Redistricting based on race is subject to strict scrutiny.

> North Carolina created a congressional district map with two majority-minority districts, intended to increase the number of representatives from North Carolina representing African Americans. (*Majority-minority* districts are those in which a more than half of voters are members of a minority group.) The new map had been drawn so as to comply with minority voting rights under the Voting Rights Act of 1965.

> The Court struck down the map, holding that although congressional district maps must comply with the Voting Rights Act of 1965, a district drawn based solely on race must pass strict scrutiny: it must be drawn with a compelling state interest in mind, be narrowly tailored to meet that need, and be the least restrictive means for achieving the goal.

6. **Campaign Finance**

It has long been recognized that financing campaigns can result in the disproportionate influence of well-funded interests, as well as political corruption.

Various federal laws have attempted to limit the influence of money in political campaigns within the limitations of the Constitution.

Citizens United v. Federal Election Commission (2010) (see chapter 13)
Campaign spending is speech protected by the First Amendment.

> Citizens United, a conservative nonprofit organization, challenged restrictions placed by the Bipartisan Campaign Reform Act on advertising intended to influence elections by corporations and other organizations.

> The Court held that the First Amendment's free speech protections apply to corporations, labor unions, and other organizations, and that BCRA restrictions violated those rights.

> Spending by organizations to influence elections may not be limited so long as there is no coordination between the organization and the candidate or campaign.

Important Laws

A. CIVIL RIGHTS ACT (1964)

1. Prohibits discrimination based on race, color, religion, or national origin in public accommodations or any place open to the public (restaurants, hotels, and businesses), government services, programs receiving federal funds, education, and employment.

2. The Supreme Court has upheld the constitutionality of the law based on the commerce power in Article I.

B. VOTING RIGHTS ACT (1965)

1. Prohibits discrimination in voting rights, including the use of literacy tests.

2. Created a preclearance requirement for changing voting procedures in jurisdictions with a history of discrimination. (The preclearance provision required jurisdictions with a history of discriminatory voting practices to obtain authorization from the Department of Justice before making significant changes to election procedures. It is currently unenforceable as a result of *Shelby County v. Holder* (2013), a Supreme Court decision which found that the formula for determining whether a jurisdiction required preclearance was out-of-date and, therefore, unconstitutional.)

C. FREEDOM OF INFORMATION ACT (FOIA) (1967)

1. Requires executive branch federal agencies to provide information about the government that is not already published in the *Federal Register* when requested by journalists, researchers, or the public.

2. Important for protecting the First Amendment freedom of the press because it forces the government to be more transparent.

3. There are some exceptions to the release of documents including those related to personal privacy, privileged communication, trade secrets, and law enforcement or national security concerns.

4. Has been amended to account for advances in technology.

D. TITLE IX OF THE EDUCATION AMENDMENTS ACT (1972)

1. Prohibits discrimination on the basis of sex in all federally funded educational activities.

2. Best known for increasing women's access to athletic activities.

3. Prohibits sexual harassment in educational environments.

E. WAR POWERS RESOLUTION (1973)

1. Also known as the War Powers Act.

2. Passed in response to congressional concern about presidential overreach in use of the military, during both the Korean and Vietnam wars.

3. Requires that the president inform Congress within 48 hours of committing military forces to action.

4. If Congress does not authorize the action within 60 days, military forces must be withdrawn.

5. An additional 30 days are allowed for troops to make a safe withdrawal.

F. FEDERAL ELECTION CAMPAIGN ACT (1974)

1. Created the Federal Election Commission (FEC), a bipartisan commission charged with enforcing campaign contribution and spending limits and monitoring disclosure compliance.

2. Places limits on individual and Political Action Committee (PAC) contributions.

3. Places limits on campaign spending.

4. Requires reporting of campaign contributions and expenditures.

5. Establishes a system for public financing of presidential campaigns, which is now rarely used because presidential candidates can raise more money outside of the public financing system.

6. In *Buckley v. Valeo*, the Court struck down limits on campaign spending (but not contributions) created by the law, ruling that spending money to influence elections is a form of constitutionally protected free speech.

G. AMERICANS WITH DISABILITIES ACT (ADA) (1990)

1. Civil rights legislation that broadly defines the term *disability* to include both physical and mental conditions.

2. Prohibits discrimination against disabled individuals by all employers with more than 15 employees.

3. Applies to private businesses, not only to entities receiving federal funds.

4. Requires all places open to the public to ensure physical access to facilities, including wheelchair access.

5. Example of an unfunded mandate.

H. NATIONAL VOTER REGISTRATION ACT (1993)

1. Also known as the Motor Voter Act.

2. Requires states to provide individuals with the opportunity to register to vote at the same time that they apply for a driver's license or seek to renew a driver's license, thus increasing voter access.

I. WELFARE REFORM ACT (1996)

1. Formally known as the Personal Responsibility and Work Opportunity Reconciliation Act.

2. Ended the entitlement status of welfare by creating the Temporary Assistance for Needy Families program (replacing the Aid to Families with Dependent Children program).

3. Creates stricter rules for Medicaid eligibility.

4. Distributes block grants to the states to use on welfare programs with some specific requirements, including no federal welfare for individuals who have not worked within two years and no federal welfare for more than five years total.

5. Example of devolution because block grants gave states more discretion with regard to management of welfare programs.

J. USA PATRIOT ACT (2001)

1. Uniting and Strengthening America by Providing Appropriate Tools Required to Intercept and Obstruct Terrorism Act

2. Enacted in response to 9/11 attacks.

3. Includes provisions expanding government power to conduct surveillance operations and allowing extended detention of immigrants.

4. Several of the provisions enhancing government search and seizure authority were subject to successful constitutional challenges.

5. Portions of the USA PATRIOT Act were extended by the USA Freedom Act of 2015.

K. BIPARTISAN CAMPAIGN REFORM ACT (BCRA) (2002)

1. Also known as the McCain-Feingold Act.

2. Prohibits national parties from soliciting or spending soft money.

3. Places specific limits on contributions to candidates, parties, and PACs.

4. Prohibits issue advertisements on television or radio that used a candidate's name, were paid for by corporations or unions, and were broadcast within 30 days of a primary election or within 60 days of a general election.

5. Includes the "Stand By Your Ad" provision requiring candidates and any group running political advertisements to disclose who paid for the ad.

6. In *Citizens United v. FEC* (2010), the Court struck down BCRA's limitations on outside spending as a violation of the free speech protections of the First Amendment.

L. PATIENT PROTECTION AND THE AFFORDABLE CARE ACT (ACA) (2010)

1. Also known as Obamacare.

2. Creates affordable health insurance for more people by creating insurance exchanges, or marketplaces, and offering subsidies.

3. Requires insurance companies to cover pre-existing conditions, offer free preventative care, allow children to remain on a parents' plan until age 26, and eliminate lifetime coverage limits.

4. Guarantees coverage for contraception, mental health, and substance abuse services.

5. Created an individual mandate requiring all individuals not covered by an employer's plan or government program to purchase health insurance. The individual mandate was repealed in 2017.

M. USA FREEDOM ACT (2015)

1. Reauthorizes several provisions of the USA PATRIOT Act, which had expired the previous day.

2. Does not reauthorize the government to collect bulk data on phone records.

PART IV

TEST-TAKING
STRATEGIES AND
PRACTICE QUESTIONS

Mastering the Multiple-Choice Questions

A. TIMING AND SCORING

1. Your score for the multiple-choice section of the exam is based on the total number of questions you answer correctly. Points are not deducted for incorrect answers, so it is important that you answer every question, even if you have to guess.

2. There are 55 multiple-choice questions with four possible answer choices (A–D). This section of the exam lasts 1 hour and 20 minutes.

B. TOP 10 TEST TIPS FOR MULTIPLE-CHOICE QUESTIONS

1. The most important tip for answering multiple-choice questions is to carefully read the question and be sure you understand what the question is asking. In other words, RTFQ (Read the Full Question).

2. When reading the question, feel free to underline, draw boxes around words, or make notes. Do whatever helps you understand the question correctly and remember helpful information.

3. Cross out answers that you feel confident are incorrect.

4. Keep in mind that you will be expected to choose the *most correct* option from among answer choices that may include a few reasonable options. Ask yourself which choice fully answers the question. If it's only partially true or true in limited circumstances, it is likely *not* correct.

5. The multiple-choice questions vary in their level of difficulty. Some will be easy, while others will be more difficult. Answer the easy ones and move on; don't waste time. Reason through the difficult questions using the strategies you know.

6. Occasionally, you may see something unfamiliar that was not covered in class. Eliminate unlikely answers and make an educated guess. Ask yourself what seems logical. No worries—you will *not* be getting 100% on the multiple-choice section. The test is designed to make this extremely unlikely.

7. Test questions may use different or slightly altered terms for concepts you are familiar with. For example, *gubernatorial* refers to something relating to the governor. Other terms for *supply-side economics* are *Reaganomics* and *trickle-down economics*. If a question seems to be asking about a familiar concept, it may just be using an unfamiliar term.

8. Make a notation next to questions you find difficult. You can come back to them if you have time.

9. Save time on text-based questions by looking over the questions before you read the passage. Then annotate or underline the excerpt, focusing only on the information being tested.

10. Familiarize yourself with the six question types (see below), and complete as many practice questions as you can. Test-taking is really a skill! Use your results to help you focus your study time on your areas of weakness.

C. TYPES OF MULTIPLE-CHOICE QUESTIONS

There are six types of multiple-choice questions. Each type is explained in detail below and followed with examples. Remember that some questions will take more time to answer than others, especially those involving reading a passage or analyzing a data set. Spend time carefully reviewing the sample multiple-choice questions in Chapter 20.

I. **Knowledge-Based Questions.** This type of multiple-choice question is probably the most familiar to you, but one you will see the *least* frequently on the test. This type of question tests your understanding of political principles, processes, policies, and behaviors. Most of the exam requires a different skill: using your knowledge of the material in the context of how political science principles apply in real-world situations.

II. **Comparison-Based Questions.** These questions require the skill of comparing and contrasting—or identifying similarities and differences—between political science concepts. They involve a specific style of chart and can be tricky. Remember that an answer must be correct as it relates to *both* sides of the chart. It is extremely helpful for you to cross off answers if you know that one side is incorrect.

III. **Quantitative Analysis.** When presented with quantitative data in graphs, tables, charts, or infographics, you will be expected to draw conclusions and make connections to course content. The first question will often require you to identify a trend, outcome, pattern, or limitation in the data. Subsequent questions will test your ability to make an inference or conclusion about the data based on your existing knowledge. You may be asked to identify the causes or consequences of a trend or the reason for a relationship within the data.

IV. **Text-Based Analysis.** This type of multiple-choice question requires analysis and application of both primary and secondary sources. Primary sources include, but are not limited to, the nine required foundational documents of the course (see Chapter 16) and opinions from the 15 required Supreme Court cases (see Chapter 17). Primary source documents in this type of multiple-choice question might also include non-required foundational documents, non-required Supreme Court opinions, speeches, or legislation. These questions might also involve a secondary source, such as writings from political scientists, economists, or historians.

V. **Visual Source Analysis.** This multiple-choice section will require you to analyze images presented in the form of maps, flowcharts, infographics, and political cartoons that may or may not contain data for related political science concepts. For example, you may be asked to interpret congressional maps or organizational charts.

VI. **Concept Application.** You will encounter multiple-choice questions that require you to analyze specific situations and explain how they demonstrate various political science concepts or theories.

Practice Multiple-Choice Questions

Practice with the following AP®-style questions. Then go online to access a timed, full-length practice exam at *www.rea.com/studycenter.*

> *Questions 1 and 2 are sample knowledge-based items.*

1. In a civilized society, citizens agree to give up or limit certain freedoms and empower a government to make rules to govern them in exchange for a level of security. The people may dismantle a government that does not respect their natural rights. Which of the following terms is the most accurate label for this idea?

   (A) limited government

   (B) social contract

   (C) popular sovereignty

   (D) republicanism

2. Which of the following serves as the basis for the implied powers of Congress?

   (A) the Establishment Clause

   (B) the Full Faith and Credit Clause

   (C) the Commerce Clause

   (D) the Necessary and Proper Clause

3. Which of the following pairs accurately represents views
    likely to be held by a liberal and views likely to be held by a
    conservative?

	Liberal	Conservative
(A)	supports extensive regulation of business to protect consumers	supports extensive regulation of industry to combat climate change
(B)	supports reduced taxation on wealthy individuals and corporations to stimulate economic growth	supports increased taxation on wealthy individuals and corporations and funding of social welfare programs
(C)	supports increased education spending	opposes federal regulation of public education
(D)	supports death penalty	opposes death penalty

4. Which of the following is an accurate comparison of the
    constitutional powers of the House of Representatives and
    the Senate?

	House of Representatives	Senate
(A)	confirms ambassadors	confirms federal judicial nominees
(B)	originates all revenue bills	brings charges of impeachment
(C)	limits debate by issuing rules	limits debate with a filibuster
(D)	determines the president if no candidate receives a majority of the electoral votes	determines the vice president if no candidate receives a majority of the electoral votes

5. Which of the following is an accurate comparison of reapportionment and redistricting?

	Reapportionment	Redistricting
(A)	conducted by the federal government	conducted by state governments
(B)	increases or decreases a state's total number of senators	increases or decreases a state's total number of electoral votes
(C)	conducted every ten years based on census data	conducted biannually based on population shifts within states
(D)	often involves gerrymandering by state legislatures	is determined by the Census Bureau

6. Which of the following is an accurate comparison of the two court cases?

	Schenck v. United States (1919)	*New York Times Co. v. United States* (1971)
(A)	established the clear and present danger test	prohibited prior restraint of the press in most cases
(B)	upheld defendants' prison sentences for encouraging others to resist the military draft	upheld prison sentence of congressional staffer who leaked the Pentagon Papers to the press
(C)	declared the Espionage Act unconstitutional	upheld prior restraint of the press in most cases
(D)	established First Amendment protections for symbolic speech	declared the Espionage Act unconstitutional

*Questions 7–12 are sample
quantitative analysis items.*

QUESTIONS 7 AND 8 REFER TO THE GRAPH.

Wide gender, race, age, education and religious differences in presidential voter preferences

% of registered voters who support...

	Clinton	Trump	Johnson	Stein
All voters	46	46	6	3
Men	39	43	8	4
Women	52	36	4	2
White	38	49	6	3
Black	81	3	6	2
Hispanic	65	18	6	4
18–29	49	28	12	6
30-49	47	34	7	3
50–64	43	47	4	2
65+	45	47	3	1
Postgrad	64	25	7	2
College grad	49	35	7	3
Some college	43	41	7	4
High School or less	40	47	5	3
White Evang Prot.	14	75	4	1
White mainline Prot.	37	48	6	2
Black Protestant	87	3	4	0
Catholic	46	44	3	2
Unaffiliated	59	21	9	6
Among whites				
College+	51	36	7	2
Non-college	31	56	5	3

Source: Pew Research Center, October 2016

7. According to the data set, which of the following is the strongest demographic indicator of support for Clinton?

   (A) being a woman

   (B) being Black

   (C) being 18–29 years old

   (D) having a postgraduate education

8. In the 2016 election, two minor party candidates drew a measurable percentage of the vote, Jill Stein, who ran as the Green Party candidate, and Gary Johnson, who ran as a Libertarian. Considering how minor parties can affect presidential election outcomes, which of the following statements is true?

(A) Stein's candidacy most likely aided Clinton by drawing voters who would otherwise have voted for Trump.

(B) Stein's candidacy most likely aided Trump by drawing voters who would otherwise have voted for Clinton.

(C) Johnson's candidacy most likely aided Trump by drawing voters who would otherwise have voted for Clinton.

(D) Neither minor party candidate drew enough voters to impact the outcome of the election.

QUESTIONS 9 AND 10 REFER TO THE GRAPH

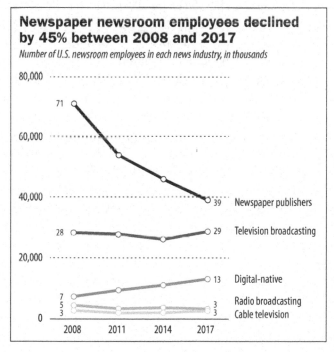

Source: Pew Research Center

9. Which of the following statements accurately describes a trend in the data set on the previous page?

    (A) Newspaper publishers are the only industry to show an overall decline in newsroom employees from 2008 to 2017.

    (B) The newspaper industry employed more newsroom employees in 2017 than any other news industry.

    (C) Newspaper newsroom employees have declined significantly since 2008 while the numbers of newsroom employees in other industries have grown overall.

    (D) Television broadcasting showed the greatest increase in newsroom employees from 2008 to 2017.

10. Given what you know about changes in the news media in recent decades, which of the following statements might accurately explain the changes in newsroom employee numbers presented in the data?

    (A) Newspaper subscriptions have declined as news consumers have gained access to increasing numbers of free or low-cost online sources of news.

    (B) Increases in newsroom hiring in the television and digital media industries have created increasing demand for newsroom employees overall.

    (C) Growth in radio broadcasting has allowed the industry to offer newsroom employees higher salaries, drawing employees away from other news industries.

    (D) Advertising revenues have increased for cable news and radio broadcasting, while declining for newspapers.

QUESTIONS 11 AND 12 REFER TO THE GRAPH.

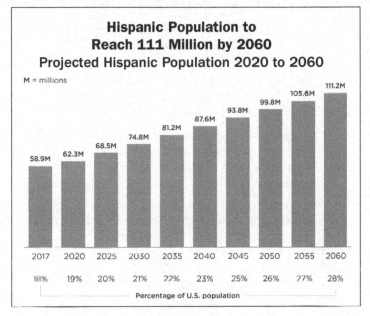

**Hispanic Population to
Reach 111 Million by 2060**
Projected Hispanic Population 2020 to 2060

M = millions

Year	Population	Percentage
2017	58.9M	18%
2020	62.3M	19%
2025	68.5M	20%
2030	74.8M	21%
2035	81.2M	22%
2040	87.6M	23%
2045	93.8M	25%
2050	99.8M	26%
2055	105.6M	27%
2060	111.2M	28%

Percentage of U.S. population

Source: U.S. Census Bureau, 2017

11. By what year will Hispanics reach one-quarter of the United States population?

    (A) 2025

    (B) 2040

    (C) 2045

    (D) 2050

12. Based on your understanding of demographics and politics, which of the following conclusions is true?

   (A) Because large numbers of Hispanic voters tend to favor Republican candidates and policies, Republicans are likely to gain political power.

   (B) Because large numbers of Hispanic voters tend to favor Democratic candidates and policies, Democrats are likely to gain political power.

   (C) Because the Hispanic population is diverse in their political views and party affiliations, the growing Hispanic demographic is unlikely to significantly affect partisan politics.

   (D) Democratic politicians should discontinue support for immigration reform measures and the DREAM Act, which are opposed by most Hispanic voters.

Questions 13–18 are sample text-based analysis items.

QUESTIONS 13–15 REFER TO THE PASSAGE.

In 1984, Congress passed the National Minimum Drinking Age Act requiring the Secretary of Transportation to withhold 5 percent of federal highway funds from states that did not adopt a 21-year-old minimum drinking age. South Dakota, a state that permitted persons 19 years of age to purchase alcohol, challenged the law, arguing that regulation of alcohol sales is an exclusive power of state government. The Supreme Court held that the threat of withholding funds as an inducement to comply with a federally promoted policy is constitutional.

The Court stated:

The Constitution empowers Congress to "lay and collect Taxes, Duties, Imposts, and Excises, to pay the Debts and provide for the common Defense and general Welfare of the United States." Art. I, 8, cl. 1. Incident to this power, Congress may attach conditions on the receipt of federal funds, and has repeatedly employed the power "to further broad policy objectives by conditioning receipt of federal moneys upon compliance by the recipient with federal statutory and administrative directives." . . .

Here Congress has offered relatively mild encouragement to the States to enact higher minimum drinking ages than they would otherwise choose. But the enactment of such laws remains the prerogative of the States not merely in theory but in fact. Even if Congress might lack the power to impose a national minimum drinking age directly, we conclude that encouragement to state action found in 158 is a valid use of the spending power.

— *South Dakota v. Dole* (1987) Majority Opinion

13. Which of the following enumerated powers of Congress allowed the Supreme Court to side with the federal government in the case of *South Dakota v. Dole* according to the majority opinion?

    (A) Supremacy Clause

    (B) Commerce Clause

    (C) Tax and spend money

    (D) Standards of weights and measures

14. In which of the following court cases did the Supreme Court decide a case in the opposite manner by upholding the rights of states in balancing power between the national and state governments?

    (A) *McCulloch v. Maryland* (1819)

    (B) *Tinker v. Des Moines* (1969)

    (C) *Marbury v. Madison* (1803)

    (D) *United States v. Lopez* (1995)

15. In *South Dakota v. Dole*, the Court upheld a requirement placed on the states by the federal government. Which of the following terms best describes the federal requirement that states comply with federal drinking age policy?

    (A) dual federalism

    (B) devolution

    (C) eminent domain

    (D) a mandate

QUESTIONS 16 AND 17 REFER TO THE PASSAGE.

> Independent of the opinions of many great authors, that a free elective government cannot be extended over large territories, a few reflections must evince, that one government and general legislation alone never can extend equal benefits to all parts of the United States: Different laws, customs, and opinions exist in the different states, which by a uniform system of laws would be unreasonably invaded. The United States contain about a million of square miles, and in half a century will, probably, contain ten millions of people; and from the center to the extremes is about 800 miles.
>
> Before we do away the state governments or adopt measures that will tend to abolish them, and to consolidate the states into one entire government several principles should be considered, and facts ascertained:—These, and my examination into the essential parts of the proposed plan, I shall pursue in my next.
>
> —*Letters from the Federal Farmer No. 1*

16. Which of the following statements best summarizes the author's argument?

    (A) Removing the authority of the state governments would make them vulnerable to invasion.

    (B) The United States is too large of a territory to be governed by a federal government because standard national laws would intrude on the rights of states to protect different traditions.

    (C) Large centralized governments are the most effective way to eliminate factions and protect personal liberties.

    (D) State government should be eliminated, and a unitary system of government established because federalism cannot succeed in the real world where states will be in conflict with each other.

17. In which of the following documents does the author make an argument that is most similar to the one presented in *Letters from the Federal Farmer No. 1*?

    (A) *Federalist No. 10*

    (B) *Declaration of Independence*

    (C) *Brutus No. 1*

    (D) *Federalist No. 51*

QUESTION 18 REFERS TO THE PASSAGE.

In the case of *Reed v. Reed* (1971), the Supreme Court struck down an Idaho law giving preference to males over females in selecting the administrator of a deceased person's estate (the person responsible for overseeing the belongings of the person who has died).

The Court stated:

In applying that clause, this Court has consistently recognized that the Fourteenth Amendment does not deny to States the power to treat different classes of persons in different ways . . . [T]hat amendment does, however, deny to States the power to legislate that different treatment be accorded to persons placed by a statute into different classes on the basis of criteria wholly unrelated to the objective of that statute. A classification "must be reasonable, not arbitrary, and must rest upon some ground of difference having a fair and substantial relation to the object of the legislation, so that all persons similarly circumstanced shall be treated alike." The question presented by this case, then, is whether a difference in the sex of competing applicants for letters of administration bears a rational relationship to a state objective.

—*Reed v. Reed* (1971) Majority Opinion

18. Based on the above excerpt and your existing knowledge, upon which constitutional clause was the Court relying in its decision to prohibit sex-based discrimination in this case?

    (A) The Supremacy Clause

    (B) The Full Faith and Credit Clause

    (C) The Equal Protection Clause

    (D) The Due Process Clause

Questions 19–22 are sample
visual analysis items.

QUESTIONS 19 AND 20 REFER TO THE MAP.

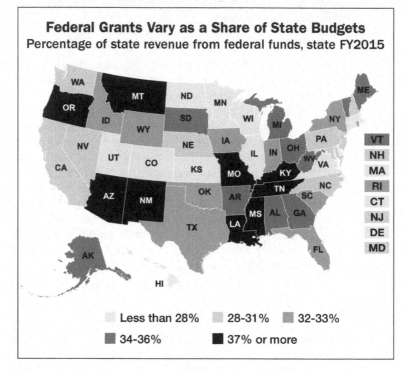

Federal Grants Vary as a Share of State Budgets
Percentage of state revenue from federal funds, state FY2015

Less than 28%   28-31%   32-33%

34-36%   37% or more

19. Which of the following correctly pairs the states with the highest and lowest groups of federal aid as a percentage of the state budget, respectively?

(A) Minnesota (MN) and Georgia (GA)

(B) Montana (MT) and North Carolina (NC)

(C) Texas (TX) and California (CA)

(D) Kentucky (KY) and Illinois (IL)

20. Which of the following statements is accurate based on the data in the graphic?

(A) Federal aid generally composes a larger share of the budget for coastal states than for interior states.

(B) Federal aid generally composes a larger share of the budget for southern states than for northern states.

(C) States that rely more and less heavily on federal aid are distributed evenly throughout all geographic regions.

(D) States that rely more heavily on federal aid generally do so as a result of natural disasters.

QUESTIONS 21 AND 22 REFER TO THE CARTOON.

Courtesy of the Jay N. 'Ding' Darling Wildlife Society

21. Franklin Roosevelt's early attempts to enact New Deal legislation were consistently struck down by the Supreme Court as exceeding Congress's constitutional powers. Roosevelt responded by proposing a plan to "pack the Court" by increasing the number of Supreme Court justices, which would allow him to nominate friendly judges who would be approved by a friendly Senate. Which presidential power allowed FDR to propose this plan?

    (A) the power to change the jurisdiction of the Supreme Court

    (B) the power to change the number of judges on the Supreme Court

    (C) the power to make recess appointments

    (D) the power to recommend legislation

22. Which of the following statements best describes the message of the cartoon?

    (A) The president is the captain of the ship, a trustworthy person, and has the moral and constitutional authority to control the Court.

    (B) The president does not have the constitutional power to change the direction of the Court, which is required to keep the country headed in the right direction.

    (C) It is the duty of Congress to support the president, and his agenda must be supported by all three branches.

    (D) Congress is a powerful co-equal branch of government and unafraid to stand up to his agenda, which is an abuse of power.

23. Which of the following is an example of judicial review?

(A) The Supreme Court hears a case to determine whether an environmental regulation applies to a specific category of manufacturers.

(B) State police agencies review the performance of criminal court judges.

(C) A federal district court in Texas strikes down parts of the Affordable Care Act as unconstitutional.

(D) The Senate conducts confirmation hearings to determine the fitness of a presidential nominee to the Supreme Court.

24. In *Riley v. California (2014)*, the Supreme Court unanimously held that the warrantless search of a cell phone was unconstitutional. Which constitutional amendment protects the right violated by the search?

(A) First Amendment

(B) Fourth Amendment

(C) Fifth Amendment

(D) Sixth Amendment

25. Which of the following options would be a tool available to the president to ensure that an independent agency is effectively carrying out its mandate?

(A) appoint the head of the agency

(B) solicit opinions from interest groups for use in formulating regulations

(C) fire and replace a large percentage of lower-level agency employees

(D) perform oversight by conducting public hearings

ANSWER EXPLANATIONS

1. **(B) is correct.** The idea of the social contract, proposed by John Locke, is foundational to the Declaration of Independence and the American Revolution itself. It is a concept you should be able to name and define. This question may challenge you because limited government (A) and popular sovereignty (C) both also relate to the broader ideas of democracy. Republicanism (D) is incorrect because it involves the unrelated principle of representative government. Answer (B) is the best choice because the statement provided is the definition of a social contract.

2. **(D) is correct.** Answers (A) and (B) are clearly wrong. The Establishment Clause (A) is the First Amendment clause that requires the separation of state and church. The Full Faith and Credit Clause (B), found in Article IV, requires that states respect official records and decisions of other states. The Commerce Clause (C) is more challenging. The Commerce Clause has been interpreted very broadly, and forms the basis for more implied powers than any other power of Congress. Choice (D), however, the Necessary and Proper Clause, actually grants Congress the authority to exercise powers that are implied and not specifically expressed in the Constitution.

3. **The correct answer is Choice (C)** because both corresponding statements are correct. Choice (A) is incorrect because the second statement is false. Conservatives generally do not support increased regulation of industry. Choice (B) is incorrect because the liberal-side statement describes supply-side economics, a theory that is generally supported by conservatives. The conservative-side statement is also false; conservatives do not favor increased taxation or support the expansion of social welfare programs. Choice (D) is incorrect because the liberal and conservative positions are reversed. Liberals are more likely to oppose the death penalty, while conservatives generally favor it.

4. **The correct answer is (D).** Remember that both parts of the answer must be correct for the answer to be correct. Choice (A) is incorrect as to the House (the Senate confirms ambassadors), but correct as to the Senate. Choice (B) is correct as to the House, but incorrect as to the Senate (the House brings impeachment charges). Choice (C) is incorrect because neither the practice of issuing rules for bills in the House, nor the filibuster in the Senate are constitutional powers. The question asks you to compare the constitutional powers of the House and Senate. This is a very difficult question. (Sorry!) Remember to

carefully read the question. If you find yourself trying to decide between two answers that both seem correct, go back and read the full question (RTFQ).

5. The correct answer is (A) because both corresponding statements are true. Choice (B) is incorrect because both statements are false. Reapportionment impacts representation in the House, and redistricting, the redrawing of district boundaries within a state, does not change the number of House seats or electoral votes. Choice (C) is incorrect because the redistricting statement is false. Redistricting occurs every ten years as a result of reapportionment. Choice (D) is incorrect because both parts are false. The "Reapportionment" side is incorrect because gerrymandering relates to redistricting, not reapportionment. The "Redistricting" side is incorrect because redistricting is carried out by states, whereas the Census Bureau is the federal agency that conducts the population census.

6. The correct answer is (A) because both corresponding statements are true. Choice (B) is incorrect because the second statement is false. The *New York Times* case did not involve criminal charges, and no one was imprisoned. Choice (C) is incorrect because both parts are false. The Espionage Act was not declared unconstitutional, and prior restraint of the press was rejected. Choice (D) is incorrect because both parts are false. *Schenck* did not involve symbolic speech and, again, the Espionage Act was not declared unconstitutional.

7. The correct answer is (B). Black voters preferred Clinton by a margin of 81 to 3 percent, a far greater difference than the other three possible demographics: women voted for Clinton by a margin of 52 to 36 percent; 18- to 29-year-olds preferred Clinton by a margin of 49 to 28 percent; and postgraduates (more than a 4-year college degree) preferred Clinton by a margin of 64 to 25 percent.

8. The correct answer is (B): the 3 percent of the voters who supported the Green Party candidate, Jill Stein, took votes away from the Democratic candidate, Clinton, thus aiding the Republican candidate, Trump. Choice (A) is incorrect because voters who supported the Green Party candidate, Stein, would have been more likely to support the Democratic candidate, Clinton, and not likely to support the Republican candidate, Trump. Choice (C) is incorrect because voters who supported the Libertarian Party candidate, Johnson, would have been more likely to support the Republican candidate, Trump. Choice (D) is incorrect because the Libertarian and Green candidates received 6 and 3 percent of the vote, respectively. Either of these percentages could affect the outcome of the election since a very

small percentage of votes could determine the winners of significant numbers of electoral votes and thus be determinative of the winner.

9. The correct answer is (C). Newspaper newsroom employees have declined significantly. The number of newsroom employees in most other industries has grown modestly, and their collective number overall has increased. Choice (A) is incorrect because radio broadcasting also showed an overall (small) decline. Choice (B) is incorrect because, although the statement is true, it describes a data point and not a trend. (RTFQ). Choice (D) is incorrect. Television broadcast news employees increased by only 1,000. Digital-native news employees increased by 6,000, the largest numeric and percentage increase shown in the data.

10. The correct answer is (A). Choice (B) is incorrect because newspapers have lost 32,000 newsroom employees, while television and digital-native media combined have increased by 7,000. Demand cannot explain the loss of the other 25,000 employees. Choice (C) is incorrect. Radio broadcasting has not shown growth in market share, and the data does not indicate an increase in newsroom employees. Choice (D) is incorrect because there is no evidence in the data set regarding revenues.

11. The correct answer is (C). While the Hispanic population may grow to 25% sometime between 2040 and 2045, according to the data it cannot be concluded that it will happen before 2045.

12. The correct answer is (B) because as a group, Hispanic voters tend to support Democratic candidates and policies by a significant margin. Choice (A) is incorrect because, overall, Hispanic voters do not favor Republican candidates and policies. Choice (C) is partly true. The Hispanic population is diverse, and certain groups within this population have historically preferred Republican candidates. However, while diversity exists within all demographic groups, Hispanic voters overall are decisively Democratic. Furthermore, the second part of the answer, that one-quarter of the voting population is unlikely to affect partisan politics, is false. Choice (D) is also false. Hispanic voters, as a group, are supportive of immigration reform.

13. The correct answer is (C). In the majority opinion of *South Dakota v. Dole*, the Court upheld the law based on the expressed power of Congress to "lay and collect Taxes, Duties, Imposts, and Excises, to pay the Debts and provide for the common Defense and general Welfare of the United States" and that Congress can attach condi-

tions to funding. Choices (A), (B), and (D) are not referenced in the opinion.

14. The correct answer is (D). In *South Dakota v. Dole,* the Supreme Court sided with the federal government over the states, but in *United States v. Lopez*, the Court sided with the states claiming that the federal government overreached with the Commerce Clause by banning guns in schools. Choice (A) is incorrect because in this federalism case the Court sided with the Federal government over the states. Choices (B) and (C) are incorrect because they are not related to federalism or the division of power between the national and state governments.

15. The correct answer is (D). An order to comply with a federal policy, as upheld in *South Dakota v. Dole,* is best described as a "mandate." Choice (A) is incorrect because the term *dual federalism* (layer cake federalism) describes an ideal in which the state and federal governments regulate in separate spheres of power, and do not interact with each other. In this case, there is clearly an overlap of authority and a clash for power. Choice (B) is incorrect because devolution refers to the move to return more reserved powers to the states and this case gives the federal government greater power. Choice (C) is incorrect because eminent domain is the name for the power held by state and federal governments to take private property for public use. It is unrelated to this case.

16. The correct answer is (B). In *Letters from the Federal Farmer No. 1,* the author argues that the proposed federal government created by the Constitution will be unable to effectively govern a large, diverse nation and that it poses a threat to state autonomy. Choice (A) is incorrect because an invasion in the form of an attack is not discussed by the author. Choice (C) is incorrect because the Anti-Federalist author argues against a large national government. Choice (D) is incorrect because the Anti-Federalist author does not support the reduction of state power.

17. The correct answer is (C). Anti-Federalists wrote both *Brutus No. 1* and *Letters from the Federal Farmer* in opposition to the ratification of the Constitution. The *Federalist Papers* in Choices (A) and (D) were both written in support of the Constitution, and *Federalist 10* makes an argument for how a large republic will protect liberty. Choice (B), the *Declaration of Independence,* does not argue for or against a federal form of government, but merely explains the justification for independence.

18. The correct answer is (C) because discrimination based on sex is a civil rights question. The Equal Protection Clause of the Fourteenth Amendment prohibits discrimination on the basis of membership in a minority group. In *Reed*, the Court applied the Equal Protection Clause to sex-based distinctions. Choice (A), the Supremacy Clause, is the basis for the requirement that states comply with the federal Constitution generally, but is not the specific basis for this decision. The Full Faith and Credit Clause (B) applies to relationships between states. The Due Process Clause (C) of the Fourteenth Amendment requires that states respect the civil liberties of their citizens. It is the Equal Protection Clause that protects civil rights.

19. The correct answer is (D). The map key divides states into five categories. States whose budgets are composed of federal funding by 37% or greater are the highest group. Those states whose budgets include less than 28% funding from the federal government are in the lowest group. Of the pairs presented, only Kentucky and Illinois are classified in the highest and lowest groups.

20. The correct answer is (B). Although there are not clear linear divisions with regard to state reliance on federal aid, southern state budgets are composed of a higher percentage of federal funds overall compared with other regions. Choice (A) is incorrect because the opposite is true: coastal states generally have budgets with a lower percentage of federal aid. Choice (C) is incorrect because states relying more heavily on state aid are clustered more heavily in certain regions. Choice (D) is incorrect because the map does not provide causal data.

21. The correct answer is (D). This question requires you to understand distinctions between congressional and presidential powers. The question asks what power the *president* used to *propose* the plan. Both Choices (A) and (B) refer to powers of Congress. Choice (C) is also incorrect. The power to make recess appointments is a power of the president, but the president cannot create new positions; he or she may only fill certain positions that become vacant. With regard to changing the number of seats on the Court, the president may only recommend that Congress do so.

22. The correct answer is (B). The Court is symbolized as a compass, a scientific instrument that points to the truth. Choices (A) and (C) are incorrect because they suggest that the cartoonist is supportive of the president's agenda, which is clearly not the case. Choice (D)

is incorrect because Congress is pictured as weak and fearful, rather than powerful and willing to challenge the president.

23. The correct answer is (C). Judicial review is the power of the courts to invalidate laws and government actions that are unconstitutional. It is not a power reserved to the Supreme Court. Choice (A) is incorrect because it does not involve a constitutional issue. Choices (B) and (D) do not describe judicial review scenarios. Choice (C) is the only answer that describes a court exercising the power of judicial review.

24. The correct answer is (B). This question is a concept application question because it requires you to identify the type of right that has been violated and place that right in the correct constitutional amendment. The right in question is the right against unreasonable searches and seizures, found in the Fourth Amendment.

25. The correct answer is (A). Choice (B) is incorrect because the president does not formulate regulations and does not make policy in the case of independent agencies. Choice (C) is incorrect because the president may only remove and appoint certain high-ranking government employees, not regular civil service employees (lower-level employees). Choice (D) is incorrect because Congress, not the president, conducts hearings as part of its oversight role.

Mastering the Free-Response Questions

A. SCORING

1. Your score on the free-response questions (or FRQ) section of the exam is based on responding to four questions. Each of the four free-response questions is equally weighted and will comprise 50% of your total score. You will have one hour and 40 minutes to complete your responses to all of the FRQ questions.

2. The free-response questions will require you to make connections between topics across the course and draw conclusions about these connections and how they apply to specific situations.

3. Below is a chart showing the breakdown of the FRQ section of the exam.

Free-Response Question Type	Suggested Time Limit	Percentage of Overall Exam Score
Concept Application	20 minutes	12.5%
Quantitative Analysis	20 minutes	12.5%
SCOTUS Comparison	20 minutes	12.5%
Argument Essay	40 minutes	12.5%

B. TOP TIPS FOR THE FREE-RESPONSE QUESTIONS

1. The most important tip for answering free-response questions is to carefully read the question and be sure you understand what the question is asking. In other words, RTFQ (Read The Full Question).

2. In reading the question carefully you should underline, draw boxes around words, make notes—whatever helps you understand the question correctly or organize helpful information. Take a few minutes to create a plan before you begin writing your answer to the question.

3. Send in a "reserve player" (an extra answer that may be able to score the point).

   ➤ On free-response questions, you may be asked to identify or explain one or more examples, similarities, or differences. In such cases, it is recommended that you include an extra idea that may earn the point in case one of your required responses is wrong. This offers you protection because, if one of your examples is incomplete or inaccurate, you might be able to score the point with your second option.

   ➤ For example, if the prompt asks you to describe one power of Congress, describe two. Even if you are confident in your original answer, take a moment to call in a reserve player!

4. Time management is essential, so take into account the suggested pacing for each question and allow more time for the argument essay free-response question.

   ➤ The College Board recommends that you budget twenty minutes for each of the first three questions and forty minutes for the last question. Because the last free-response question, the argument essay, is the most complex it is recommended that you allow yourself additional time on that question.

   ➤ Remember you are free to move between the free-response questions at any time. So, if you finish one question early, you may move ahead to the next question. If you have any time left at the end, you should go back and review your answers and add in "reserve players" if you have any.

5. Order and spacing should reflect the format of the question. Answer the questions in order using complete sentences. Leave three to five blank lines of space between each part of your answer in case you need to add more to your response later. It will also make it easier for you to assess that you have answered all parts of the questions.

Sample Spacing

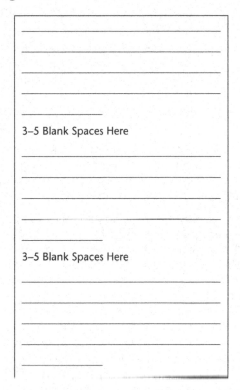

3–5 Blank Spaces Here

3–5 Blank Spaces Here

6. Remember to "close the loop." Your answer must be relevant to the prompt, so it helps to begin your response to each section of the question with the specific wording from the prompt. Also, after finishing your response to a section, be sure to indicate how you answered what was asked in the stimulus. For example, you might say, "and that explains how Congress uses the power of oversight to influence bureaucratic regulations."

7. Answer questions using political science terminology. When describing the balance between state and federal power, use the term *federalism* or mention *division of powers*. When discussing a case in which the Supreme Court has overturned a law, use the term *judicial review*. Show the reader that you understand the technical language of the subject to be sure you earn every possible point.

8. Use specific examples of each important concept in your answer. Sometimes you may have a general idea of an answer, but may not be able to articulate it exactly.

> ➤ If you are not sure of the name for a concept or can provide only a general description, an example may save the point.

> ➤ For example, if the answer is the "oversight power of Congress" and you describe it without naming it, the reader may not be sure you are talking about oversight. If you give, as an example, Congressional hearings on enforcement of environmental regulations, your example makes clear that you are discussing oversight.

9. Answer questions in neutral terms. It's great to have political opinions, but the AP® reader evaluating your answer may not share them. Avoid value judgments and expressions of personal political ideology, and answer in factual, straightforward language.

10. Be aware of what is being asked of you based on the verb used in each part of the question. Notate the verb in each question by drawing a box around it so that you are conscious of the directive. Some of the most commonly used verbs on the free-response questions and what they mean in terms of your response are provided in the chart below. Generally, you are expected to write a brief paragraph of three to five sentences in response to each of these prompts, with the exception of "identify" prompts, which typically require only one to two sentences to list and define.

FRQ Verb	Expected Response
Identify	Provide a specific example of a political science concept using a complete sentence. This is a perfect place to add a "reserve player."
Describe	Define, illustrate, and outline what is being asked about by providing specific details. These questions require you to depict a phenomenon or idea by illustrating its key characteristics. Remember to demonstrate your knowledge by utilizing political science terminology and be specific.
Explain	Address possible causal relationships by defining all relevant terms and making logical connections using specific examples. Make sure that you close the loop and indicate clear cause and effect relationships by using a "because" or "therefore" in your response.
Identify a Trend	A trend is a clear movement or tendency that can be seen in a data set. Trends are those things that can be identified using words that describe change or stability over time. For example, words like *increase, decrease, grow, shrink,* or *stability*. Trend questions relate to data sets. A single data point is not a trend!

FRQ Verb	Expected Response
Draw a Conclusion	This verb is most likely to show up when you are asked to examine data presented in a chart or graphic. Indicate the broader meaning or outcome of findings that can be determined based on the data. Consider why the results are important and how they illustrate political science concepts.
Compare (Similarities and Differences)	Clearly show the relationship between two concepts by highlighting similarities and differences. It helps if you can define each term first, but you must indicate how the concepts are alike and how they are different. Write about both concepts and cross-reference them.
Articulate a Claim	Expect to see this verb in the argument-essay FRQ where you will need to make a defensible statement or thesis using one to two sentences. A helpful format for this is to write an "I believe . . . . because" statement. "I believe that (choose a side or one of the options from the prompt) because (explain your reasoning which you will support with evidence in your response)."
Support	Provide specific evidence to prove the truth of a statement.
Use Reasoning	Make specific connections between the evidence you cite and your thesis by clearly explaining how each piece of evidence supports your claim.
Refutation or Rebuttal (Argument Essay)	Use reasoning to explain how evidence contradicts or disproves a claim. Make a clear comparison by stating your original claim with reasoning and indicating why your claim is superior to the counterclaim.
Concession (Argument Essay)	Use reasoning in admitting that an opposing viewpoint is correct based on an examination of evidence. Make a clear comparison by stating your original claim with reasoning and then indicating why the counterclaim is also correct or valid.

Test Tip

The readers who will be evaluating your free-response questions are "gatherers," not "hunters." They will be glad to pick up the points that are apparent in your answer, but they will generally not chase them down.

C. THE FOUR TYPES OF FREE-RESPONSE QUESTIONS

Section II of the exam consists of four distinct types of free-response questions that are all weighted equally in terms of your overall exam score. The four types of questions are concept application, quantitative analysis, SCOTUS comparison, and argument essay.

1. **Concept Application:** In one of the FRQs you will be asked to evaluate a political scenario and indicate how it illustrates or explains political science concepts, public policy, government institutions, or political behavior. This style of free-response question will be worth three points (parts A, B, and C will each be worth one point) and it is suggested that you spend about 20 minutes on this question. The question prompt will begin with a provided scenario.

Part (A) will likely ask you to describe a political institution, behavior, or process connected with the scenario described. (1 point)

Part (B) will likely ask you to explain how your response in Part (A) affects or is affected by a political process, government entity, or citizen behavior as related to the scenario. (1 point)

Part (C) will likely ask you to explain how the scenario relates to a political institution, behavior, or process in the course. (1 point)

> ➤ Each part of your answer should be a short paragraph of 3–5 sentences. Remember to leave several blank lines between each section.

> ➤ Be sure to answer in context. For each part of the question, be sure to make clear how your answer relates to the scenario you are being asked to analyze.

SAMPLE CONCEPT APPLICATION QUESTION

1. The following is from a 2012 speech by President Barack Obama on immigration issues.

> Good afternoon, everybody. This morning, Secretary Napolitano announced new actions my administration will take to mend our nation's immigration policy, to make it more fair, more efficient and more just, specifically for certain young people sometimes called DREAMers.

> Now, these are young people who study in our schools, they play in our neighborhoods, they're friends with our kids, they

pledge allegiance to our flag. They are Americans in their heart, in their minds, in every single way but one: on paper. They were brought to this country by their parents, sometimes even as infants, and often have no idea that they're undocumented until they apply for a job or a driver's license or a college scholarship.

Put yourself in their shoes. Imagine you've done everything right your entire life, studied hard, worked hard, maybe even graduated at the top of your class, only to suddenly face the threat of deportation to a country that you know nothing about, with a language that you may not even speak.

President Barack Obama, June 15, 2012

After reading the scenario, respond to parts A, B, and C below:

(A) Describe a power the president could use to address the concerns outlined in the scenario.

(B) In the context of the scenario, explain how the use of executive power described in Part A can be affected by its interaction with Congress.

(C) In the context of the scenario, explain how the interaction between Congress and the presidency can be affected by the judicial system.

SCORING GUIDELINES—CONCEPT APPLICATION QUESTION

PART A POSSIBLE POINTS

Clearly describe one of the following as a power the president could use in this situation.

> ➤ Issue an executive order to create a system under which DREAMers could legally remain in the United States.

> ➤ Recommend legislation urging Congress to create an amnesty program for DREAMers.

> ➤ Use the power to execute the law to selectively enforce existing deportation requirements.

> ➤ Use the president's informal powers and media access to persuade the public to pressure Congress to take action (bully pulpit).

PART B POSSIBLE POINTS

Clearly explain, in the context of the scenario, how the use of executive power described in Part A can be affected by its interaction with Congress.

➤ If the president issues an executive order creating a system under which DREAMers could legally remain in the United States, Congress could pass a law that either strengthens or eliminates the policy.

➤ If the president recommends legislation to create an amnesty program for DREAMers, Congress can pass a law that specifically addresses this policy issue and provides funding for its implementation.

➤ If the president uses the "executing the law" power to limit enforcement of existing deportation requirements, Congress can pass stricter laws with more specific requirements or use the oversight power to investigate.

➤ If the president uses the informal power of the president to appeal to the people to pressure Congress to take action (bully pulpit), members of Congress may feel pressure from their constituents to pass laws related to DREAMers or to hold hearings and investigate the issue using the oversight power.

PART C POSSIBLE POINTS

Clearly explain in the context of the scenario how the interaction between Congress and the presidency can be affected by the judicial system.

➤ If the president issues an executive order creating a system under which DREAMers could legally remain in the United States, the courts could potentially strike down or uphold the action using the power of judicial review.

➤ If the president recommends and Congress passes legislation to create an amnesty program for DREAMers, the courts could strike down or uphold the law.

2. **Quantitative Analysis:** In this type of free-response question, you will be required to identify a trend or pattern or make a conclusion from a specific data set. Additionally, parts of this question will require you to relate the data to a specific political science principle or process, institution of government, linkage institution, public policy, or political behavior. This style of free-response question will be worth four points, typically having parts A, B, C, and D. It is suggested that you spend about 20 minutes on this question.

Part (A) will likely ask you to identify or describe the data in the quantitative visual. (1 point)

Part (B) will likely ask you to describe a pattern, trend, or similarity/difference as prompted in the question. (1 point)

Part (C) will likely ask you to draw a conclusion and explain how the pattern, trend, or similarity/difference in the data supports your conclusion.

Part (D) will likely ask you to explain how specific data in the quantitative visual demonstrates a political principle, institution, process, policy, or behavior. (1 point)

> ➤ Write a brief paragraph in response to each part of the question and leave several blank lines between each section. Identification questions may require a shorter response.

> ➤ Read the title, headings, legend or key, and any notes or descriptions provided to help you interpret the data.

> ➤ Quantitative data may be presented in a variety of ways. Carefully examine the format of the graphic to be sure you understand the relationships between data categories.

> ➤ Do not confuse trends with data points. Trends show changes or consistencies over time, while data points represent individual pieces of information. Simply pointing out specific data points does not show a trend.

> ➤ Be sure to use the data in the form it is given to you. For example, don't confuse percentages with raw numbers. Be sure to label any numerical conclusions you draw according to the labels given in the data.

SAMPLE QUANTITATIVE ANALYSIS QUESTION

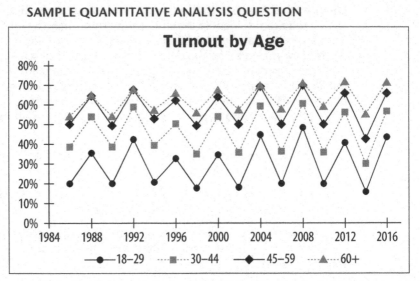

Turnout by Age

This chart is taken from the United States Election Project (electproject.org).

2. Use the information in the graphic to answer the following questions.

(A) Identify a pattern in voter turnout related to age.

(B) Describe a trend in voter turnout relative to presidential and midterm election years.

(C) Explain a possible reason for the trend in voter turnout in presidential and midterm election years.

(D) Explain how the trend in voter turnout relative to presidential and midterm election years impacts policymaking interactions between the president and Congress.

SCORING GUIDELINES—QUANTITATIVE ANALYSIS QUESTION

PART A POSSIBLE POINTS: Identify a pattern.

➤ Voting participation increases as people age.

➤ Younger people vote at lower rates than older people.

PART B POSSIBLE POINTS: Describe a trend.

➤ Voter turnout increases in presidential election years and decreases in midterm election years.

> ➤ Voter turnout increased in every presidential election and decreased in every midterm election relative to the previous election.

PART C POSSIBLE POINTS: Explain a possible reason.

> ➤ Presidential elections motivate voters more than midterm elections because the Office of the President has a higher profile than those of lower-level politicians, and people care more about voting for this office.

> ➤ Considerably more money is spent by presidential campaigns than other types of campaigns. As a result, voters are more informed and motivated in presidential election years than in midterm election years.

> ➤ Presidential elections generate more media coverage than midterm elections, which leads to greater voter interest and turnout.

PART D POSSIBLE POINTS: Explain how the trend affects policymaking interactions.

> ➤ Gridlock tends to increase following midterm elections, since the president's party almost always loses seats in the midterm.

> ➤ The president may be more able to claim a mandate as a result of the higher turnout associated with presidential elections and may consequently hold an advantage in public perception.

> ➤ The honeymoon period following presidential elections in which a president is elected to his or her first term gives the president leverage over Congress during the policymaking process.

3. **SCOTUS (Supreme Court of the United States) Comparison:** This free-response question will involve explaining how aspects of one of the fifteen required Supreme Court cases are relevant to another, non-required Supreme Court case. This style of free-response question will be worth four points (typically parts A, B, and C) in which part B is worth two points. It is suggested that you spend about 20 minutes on this question.

Part (A) will likely ask you to identify a similarity or difference between the two Supreme Court cases, as specified in the question. This part of the question often focuses on a specific constitutional clause (e.g., the Commerce Clause). (1 point)

Part (B) will likely ask you to provide factual information from the specified required Supreme Court case (1 point) and explain how or why that information is relevant to the non-required Supreme Court case described in the question. (1 point) Note: Part B is typically worth 2 points.

Part (C) will likely ask you to describe or explain an interaction between the holding in the non-required Supreme Court case and a relevant political institution, behavior, or process. (1 point)

➤ Write a brief paragraph in response to each part of the question and leave several blank lines between each section.

➤ When identifying similarities or differences, focus on constitutional clauses or principles, such as freedom of religion or due process.

➤ Don't just name the constitutional clause or principle— explain or describe it.

➤ Be sure to know your fifteen required cases—the facts, constitutional issue(s), holding(s) and reasoning. You will always be asked to relate a required case to a non-required case.

➤ Cases that have the same legal outcome are often based on similar factual scenarios.

➤ When cases based on similar factual situations have different legal outcomes, there are two possibilities. First, the Court may have overturned precedent (which will have been pointed out to you, because it is a big deal). More often, there is a factual difference that distinguishes one case from the other and leads to a different legal outcome.

SAMPLE SCOTUS COMPARISON QUESTION

3. In 1996, California voters passed a referendum legalizing the use of marijuana for medical purposes. The possession and use of marijuana remained illegal under the federal Controlled Substances Act. Angel Raich and Diane Monson were California residents who produced and used marijuana to treat their own serious medical conditions. In the case of *Gonzales v. Raich* (2005), they sued the Attorney General of the United States and the head of the Drug Enforcement Administration, demanding that federal agents refrain from enforcing federal marijuana law against them in the state of California.

Gonzales required a determination of whether states or the federal government had constitutional authority to regulate the medical use of marijuana. The question presented was whether Congress's power to regulate interstate markets for medicinal substances includes the power to regulate drugs that are produced and consumed locally. The Court held that:

> the diversion of homegrown marijuana tends to frustrate the federal interest in eliminating commercial transactions in the interstate market in their entirety. [T]he regulation is squarely within Congress's commerce power because production of the commodity meant for home consumption . . . has a substantial effect on supply and demand in the national market for that commodity.

Based on the information above, respond to the following questions.

(A) Identify the congressional power upon which the Court based its rulings in both *Lopez v. United States* (1995) and *Gonzales v. Raich* (2005).

(B) Explain how the facts of *United States v. Lopez* and *Gonzales v. Raich* led to different outcomes.

(C) Describe an action that Congress could take to respond to the holding in *Gonzales v. Raich* if it disagreed with the decision.

SCORING GUIDELINES—SCOTUS COMPARISON QUESTION

PART A POSSIBLE POINTS

➤ Both the *Lopez* and *Gonzales* holdings are based on the commerce power or the authority of Congress to regulate interstate trade.

PART B POSSIBLE POINTS

➤ Clearly state the facts of *Lopez* to ensure you earn the point for this requirement.

> Alfonso Lopez, a twelfth grade student, was arrested for carrying a gun into his high school. He was charged with violating the federal Gun Free School Zones Act of 1990, which prohibited possession of a gun in a school zone. Lopez appealed, arguing that regulation of guns in school zones was a state matter and not within the scope of Congress's commerce power.

➤ Clearly explain how the facts in these cases led to different outcomes.

> Both *Lopez* and *Gonzales* centered on the limits of Congress's commerce power. In *Lopez*, the Court struck down the Gun-Free School Zones Act of 1990, holding that the commerce power could only be exercised to regulate economic or interstate activity. Because possessing a gun in a school zone was neither an economic activity nor related to interstate commerce, the federal government could not make it a federal crime. However, in *Gonzales*, the Court held that federal regulation of marijuana production was a legitimate exercise of the commerce power because it is an economic activity that affects interstate commerce.

PART C POSSIBLE POINTS

➤ Congress could decriminalize or legalize medical marijuana by passing a federal law.

➤ Congress could amend or change the Controlled Substances Act to exempt states that have decriminalized medical marijuana from enforcement.

➤ Congress could propose a constitutional amendment with a two-thirds vote of both chambers to legalize marijuana or to allow states the discretion to regulate marijuana.

➤ Congress can refuse to fund enforcement agencies, or refuse to confirm justices who oppose expansive states rights and individual liberties (particularly on drug or commerce issues).

4. **Argument Essay:** The final free-response question involves forming a well-reasoned argument that is supported by evidence from one of the nine foundational documents as well as addressing an alternative perspective. This free-response question will be worth six points, and because it involves more sophisticated thinking, it is suggested that you allow about 40 minutes to answer this question. However, it still carries the same weight in your overall exam score as the first three FRQs. The argument essay has four main sections: claim, evidence, reasoning, and a response to an alternative perspective. Remember to leave several blank lines between each section.

CLAIM/THESIS SECTION (1 point)

This part of the question will ask you to articulate a defensible claim or thesis that responds to the question and establishes a line of reasoning (1 point). In order to ensure that you can earn all of the later points make sure that you establish a line of reasoning and do not merely repeat the prompt.

> ➤ To earn the thesis/claim point, you must take a position, so begin with a straightforward statement of your position and explain why you believe it is correct. Your thesis must state a causal relationship. You must pick a side. Two possible forms this statement could take are:
>
> "I believe . . . because . . . "
>
> "The argument that . . . is true because . . . "
>
> ➤ Be sure your thesis responds to the question that is being asked (RTFQ).

EVIDENCE SECTION (3 points)

This part of the question will likely ask you to support your claim by describing two pieces of evidence that are accurately linked to the topic of the question (2 points). Clearly use each piece of evidence to support your argument (1 point). Note that the evidence section is worth a total of 3 points.

> ➤ The evidence you cite must logically relate to your thesis statement.
>
> ➤ You will likely be expected to draw on your understanding of the required foundational documents to defend your argument. The Constitution, including the Bill of Rights, is the most likely document to be encountered and/or useful.

REASONING SECTION (1 point)

This part of the question will likely ask you to explain how or why the evidence supports the claim or thesis. (1 point)

> ➤ Clearly and explicitly make connections to explain how the pieces of evidence you have presented support your argument.

RESPONSE TO ALTERNATIVE PERSPECTIVES SECTION (1 point)

This part of the question will likely ask you to respond to an opposing or alternate perspective, using refutation, concession, or rebuttal, that is consistent with the argument. (1 point)

> ➤ Be sure to state **and** respond to an opposing viewpoint by refuting, conceding, or rebutting.

> ➤ In your response to an alternative perspective, be sure to "close the loop" by restating your claim and reasoning and indicating how it is either superior to a counterclaim or how the counterclaim is also valid.

SAMPLE ARGUMENT ESSAY QUESTION

Congressional effectiveness is influenced by several factors, including the different views of the role of a member of Congress. Various roles for a member of Congress, i.e., "trustee," "delegate," or "politico" are related to a congressmember's accountability to constituents.

Present an argument about which role best achieves the goal of constituent accountability, or the duty of elected officials to act in the best interest of the citizens they represent.

Use at least one piece of evidence from one of the following foundational documents:

- The Constitution

- *Brutus No. 1*

- *Federalist No. 51*

In your essay, you must:

- Articulate a defensible claim or thesis that responds to the prompt and establishes a line of reasoning.

- Support your claim with at least TWO pieces of accurate and relevant information.

  - One piece of evidence must come from one of the foundational documents listed above.

  - A second piece of evidence can come from any other foundational document not used as your first piece of evidence, or it may be from your knowledge of course concepts.

- Use reasoning to explain why your evidence supports your claim or thesis.

- Respond to an opposing or alternate perspective using refutation, concession, or rebuttal.

SCORING GUIDELINES—ARGUMENT ESSAY QUESTION

CLAIM/THESIS SECTION POSSIBLE POINTS

➤ The delegate model best achieves congressional accountability to constituents because, in a representative democracy, elected officials are chosen to vote on behalf of those they represent and, in this case, the member of Congress would vote along with the wishes of the majority of their constituents.

➤ I believe the trustee model is the best way for members of Congress to act in the best interest of those they represent. Voting based on conscience is effective because politicians have greater access to information about issues than the people they represent and can therefore make more informed decisions.

➤ The politico model best achieves the goal of congressional accountability to constituents because it combines both the preferences of the professional legislators and the preferences of the members of their district/state, allowing them to make the most informed decisions for the citizens they represent.

EVIDENCE SECTION POSSIBLE POINTS

➤ By placing responsibility for selecting senators in the hands of state legislatures, the original Constitution supported the argument that the trustee model of representation is superior. Legislators are likely to be more sophisticated than lay people, and are therefore in a better position to make informed choices on important issues.

➤ The delegate model, by emphasizing the responsibility of elected officials to act in accordance with the will of their constituents, is supported by *Brutus No. 1*, in which it is argued that power should be dispersed and concentrated in lower levels of government, where voters hold more power.

REASONING SECTION POSSIBLE POINTS

➤ The delegate model is best because, in a democracy, policy choices must be informed primarily by the will of the voters. The Constitution's scheme of electing Representatives based on popular vote for two-year terms reflects the Framers' belief in the delegate model.

Representatives who fail to act on the preferences of their voters may be replaced at the ballot box.

➤ The politico model is best because it allows elected officials to rely on their own expertise while ensuring that the will of the voters is considered. The importance of voter preferences in making political decisions is seen in the Constitution's scheme of House elections, as well as in *Brutus No. 1*'s argument in favor of local control of government. The value of expertise and information is stressed in the Electoral College, as well as in the original constitutional provision placing responsibility for selection of senators with state legislatures.

RESPONSE TO ALTERNATIVE PERSPECTIVES SECTION POSSIBLE POINTS

➤ Some may say that the trustee model is the best method for optimizing constituent accountability because, when representatives vote in this manner, they are using their expertise and are more informed than the public. However, the trustee model is flawed because it is not consistent with a representative democracy, in which elected officials should represent the will of their constituents, as they do in the delegate model.

➤ The delegate model is the best method for achieving constituent accountability because in a democracy elected officials should vote according to the wishes of those they represent. Those who suggest that the politico model is best have a valid point because they argue that representatives should vote according to the majority of their constituents in most cases (delegate), but that they may at times need to vote based on their conscience based on greater access to information or to do what is best for the nation as opposed to his or her district only (trustee). The politico model thus may be superior to the delegate model because it offers more flexibility for representatives who, either way, may be voted out of office if the constituents do not agree with their decisions.

Notes

Notes

Notes

Notes

Notes

Notes

Notes

Notes

Notes

Notes